PUBLICATIONS OF THE
DEPARTMENT OF SOCIAL AND ECONOMIC RESEARCH
UNIVERSITY OF GLASGOW

GENERAL EDITOR: A. K. CAIRNCROSS

SOCIAL AND ECONOMIC STUDIES

5
FACTORY WAGE STRUCTURES
AND
NATIONAL AGREEMENTS

FACTORY
WAGE STRUCTURES
AND
NATIONAL AGREEMENTS

BY

D. J. ROBERTSON, M.A.
*Senior Lecturer in Political Economy in the
University of Glasgow*

CAMBRIDGE
AT THE UNIVERSITY PRESS
1960

CAMBRIDGE UNIVERSITY PRESS
Cambridge, New York, Melbourne, Madrid, Cape Town,
Singapore, São Paulo, Delhi, Mexico City

Cambridge University Press
The Edinburgh Building, Cambridge CB2 8RU, UK

Published in the United States of America by Cambridge University Press, New York

www.cambridge.org
Information on this title: www.cambridge.org/9781107669130

First published 1960
First paperback edition 2013

A catalogue record for this publication is available from the British Library

ISBN 978-1-107-66913-0 Paperback

CONTENTS

LIST OF TABLES

vii

LIST OF FIGURES

PREFACE

Anyone who is acquainted with the friendly and helpful atmosphere of the Departments of Political Economy and of Social and Economic Research in the University of Glasgow will readily understand why I find it difficult in writing this preface to select those of my colleagues to whom I should record my thanks for assistance in the writing of this book. If, therefore, I name some, this should not be held to exclude the others, but merely to indicate a greater degree of obligation. I am indebted for criticism, comment and encouragement to Professor A. K. Cairncross, Professor A. D. Campbell, Mr E. B. Gibb, Professor A. L. Macfie, Dr S. C. Orr, and Mr J. R. Parkinson. I am specially indebted to Miss Moira Dickson who carried out much of the work for Chapter 3. I have been discussing industrial relations problems with Dr T. T. Paterson for some years now. At many points I just do not know whether the ideas are his or mine, and so I cannot quantify my debt to him. His book *Glasgow Ltd* is in some respects a companion volume to this one. I have to thank Miss C. M. MacSwan and Miss Rona Plumpton for secretarial assistance and Miss Cathic Wilson for her great help in the computation of the material used in Chapter 6. I should also like to express my gratitude for the co-operation of the firms who provided the data used. I am indebted to the Carnegie Trust for the Universities of Scotland for a guarantee which has enabled this volume to be published Finally, I owe a much more than formal debt to my wife for her patience and encouragement.

D.J.R.

University of Glasgow
July 1958

CHAPTER 1

INTRODUCTION

In recent years those who have studied wages in this country have devoted most of their attention to nationally agreed rates rather than to arrangements made between individual firms and their own employees. This has meant concentration on institutional studies, especially of trade unionism operating at the national level, while the problems analysed have been those of national negotiations. The issues that arise when national wage agreements are interpreted at local level, and supplemented by individual employer's own arrangements, have been neglected, though this is the level at which the size of the worker's pay-packet is actually determined. Moreover, at this level forces other than institutional, and payments other than national rates, are involved.

There are obvious reasons for this concentration of attention at national level and on trade union matters. The decisions made nationally affect everybody, and, whatever special circumstances may apply at local level, decisions recorded at national discussions are applied at all levels. This means, for example, that the general economist considering the broad trends of our economy finds an index of national wage rates a useful, if not an ideal, instrument. Moreover, trade unions have for many years now exerted considerable pressure on wage movements and put forward as one of their most important aims the enforcement of the 'common rule'. This has found expression in a drive for national negotiating machinery, in the reduction of regional anomalies in wage rates, and in an apparent fostering of every attempt to reduce discrimination between workers who can be classified as being of the same grade and type of labour.

Each of these objectives has in some measure been achieved in wage rate negotiations and in national wage rate structures; but this achievement has led to a widespread belief that national decisions are most important, that actual wage structures at factory level are in broad conformity with national structures, and that variations in earnings levels are simply the result of differences in individual abilities and preferences. The truth is that investigation of national wage rates and wage agreements is not a satisfactory experience for the research worker who wishes to know what people are actually paid in British industry, and to understand the principles which determine such payments. The trend of research work in wages problems in Britain in recent years has tended to bear out this generalization. Those who have been integrating wage movements into wider studies of trends in the economy, and of broad distributive patterns, have generally been content with national

1

indices of wage rates or earnings, or with the aggregates of the *National Income and Expenditure* Blue Book. But, those research workers whose interests have been more specifically turned to wages problems, have been less certain of the validity of broad aggregates and have been reluctant to accept their import. As a result, several studies of particular industries,[1] of earnings patterns as against wage rates, and of detail as against average, have investigated the differences between the broad general pattern of national wage rates and 'common rule' and the actuality of wage-payment in industries, and have produced growing scepticism about the meaning to be attached to national indicators.

The evidence which has suggested the breakdown of the assumption of uniformity in wage structures can be briefly summarized.

(1) Considerable divergences between rates and earnings have appeared in studies of national averages in different industries, and marked irregularities have emerged in the degree of such divergence in different types of occupation and different types of industries.

(2) There is a growing body of knowledge which emphasizes the differences in earnings, which exist between different regions of the country. These discrepancies cannot be readily explained away as due solely to difference in industrial structure, in occupational structure, in sex-structure, in hours of work, or in age-structure between workers in one region as against another. The evidence leads almost inescapably to the conclusion that, despite apparent uniformity produced by nationally negotiated wage rates in many industries, people in comparable occupations in different parts of the country have different earnings opportunities and receive unequal returns for comparable effort.[2]

(3) In very many industries, though perhaps most noticeably in engineering, the extending use of machinery has brought a growth in the numbers of occupations. This increase in detail and difference in the occupational structure of industry has not always been matched by increased detail in national agreements.

(4) There has been a growth in the numbers of workers affected by payment-by-results schemes, a growth in time-study, and in the use of industrial consultants and the like. These developments have been connected with factory rather than national settlement of wages. Indeed their essential character dictates independent adjustment in each factory.

(5) The persistence of inflationary trends over the last fourteen years has

---

[1] See, for example, studies published in the *Bulletin* (of the Oxford University Institute of Statistics) *passim* since 1951, and G. Evans, 'Wage-Rates and Earnings in the Cotton Industry from 1946 to 1951', *Manchester School*, September 1955.

[2] Cf. Chapter 11, by D. J. Robertson, of *The Scottish Economy*, ed. A. K. Cairncross, Cambridge, 1954; and C. E. V. Leser, 'Earnings in British Regions in 1948', *Scottish Journal of Political Economy*, October 1954.

brought a consequent tendency for managements to bid above the level of negotiated rates to secure labour from competitive demands for its services.

Two major themes can generally be distinguished in the various enquiries which have been mentioned. The first is to point out the distinctions between wage rates and earnings, and the pitfalls that await the unwary who stumble from the one to the other without noticing their movement; while the second is to emphasize and to elaborate the very great complications and difficulties that exist in study of actual wage payments, in contrast to the seeming simplicity of many national agreements. Unfortunately those who have been concerned in work of this kind, and who have immersed themselves in it, have tended to come to the surface again so thoroughly aware of complexity as to be almost unable to venture upon any generalizations. Yet, if the generalizations based on wage rates are to be held unsatisfactory, it is necessary to construct some alternative, though more involved, guides to those who lack the time to sift the evidence on their own account, and who seek guidance from those who have. It is out of this background that this study emerged.[1]

THE GENERAL PATTERN OF THE BOOK

This book began with an attempt to add to our knowledge of wage determination in Britain by studying the pattern of wages in factories; and the first result was the case-study that now appears as Chapter 3. The weakness of the case-study method early became apparent with the realization that factory wages were so radically different from national wage rates as to require a general restatement of the principles of wage settlement in Britain. Generalizations aimed at the whole structure of wage payments in an economy would normally require to be backed by information on wages of a similar degree of generality. Yet, since the burden of the reformulation of attitudes to national wage payments which was to be attempted rested on a contrast between the pattern of wages which is revealed by factory studies and that settled by national negotiations, the factual background had to get down to the detail of factory wage structures and, at this level, no complete picture could possibly be presented. The large number of factories and companies in Britain makes adequate study of them all impossible, while the bewildering variety of the material makes even a satisfactory case-study of one factory a difficult matter. On the other hand, studies at the industry level miss many of the issues and are finally inconclusive, since the wage payments to individuals and at factories can only be inferred, and their effects deduced, at second-hand. Thus, even though case-studies cannot fail to give a very incomplete picture, there

---

[1] The present writer has taken part in some of the earlier earnings enquiries. Cf., for example, K. G. J. C. Knowles and D. J. Robertson 'Earnings in Engineering, 1926–1948', *Bulletin*, June 1951; and *Scottish Economy*, op. cit.

was really no substitute for this type of approach. Its inadequacies are, however, freely admitted.

Part I

Part I contains the factual basis of the book, and consists of five chapters. Two of these are general discussions of wages in the engineering and ship-building industries; the other three are studies of wages in two engineering works and a shipyard. It is difficult to justify this particular selection of case-studies; but the engineering industry is quite the largest industrial grouping in Britain, and is characterized by a very general national agreement for a very large industry. The shipbuilding industry raises payment-by-results problems in a particularly acute fashion, and the two engineering case-studies are drawn from the heavier section of the industry where, also, payment-by-results problems can be specially difficult. Thus the case-studies do give evidence for the most important sector of British industry and do highlight the problems discussed in this book. It would certainly be too much to claim that the case-studies are representative of British industry (case-studies are probably never representative anyway), but they show, perhaps in a slightly exaggerated way, the general state of affairs within the engineering and ship-building industries, while the engineering industry can be regarded as showing, again possibly in a slightly exaggerated way, the difficulties that occur when, with national wage rate determination, other payments grow to fill the gaps between national rates and factory earnings.

Part II

The two major points that emerge from the case-study section are that wages in factories do not conform to national agreements and that payment-by-results and overtime play a very important part in determining factory wage structures. These combine to suggest an analysis of the elements of wage structure at the factory level. This is undertaken in Part II with discussions of payment-by-results, overtime, and rewards for skill.

If the formal and distant character of national agreements is remembered, then the growth of payments extra to national rates, and the part such extra payments play in fashioning diverse factory wage structures, are hardly to be wondered at. But the use of payment-by-results and overtime as such extra payments need not necessarily follow; they require their own positive justification, since they are used as alternatives to factory-settled additional wage rates.

The general approach adopted in the discussion of payment-by-results in this book is to consider the number of conditions which ought to be satisfied before payment-by-results is used as a method of payment; to suggest that such payment systems are used much too frequently; and to indicate the practical consequences of excessive reliance on payment-by-results and of its use in unsuitable circumstances.

Overtime payments were originally intended to be extra rewards to workers required to undertake work at unsuitable times, and to be extra cost burdens laid upon employers to discourage the practice of constant overtime. In the post-war period overtime has been constantly used, and has been an important force in the formation of factory wage structures. Chapter 9 considers the costs and benefits of overtime in the light of these changes, and concludes that constant overtime working is costly from the point of view of the employer and is not the best form of payment for the worker.

One particularly important disadvantage of both payment-by-results and overtime is that they are uncertain and can lead to considerable variations in the size of pay-packets. This topic is elaborated in Appendix 1 on Variable Earnings and Wage Earners' Expenditure, where an attempt is made to relate different forms of expenditure to different types of payment.

The idea of wage structure evokes a direct reference to the use of wages in determining labour mobility—'that intermediate level of analysis which classical and neoclassical economists had regarded as the proper province of wage theory . . . the study of relative wage rates, or what it is now fashionable to term "wage structure" '.[1] Such a study has to do with the determination of relative wage levels for all the differing circumstances of workers. Many 'differentials', age, sex, regional and occupational differentials being the most important, can find their place in studies of wage structures. In this study the skill differential, the relationship between the payment of skilled and less skilled workers, is the only one discussed. There are two reasons for restricting the discussion to this differential only. First, certain differentials are not relevant at factory level, especially regional differentials. Secondly, data on age and sex differentials were not readily available in the cases studied. The discussion of rewards for skill in Chapter 10 argues that the patterns of demand and supply of skill have been altering, that nevertheless a positive skill differential is required though its amount cannot be determined, and that payment systems must be arranged so as to make a clear-cut skill differential.

Part III

The wisdom of the present policy of trade unions and employers' associations with regard to national negotiations is brought in question by the wide gap

[1] Lloyd G. Reynolds and Cynthia H. Taft, *The Evolution of Wage Structure*, New Haven, 1956.

between nationally settled wage rates and actual factory payments. The existence of this wide gap, and the suggestion that different forces operate to determine earnings from those that fix national rates, also force consideration of the foundations of 'wage policy' suggestions designed to control wage inflation.

The discussion of trade unions and employers' associations in Chapter 11 is designed to emphasize the extent to which these institutions are responsible for the present divorce of factory earnings from nationally negotiated wage rates. The trade unions have devoted much time and energy to securing the right to negotiate with employers, and have favoured the development of national negotiations. In so doing they have left many differentials to flourish uncared for, and have appeared to sacrifice the substance of actual payment-levels at the factories for the dream of complete uniformity at the national level. It is argued that a development towards more local bargaining would be in the long-term interests of the trade unions, and would be specially useful in curing present tendencies towards apathy at branch level. The parallel development of employers' associations has increased the tendency to separation of national rates and actual payment-levels. Such associations have had a largely defensive role which has caused them to persuade employers into accepting and conforming to the nationally negotiated standard rates. As a consequence employers faced on the one hand by the obligation to conform to standard payments, and on the other by the needs of their labour supply situation have taken to maintaining standard payments while increasing the pay-packet by the use of extra earnings. It is suggested that employers' associations at present frequently carry too heavy a load of responsibility and authority.

The relevance of this study to discussions of wage policy lies in its emphasis on the divorce of rates from earnings. This implies that any attempt to control wage movements must result in the control of each of these payments, and must be able to construct an acceptable wage structure based on the whole complex of wage payments and not just on wage rates. It is suggested in Chapter 12 that this result can only be achieved if national negotiations are reduced in importance and if negotiations are generally transferred to the local or factory level. If this were done the major source of the gap between wage rates and earnings would disappear since there would no longer be two settlements of wages, of wage rates at the national level, and of earnings at the local level. Only one wage structure would then exist and only one level of wage payments would require to be controlled. Moreover, a shift from national negotiations to local would tend to move wage bargaining away from a quasi-political atmosphere which is difficult to control or to influence towards a level which is much more directly affected by economic circumstances.

6

It is, perhaps, unlikely that such a movement from national bargaining to a purely local level would take place all at once. Even if it did not happen, considerable improvements in wage structure could be achieved by more detailed national agreements which attempted to take account of as many differential circumstances as possible. Appendix 2 tries to work out some of the detail of this idea for the engineering industry agreements.

Part IV

Economists have generally elected to follow either a strictly theoretical approach to wages, using marginal productivity techniques, or an institutional approach, through understanding the operations of trade unions, but have not usually attempted to combine these approaches. One of the merits of a study which is directed at discerning the source of differences between factory wage levels and national agreements is that it brings out a number of different aspects of wages, to which different types of wage theory are applicable. Instead of a formal conclusion summing up each of the chapters, the final chapter of this book tries to show that several quite distinct explanations of wage movements can acceptably be employed in understanding wages in Britain, provided that the separate components of wage payments are kept apart. Especially it tries to show that the major elements in wage payments, national rates and factory earnings, are best understood by reference respectively to institutional and to economic explanations of wage movements.

PART I. WAGES IN PRACTICE

CHAPTER 2

WAGES IN THE ENGINEERING INDUSTRY

THE ENGINEERING INDUSTRY IN BRITAIN

The engineering industry is without doubt the most important of British industries. It is the largest British industry or industry group; it has been steadily growing in relative size as the industrial age has developed, indeed, the history of technical change is to a large extent the history of the engineering industry, and may well continue to be so in the future; and the industry has been of increasing importance in our export trade. On all these grounds it is the most useful single industry in which to study British wage problems. But, though all this is true, the term 'the engineering industry' is a massive over-simplification which conceals innumerable problems of definition and of classification that make any more detailed statement extremely difficult. The industry is not one single unit, but a group of industries with a highly complex pattern of inter-relationships.

The Standard Industrial Classification, which is used to differentiate industries and sections of industries for statistical purposes, has parts of what is commonly regarded as the engineering industry grouped under five different headings, namely 'metal manufacture', 'engineering, shipbuilding and electrical goods', 'vehicles', 'metal goods not elsewhere specified', and 'precision instruments, jewellery etc.' Of these five headings the two most obviously forming part of the complex of engineering industries are 'engineering, shipbuilding and electrical goods', and 'vehicles'; but neither of them can be accepted in their entirety as part of the engineering industry. The shipbuilding industry, while a close ally and associate of the engineering industry—and discussed in this book in that light—cannot be accepted as part of the engineering industry, except in its marine-engineering activities. The manufacture of electrical wires and cables is a process so different from those commonly found in engineering that, though it appears under 'electrical goods', it has to be left out of engineering. Under 'vehicles' the S.I.C. includes 'motor repairers and garages' and these can hardly be regarded as forming part of the *manufacturing* activities of engineering. Each of the categories of 'metal manufacture', 'metal goods not elsewhere specified', and 'precision instruments, jewellers etc.' has parts of the engineering industry.

'Metal manufacture' includes those iron foundries which provide castings for engineering products; this process involves the use of engineering drawings, and of tradesmen, such as moulders, who are commonly found in general engineering establishments, and so the trade is generally thought to be part of the engineering industry. Under 'metal goods not elsewhere specified' the S.I.C. lists, for example, iron-and-steel forgings, which would be quite generally accepted as part of engineering. Under 'precision instruments, jewellery etc.' the S.I.C. gives scientific instruments, and watches and clocks—both of which are generally regarded as examples of light engineering. But the last three categories above include activities which do not form part of the engineering industry.

It will be evident that any statistical definition of the engineering industry must be a compromise of some kind, and that no estimate of numbers employed can be more than approximately correct. In these circumstances it is best to rely on the estimate of some authorities. The Court of Inquiry, which met to consider engineering wages in January 1954, produced what appears to be a reasonable estimate. It aggregated a number of groups from the S.I.C. and estimated, from the Ministry of Labour's figures of numbers employed in these groups, that the total number of *male* workers in engineering was 2,298,000. The comparable figure for February 1955 was 2,498,000, which with a total of 714,000 female workers, calculated in the same way, made the total number of engineering workers to be 3,212,000.[1] The figure for the allied shipbuilding industries was 206,000.

If these figures are accepted, then the immense importance of engineering as part of British industry is clear. 'Engineering' employs over a third of all those engaged in British manufacturing industry.[2] Moreover, goods generally classifiable as engineering products have been amounting to more than half of British exports of manufactured goods in recent years, a proportion which has grown greatly since before the war.

But neither these estimates of numbers employed, nor the general statement that engineering products are important, and, especially, important exports, give an answer to the important question: what is the engineering industry? It is not a single unified industry but a composite one. It is difficult to define and sometimes sections included in it by one estimate are left out by another. Fortunately one of the more obvious unifying influences is provided by the wage bargain. One definition of the engineering industry could simply be: that group of firms to whom the nationally negotiated wage rates for the engineering industry could be held to apply. Alternatively, the engineering industry could be described as being composed of all those firms

[1] Cmd. 9084, H.M.S.O., February 1954. A list of the groups included appears in Footnote 1, p. 17, in this chapter.
[2] Total employment in manufacturing industry at February 1955 was 9,216,000.

9

who are members of the Engineering and Allied Employers' National Federation, or who would be regarded as being eligible for membership. (The same remark cannot, however, be applied to the unions concerned in the industry, since their activities are rarely coterminous with one industry.)

This emphasis on the wage bargain as a unifying factor suggests that firms in the engineering industry can be characterized by the types of labour employed. There are a number of trades which are generally thought to be engineering trades. The most important are those of the fitters, who assemble and construct machinery from shaped pieces of metal; the turners, who fashion metal to particular shapes by turning it on lathes of various types; the patternmakers, who make patterns of the final metal part in wood; the moulders (and coremakers) who cast metal in sand-moulds which have been shaped from the wooden patterns; and the sheet-metal-workers, who make metal parts from metal sheets. The work of these trades is all directed towards shaping metal and assembling it into working-parts in accordance with previously laid-down specifications. It therefore follows that the products of the engineering industry are entirely, or largely, of metal—mainly iron and steel—and of metal fashioned into a working-unit, such as any form of machinery or power-unit.

Thus, in common, engineering factories use skilled tradesmen who work with metal; and their products are primarily of metal, generally some kind of machinery or power-unit. But, despite these unifying features, it is necessary to stress again the diversity of the industry. It differs greatly as to size of product, for example: the engines made range from very large marine- or land-turbines to fractional-horse-power motors or wrist-watch movements. While an essential feature of the industry is the presence of the skilled engineering tradesmen, there is great variety in the extent to which they are used and the way in which they are used. A new group of semi-skilled operatives has been growing fairly rapidly and displacing skilled tradesmen. These semi-skilled operatives, unlike the old-style tradesmen, are not fully qualified to move from job to job or from machine to machine as required, but are tied to one machine, or even to one operation. Their coming can be traced to two changes, namely, the introduction of more efficient machinery which can perform relatively intricate operations without the same degree of skilled attention, and the increasing tendency to seek 'long runs' in production.

The types of factory to be found in the engineering industry vary according to the extent to which the use of semi-skilled operatives and more specialized machinery is achieved in 'long run' production. Three types may usefully be distinguished; these are jobbing, batch and mass production. Each of the types implies a different composition of the labour force as between skilled and semi-skilled, and between men and women, a different type of specialization in machinery, and a diversity of factory type and organization.

The 'jobbing' type of production occurs where each product is individually made to its own specification. In such production both machinery and men must be adaptable, which implies relatively less complex and more general-purpose machinery, and more highly skilled tradesmen who can work individually to plans. This type of production therefore requires all the old engineer's skills and employs relatively few semi-skilled workers. Because of the size, individuality, and expense of the product, jobbing is especially common in heavy engineering where orders are for 'one off' and 'long runs' are not usual.

Batch production occurs where a number of the same product can be expected to be ordered and produced at the same time, but where, nevertheless, the factory may expect, over a long period, to have variation in its orders and variation in the types of its finished products. In such a case it is possible to plan a flow of production of any one article and to use machines to repeat the operation necessary to make each component part of the final article. Machines can be 'set up' to do a 'batch' operation, and semi-skilled operatives can be employed in machining parts after the planning and setting have been attended to. A factory engaged on this type of production will therefore tend to employ numbers of semi-skilled machinemen and to use its skilled men in fitting the final product and in 'setting up' jobs for semi-skilled workers. If the work is 'light' women may be employed in the machinery process.

'Mass' production is the other extreme to jobbing. Here the factory is laid out to produce a large number of the same product in a continuous flow. Much thought is given to planning the sequence of operations, the line which the product will follow through the factory, and its flow through the factory. In such a case specialized machinery comes fully into use. Each machine is designed for a specific operation. The operative is required to be proficient in one operation and on one machine only. Semi-skilled operators therefore form a high proportion of the workers in such a factory, women are quite commonly employed, and the role of the skilled man is one of supervision and maintenance. There is a very considerable difference between this type of factory and the 'jobbing' factory, yet both may be found as part of the engineering industry.

THE WAGE RATE STRUCTURE OF THE INDUSTRY[1]

Agreements in the engineering industry in Britain are negotiated between the Engineering and Allied Employers' National Federation and the Confedera-

---

[1] A rather longer discussion of this—though worked out in a rather different way—will be found in Knowles and Hill 'The Structure of Engineering Earnings' (*Bulletin*, September/October 1954).

tion of Shipbuilding and Engineering Unions. The former is a federation of forty-six regional employers' associations, and is the chief employers' organization in the industry; the latter is a confederation of thirty-nine unions who are affiliated on the basis of the estimated number of their members who work in the engineering industry. The Confederation does most of the negotiating in the industry on behalf of the unions. It is almost certainly a more loose-knit body than the Federation, if only because many of the unions in the Confederation have interests outside the industry, while the employers' associations are specific to the industry. The central organization of the Federation is on a larger scale than that of the Confederation.

In January 1954 1,054,000 adult male manual workers were employed in establishments of the Federation, while about one and a quarter million workers were represented by the Confederation.[1] It is difficult, as has been explained, to say just what proportion of the manual workers in the industry figures of this order represent. The estimate of male employment given at January 1954 by the Court of Inquiry was 2,298,000 male workers. If it is remembered that this will include staff employees and boys, then a comparison of this with the membership figures suggests that negotiations between the Federation and the Confederation affect directly more than half of the employees in the industry.

There are, however, a good number of firms outside the Federation, and therefore not direct participants in the collective bargains which are made. Some of these firms are very large and well-known, and negotiate quite separate agreements, which fix different terms and conditions. Generally these large firms offer a rather better agreement than that negotiated by the Federation. The other non-members are generally small firms. In either case, however, the agreements fixed by the Federation and the Confederation have an indirect effect. In the case of those large firms negotiating more favourable agreements, the conclusion of a new general bargain is made the occasion for reviewing their agreement. Other firms, while not directly subscribing to the agreement, must almost certainly observe it since it is the principal agreement for the industry, and constitutes the 'recognized terms and conditions' of employment in the industry. The 'fair wages clause' would prevent Government contracts going to those not observing it. If a dispute with a non-federated firm resulted in reference to arbitration, it seems certain that an arbitrating body would regard the general agreement as the standard reference point for what wages should be in the industry.

Agreements negotiated by the Federation and the Confederation are, therefore, the direct bargain struck on wages and conditions for manual workers in all Federated establishments, and are the point of reference for workers employed by firms outside the Federation. The agreements are

[1] Figures given in Cmd. 9084, op. cit.

negotiated by a special conference of Federation and Confederation representatives, which is called on receipt of a wage application made by letter from the Secretary of the Confederation to the Secretary of the Federation. These conferences, however, have failed to agree on a number of occasions, when the claim has been settled by arbitration or after a Court of Inquiry has made its recommendations.

The agreements are drawn up mainly in terms of two occupations: fitters and unskilled workers. Hence there is an assumption in the agreements that, if rates are arranged for fitters and for unskilled workers, then it will be possible to grade the rates for all other workers with reference to those for these two groups (the fitters being regarded as the 'representative' skilled grade); the rates for other occupations are alined to them in accordance with the extent to which the occupation in question is judged 'skilled' or 'unskilled'.

Most of the differential relationships between other occupations' rates and those of fitters or labourers are governed merely by local habits or by factory decisions; but some are based on more specific national agreements between the Federation and the union representing the occupation in question. The position of the patternmakers is governed by separate agreements which fix (a) a differential rate of a few shillings above the current fitters' rate, and (b) a supplementary bonus, which was originally calculated as a percentage on basic rates but is now a fixed sum.[1] Foundry workers have nationally agreed amounts as differentials between their rates and those of fitters and labourers. Therefore even where specific national arrangements are made for other occupations the rates thereby established are not independent of, but are related to, those of either fitters or labourers. In the occupations where no specific arrangement for differentials is established, the relationship to be determined is a matter for the factory management. The latest agreements have provided an increase for 'intermediate' grades between unskilled and skilled but have not specified the rate from which the increase is to be calculated in the occupations which fall into the 'intermediate' categories. Rates for 'semi-skilled' are, therefore, quite largely left to the factory to decide.

The agreements refer to two general categories of payments: payment on time-work, and payment-by-results. Time-workers are paid according to the amount of time they have put in during the week, while the wages of payment-by-results workers are related in some way to their output. The basic facts relating to national wage arrangements for the industry can therefore be put by giving the arrangements for four categories; namely time-working fitters, time-working unskilled workers, fitters paid under payment-by-results schemes, and unskilled workers paid under payment-by-results schemes.

Time-workers in the industry have a Consolidated Minimum Time Rate

---

[1] In 1955 the differential was 4s. 8¼d. and the supplementary bonus was 12s. 9¼d. making a total differential (outside London) of 17s. 5½d. over the fitters' rate.

for forty-four hours work, which was consolidated after negotiation in November 1950. The rates fixed then and alterations up to May 1957 are given in Table 1. There are also a number of district additions to these rates. These are generally only of a few pence per week, though in a few cases they amount to as much as a few shillings per week. Such district additions can be ignored here. Payment-by-results workers are paid, according to agreement, (1) a basic rate of 66s. for fitters and 51s. for unskilled workers, and (2) a payment-by-results workers' national bonus (or 'piece-work supplement'). The agreement of November 1950, which consolidated time rates, put the payment-by-results workers' bonus at 9d. per hour or 33s. per forty-four-hour week. Additions since that date are shown in Table 1. There is also what is known as a 'minimum piece-work standard', which from November 1950 has specified that 'piece-work prices or times must satisfy the condition that a worker of average ability will be in a position to earn at least 45 per cent on the existing basic rate' (that is, 66s. or 51s. plus 45 per cent). In all cases payment-by-results workers are guaranteed a minimum payment of the consolidated time rate for all hours worked, so that a payment-by-results worker's wage cannot fall below the entitlement of a time-worker for similar hours.

Table 1. *Consolidated minimum time rates and payment-by-results workers, supplements for skilled fitters and unskilled workers in the engineering industry, as laid down by national agreements from November* 1950 *to May* 1957

Date of agreement	Consolidated minimum time rates		Payment-by-results workers' supplements	
	Skilled fitters	Unskilled workers	Skilled fitters	Unskilled workers
	s. d.	s. d.	s. d.	s. d.
November 1950	118 0	100 0	33 0	33 0
November 1951	129 0	111 0	44 0	44 0
November 1952	136 4	118 4	51 4	51 4
April 1954	144 10	124 10	59 10	57 10
March 1955	155 10	132 10	70 10	65 10
March 1956	168 4	142 4	83 4	75 4
May 1957	179 4	151 4	94 4	84 4

Hours of work in the industry were fixed at forty-four per week in January 1947 and time rates are based on this length of week. According to agreement, overtime on weekdays is paid at 'time and a third' for the first two consecutive hours and 'time and a half' for additional hours. The five-day week is now widespread in the industry and involves an obligation to pay 'time and a half' for Saturday work. 'Double time' is paid for Sunday work. Since the system of paying premia for overtime is based on the granting of *additional* hours or fractions of hours of payment, overtime premia are sometimes described as 'given time' or 'allowance hours'. All premium payments for overtime (that is the extra third, half or one hour) fall to be paid at the consolidated minimum time rate—this applies to time-workers and payment-by-results workers alike. In the case of time-workers this means, for example, that a time-worker, whose week consisted of fifty hours, forty-four hours 'ordinary' time plus six hours overtime, of which three hours were worked consecutively on a week night and three hours were Sunday work, would be paid according to agreement fifty-four and one sixth hours at the consolidated time rate $[(44 \times 1) + (2 \times 1\frac{1}{3}) + (1 \times 1\frac{1}{2}) + (3 \times 2)]$. A payment-by-results worker working the same six hours overtime would receive four and a sixth hours payment at the consolidated time rate in addition to all his payments as a payment-by-results worker.

The national wage structure as laid down by agreements may now be summed up. The skilled fitter on time-work will receive (on the May 1957 agreement) 179s. 4d. for forty-four hours' work, and he will receive additional pay for the number of 'extra hours' to which his overtime working is equivalent. The unskilled time-worker's rate will be 151s. 4d. The skilled fitter on payment-by-results will receive for his forty-four hours' work a basic rate of 66s., a national bonus of 94s. 4d. and an amount of payment-by-results earnings based on a scheme which is designed to give a man of average ability 45 per cent on his basic rate. If, therefore, he is of 'average ability' he will get for forty-four hours' work a wage of 66s., plus 94s. 4d., plus 29s. 8d. (45 per cent of 66s.) which equals 190s. At the worst he will not fall below 179s. 4d. since he is guaranteed at least the time-worker's rate. A similar calculation for unskilled payment-by-results workers would be 51s. plus 84s. 4d. plus 23s. (45 per cent of 51s.) which equals 158s. 4d. During overtime hours payment-by-results workers would receive, in addition to normal hourly payments and payment-by-results earnings, an amount of 'given time' as an overtime premium calculated on the hourly consolidated time rate. The agreements deal principally with the rates for fitters and unskilled workers only. There are agreements which formally lay down the differentials to be maintained between these two occupations and one or two others (principally the patternmakers and foundry workers); but, with these few exceptions, occupations other than fitters and labourers have no specific rates or differentials prescribed by national agreement. The agreements fix the differential between skilled fitters and unskilled workers such that unskilled workers have time rates which are 84 per cent of those of skilled fitters, and unskilled payment-by-results workers of 'average ability' may expect 83 per cent of those of skilled workers. Skilled payment-by-results workers are intended to average 106 per cent of skilled time-workers.

It is important to see how much or how little resemblance there is between the original *formal* arrangements as described above, the actual situation in the industry as it appears in the industry's average earnings, and the actual situation in the factory as it appears in factory wage rates and earnings. It will be the task of the remainder of this chapter—and of the case studies in the two following chapters—to look more closely at the reality which lies beneath the simplicity of these national agreements.

THE EARNINGS STRUCTURE OF THE INDUSTRY[1]

The earnings of workers in the engineering industry (or industries) in Britain may be found, grouped in various averages, from two sources—the enquiries of the Ministry of Labour, conducted at six-monthly intervals, and the enquiries which have been undertaken from time to time by the Engineering and Allied Employers' National Federation, who have collected large quantities of information from their members.

Before this earnings material is discussed, however, it is worth noting that the rates prescribed by the agreements and discussed above would appear to be, very definitely tending to become 'minimum' rates, rather than rates normally paid as 'standard' in the industry—a fact for which there is now some recognition. According to evidence collected by the Federation from their members and submitted to the Court of Inquiry which met in January 1954, the workers who are on the negotiated rates are in a substantial minority. The Federation suggested that their enquiries had shown that in May 1950 only 3 per cent of skilled fitters employed in Federated firms were on the minimum (time) rate: the rest were either on payment-by-results or getting some form of additional rate. If time-workers only are considered, then the Federation enquiries shows that only 10 per cent received the minimum rate, 21 per cent received additions ranging from 1 to 13s. per week, and 69 per cent received additions of more than 13s. Only 13 per cent of unskilled labourers were on the minimum rate, all the rest had something extra; while, among time-working unskilled, 16 per cent received the bare rate, 55 per cent additions of from 1 to 13s. and, 29 per cent received additions of more than 13s. It would be difficult to determine without further investigation the exact form taken by these additional payments (the following case-studies give some examples). For time-workers, however, there must presumably be some form of additional rate. Whatever the exact form of the additional payments, however, the 1954 evidence indicates that earnings in the industry are well in excess of rates.[2]

[1] Much of the discussion in this section parallels and brings up to date material already used in two articles published in the *Bulletin* for June 1951 and July 1951 by Knowles and the present author 'Earnings in Engineering, 1926–1948' and 'Some Notes on Engineering Earnings'.

[2] The Court of Inquiry Report of May 1957 (Cmd. 159) stated that, according to information provided by the Federation, a survey taken in June 1956 indicated that only 2·3 per cent of fitters were on the minimum rate.

The major official source of data on earnings in British industry is the six-monthly Earnings and Hours Enquiries of the Ministry of Labour. These enquiries are recorded in terms of the S.I.C. Table 2 gives data relating to earnings and hours in the industry at April 1954 aggregated on the basis accepted by the Court of Inquiry of January 1954, and divided into four broad groups.[1]

Table 2. *Average earnings, hours and hourly earnings of adult males in the engineering industry, April* 1954 (*Ministry of Labour*)

Groups	Average weekly earnings	Average hours	Average hourly earnings
	£ s. d.	—	s. d.
Non-electrical engineering	10 10 2	49·1	4 3
Electrical engineering	10 9 6	48·1	4 4
Vehicles and aircraft	11 16 7	47·8	4 11
Other engineering and iron working	10 10 8	47·6	4 5
All engineering	10 17 4	48·4	4 6

This Table allows three general points to be made. First, average hours in the industry are well in excess of forty-four per week for adult males—though forty-four is the 'standard' working week. Secondly, there is a tendency for different sections of the industry to have rather different earnings prospects. It is not possible to be dogmatic about this, however, because of the influence of possible differences in the proportions of different types of worker (at different levels of payment) in each section.[2] Thirdly, average earnings in the

[1] The sub-headings in the S.I.C. included in 'engineering' by the Court of Inquiry were marine engineering, agricultural machinery, boilers and boilerhouse plant, machine tools, stationary engines, textile machinery, ordnance and small arms, constructional engineering and non-electrical engineering—all included in 'non-electrical engineering' in Table 2: electrical machinery, telegraphs and telephones, wireless apparatus, valves and electric lamps, batteries and accumulators, and other electrical goods—all included in 'electrical engineering' in Table 2: motor vehicles and cycles, aircraft manufacture, motor and aircraft parts and accessories, locomotive building, and railway carriages and wagons—all included in 'vehicles and aircraft' in Table 2: iron foundries, iron-and-steel forgings, wire manufacturers, other metal industries, scientific and other instruments, watches and clocks—all included in 'other engineering and iron working' in Table 2.

[2] Knowles and Hill ('Structure of Engineering Earnings', *Bulletin*, September/October 1954) discuss sectional earnings at some length. Their analysis shows considerable variation between earnings in different sections of the industry. This variation cannot be wholly accounted for by differences in hours worked in different sections, by differences in the proportions of different types of occupation, or by differences in regional location, though the variation is of course affected and modified by such factors. A further article by the same authors ('The Variability of Engineering Earnings', *Bulletin*, May 1956) takes this discussion further, and also makes a detailed study of the variability of earnings levels as between firms in the industry.

industry are well in excess of the levels fixed in the agreements. The skilled worker according to agreement had a minimum rate at this date of 144s. 10d. (3s. 3½d. per hour) if a time-worker; and, if of average ability as a payment-by-results worker, had a minimum level of 155s. 6d. (3s. 6½d. per hour). These averages are much in excess of what the agreements would suggest as the level of earnings even if all those included are skilled, whereas, in fact, the averages include semi-skilled and unskilled workers.

When we turn to the other principal source of information on earnings and hours in the engineering industry—the enquiries conducted by the Engineering and Allied Employers' National Federation—it is possible to take the story of the relation of earnings to rates several stages further.[1]

Table 3 analyses some of the Federation's figures for September 1956. These are set out to show the relation between wage rates and actual earnings for the two best-known occupational categories—fitters and labourers. The estimates of 'forty-four-hour earnings' were worked out by the Federation from returns made by member firms on a forty-four-hour basis.

Table 3. *National agreement wage rates, earnings, hours and 44-hour*
earnings of fitters and labourers, September 1956

	Fitters		Labourers	
	'Time'	'Payment by results'	'Time'	'Payment by results'
Average hours worked	49·4	47·5	49·4	49·6
Average weekly earnings	£13 8 7¼	£14 3 0¼	£9 18 7¼	£10 18 0¼
44-hour earnings	£11 4 7	£12 11 2	£8 5 0	£9 7 0
National agreement wage rates* (for 44 hours	£8 8 4	£8 19 0	£7 2 4	£7 9 4
44-hour earnings as percentage of wage rates	133%	140%	116%	125%

* For payment-by-results workers = basic rate plus national bonus plus 'minimum piece-work standard'.

This Table leaves no doubt that earnings are much higher than wage rates. Even if all money made on overtime is excluded, and earnings for forty-four hours only are considered, time-working fitters can earn on average 33 per cent above the rates and time-working labourers can make 16 per cent more than their rates. For payment-by-results workers the excess of earnings over 'rates' is even more marked, though the basis of calculation used here for the payment-by-results 'rates' is one that includes in the 'rate' the 'minimum

[1] Except where otherwise stated, figures up to 1948 are from K. G. J. C. Knowles and D. J. Robertson, 'Earnings in Engineering, 1926–1948', *Bulletin*, June 1951 (or the material used for it). Since 1948 figures are calculated from later Federation enquiries.

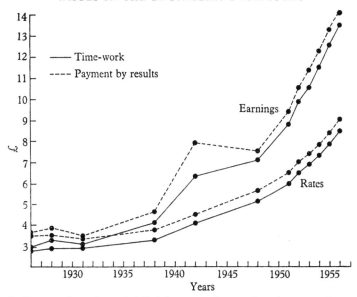

Fig. 1. Rates and earnings of skilled fitters on time-work and payment-by-results,
at various dates.

piece-work standard' (the amount—45 per cent— by which the piece-work
earnings of a worker of average ability should, according to agreement,
exceed the basic rate).

There are a number of other points of importance to be noted from Table
3. The actual earnings of skilled payment-by-results workers are larger, and
their hours of work shorter, than time-workers. Unskilled workers are less
fortunate than the skilled (fitters) in their ability to earn in excess of rates,
and they tend to have to work longer hours than skilled. For both fitters and
labourers, however, average hours are much in excess of forty-four hours,
which is the supposed standard working week (by negotiation).

The course of the relationship between rates and earnings of skilled fitters
may be traced in Figure 1. In the late 1920's and early 1930's earnings and
rates were close together; by 1938 the gap had widened, but the Figure makes
it clear that the big differences between rates and earnings in the industry
have arisen since the beginning of the war. While the gap between wage rates
and earnings is not entirely a war and post-war phenomenon, it is quite
largely so. This may be put down to full employment and its attendant labour
shortages, causing employers to pay wage rates in excess of those agreed
nationally, and causing an increase in overtime working. For payment-by-
results workers, the diagram also suggests a growing generosity in the reward
from incentive schemes.

The engineering industry has experienced a very considerable growth in

19

Table 4. *Wage rates and average weekly earnings of unskilled workers in* 1926, 1938, 1948 *and* 1954, *as percentage of fitters'*

Year	Unskilled as percentage of fitters'	
	Wage rates (Time-workers)	Average weekly earnings (Time and Payment-by-results together)
	%	%
1926 (October)	71·4	68·3
1938 (July)	75·8	68·8
1948 (January)	84·4	79·1
1954 (September)	86·2	75·0

the numbers of its semi-skilled workers. The presence of these intermediate grades has inevitably confused the nature of the relationship of the wage rates of unskilled to those of the skilled, by creating a number of steps between the quite unskilled worker and the fully skilled. But the gap between unskilled and skilled wage rates within which the semi-skilled rates have to be fixed has also diminished. Table 4 shows that the percentage gap between unskilled and skilled wage rates has been getting steadily smaller. The premium given for skill in the industry's wage rates is now much less than it was. The actual extent of the gap is however somewhat larger when earnings opportunities are taken into account. The skilled men have many more

Table 5. *Average weekly earnings of a number of occupations in relation to those of fitters, September* 1954

Occupation	Average weekly earnings			As percentage of fitters		
	Time	P. by R.	Time and P. by R. together	Time	P. by R.	Time and P. by R. together
	£ s. d.	£ s. d.	£ s. d.	%	%	%
Sheet-metal-workers (skilled)	11 9 11¼	12 19 6	12 12 7¼	99·8	105·8	105·3
Toolroom fitters and turners	12 13 0	13 1 0	12 15 6½	109·8	106·4	106·5
Moulders (loose pattern)	10 3 4¼	12 4 6½	11 13 10¼	88·3	99·7	97·5
Patternmakers	11 11 2	11 9 6¾	11 10 4	100·3	93·6	96·0
Turners and machinemen (rated at or above fitters' rate)	11 2 0¾	12 5 2¾	11 19 8	96·4	100·0	99·9
Fitters (other than toolroom)	11 10 4½	12 5 3¼	11 19 10¼	*100*	*100*	*100*
Platers, riveters and caulkers	11 2 7¼	12 2 10¼	11 17 2	96·6	99·0	98·9
Turners and machinemen (rated below fitters' rate)	9 6 1¼	11 2 0¾	10 17 4¾	80·8	90·5	90·6
Labourers	8 16 4	9 14 1	9 0 1¼	76·5	79·1	75·1

opportunities for increasing their income through incentive scheme payments than the unskilled, so that, despite the fact that the unskilled tend to work longer hours, a circumstance which is evident in Table 3 and in all statistics of the industry, there is a wider difference between their earnings and those of the skilled than there is between their rates. Of all groups, the semi-skilled tend to be most frequently on incentive payment. In consequence the gap between them and the skilled, which is already small in terms of rates, is very small if not (on occasion) non-existent in earnings.

So far the statistics have been for only two occupational groups—fitters and labourers. As Table 5 indicates, the average earnings of other occupational groups do not always correspond to those of the two groups mentioned so far.

The information set out in this Table requires little verbal amplification. The semi-skilled group corresponds very roughly indeed to that labelled 'turners and machinemen (rated below fitters' rate)'. The rather narrow differential between these people and the skilled groups in these industry-wide averages is evident. The somewhat lowly position of the patternmakers in these figures, despite their having the longest apprenticeship, is worthy of attention.

The proportion of payment-by-results workers in the engineering industry is increasing due to marked extensions in the use of and the popularity of incentive schemes. The contrast between the earnings of payment-by-results workers and those of time-workers has already been mentioned: in view of the extension of payment-by-results schemes it is worth elaborating this earnings relationship.

Table 6. *Average weekly earnings and hours worked of fitters on payment-by-results, as percentage of earnings and hours of time-workers in 1926, 1928, 1938, 1948 and 1954*

| Year | Payment-by-results workers as percentage of time-workers | |
	Average weekly earnings	Average hours worked
	%	%
1926 (October)	122	98
1928 (October)	117	97
1938 (July)	115	98
1948 (January)	107	96
1954 (September)	106	97

Table 6 makes it clear that the differential of the earnings of payment-by-results workers over those of time-workers is diminishing at least for fitters,

c

though it has been consistently true that these earnings have been obtained for fewer hours of work. Two possible explanations for this partial coming together of the time-workers' and payment-by-results workers' earnings can be suggested. In the first place an increase in the proportion of those on payment-by-results has meant that incentive schemes have been extended beyond those for whom they were originally thought suitable, and this may possibly have led to a diminution in the average ability of the men to earn bonus, and in the average ability of the work to provide bonus.

This explanation is doubtful, however, and the second possibility is the much more relevant and important one. It is that the distinction between time-workers and payment-by-results workers has itself become blurred. Along with the shift in emphasis from time-work to payment-by-results work in engineering factories, which has accompanied the growing use of incentive schemes, has gone a tendency to think up ways of compensating the time-worker who misses the extra earnings opportunities of payment-by-results. This process sometimes takes the form of considerably enhancing the time-worker's rate above the national level, but probably the major item is the enhancement of the time-worker's earnings by some form of indirect bonus, so that it has now become broadly true that the payment-by-results worker receives a direct bonus, while the time-worker is a man who gets time rates plus some less direct kind of extra bonus. It would be impossible without vastly more detailed knowledge to take this statement further: the bonuses paid to time-workers in practice may take all sorts of forms. The most formal recognition of the need to enhance time-workers' earnings is the 'lieu' bonus—a bonus payable in lieu of payment-by-results earnings—but there are innumerable less formal ways of paying indirect bonuses.

Table 6 is drawn up for fitters only. The same tendency for the differences between the earnings of payment-by-results workers and time-workers to diminish exists also for unskilled workers, but not for the semi-skilled. The explanation for its non-appearance in the case of the semi-skilled group may almost certainly be traced to the distinctions between the two principal types of workers who compose the semi-skilled engineering category. These groups are the semi-skilled machine operators, who are almost universally on bonus work, and the storemen, progress men, cranemen, drivers and other such workers whose functions are auxiliary to the production process and who tend to be largely on fixed time rates and, compared to the machine operators, relatively badly paid.

One further general point about earnings in the engineering industry, based on the Federation's data, remains to be made, namely, that earnings vary considerably between areas. Table 7 shows earnings averages in a number of areas.

The range of averages between £12 7s. 8d. for the West Midlands area and

22

£10 1*s.* 4*d.* for the Yorkshire area is an adequate illustration of the diversity of area earnings. The areas shown here, and the method of calculating their averages are the same as those in an earlier article by Knowles and the present author.[1] In that article will be found an historical account of these area differences. Area differences are by no means new, and while the exact order

Table 7. *Average weekly earnings by area, September* 1954

Area	Average weekly earnings	Area	Average weekly earnings
	£ *s.* *d.*		£ *s.* *d.*
Western Area	11 0 1	Yorkshire	10 1 4
Southern Area	11 6 5	N.W. Coast	10 9 1
London	11 11 2½	N.E. Coast	10 19 1
West Midlands	12 7 8	Scotland	10 10 5
East Midlands	11 4 7	N. Ireland	10 7 2
Eastern Area	10 19 5		
Lancs. and Cheshire	10 18 5		
		Area average	11 4 8

of areas has altered, there is a certain constancy about their relationship. Broadly speaking, higher earnings are now usual in the London and Midlands areas as against other parts of the country.

To some extent this difference in the level of area averages of earnings reflects the section of the industry which is at work in the area.[2] Certainly the level of earnings in the highest earnings district of the Federation has been closely related to its being connected with the well-paid motor car section of the industry.[3] But the general level of the activity and of the capacity to pay high wages of the regional economy in which any engineering factory finds itself must be taken into account in considering the level of earnings in the engineering industry. For example, since the general level of earnings in Scotland is some 5 or 6 per cent lower than the average for England and Wales,[4] it is not surprising that engineering factories in Scotland, whatever branch of the industry they may belong to, can obtain workers at an earnings level which is lower than the English average.

[1] K. G. J. C. Knowles and D. J. Robertson, 'Earnings in Engineering, 1926–1948', loc. cit.
[2] This point is discussed at length in Knowles and Hill, op. cit.
[3] The figures for this district are illustrated in Knowles and Robertson, 'Some Notes on Engineering Earnings', op. cit.
[4] Cf. chapters on 'Wages' and on 'Incomes' by D. J. Robertson and A. D. Campbell respectively in *The Scottish Economy*, op. cit., and D. J. Robertson, 'Incomes in the United Kingdom and Scotland 1949–1950 and 1954–1955.' *Scottish Journal of Political Economy*, October 1957.

CONCLUSIONS

The more important points made in this chapter may now be summarized.

1. 'The engineering industry' is statistically most difficult to define.

2. The most useful indicators to whether a factory is part of the engineering industry or not are

(*a*) whether it is working with metal,

(*b*) whether the product can be broadly described as machinery or power unit (or as part of these),

(*c*) whether the factory is, or could be, covered by the wage agreements of the industry, and the industry's Employers' Federation.

(*d*) whether the 'engineering trades' are employed in the factory.

3. Despite some unifying principles as mentioned above, the industry is extremely diversified, not only by product (and especially size of product), but also by methods of working (jobbing, batch and mass production) and by the composition of the factory labour force (especially the proportions of semi-skilled and women).

4. The engineering industry's national agreements on wages, negotiated by the Employers' Federation **and** the Confederation of Shipbuilding and Engineering Unions, are framed mainly in terms of time rates for skilled fitters and unskilled workers, and of basic rates, national bonuses, and 'minimum piece-work standards' for payment-by-results workers in the same occupations. Forty-four hours is the standard working week.

5. Earnings enquiries suggest that extra payments of all kinds are very common. Earnings are considerably above rates.

6. Hours worked in the industry tend at present to be in excess of forty-four.

7. Different sections of the industry have different earnings prospects.

8. The gap between earnings and rates has grown considerably since before the war.

9. The difference between the earnings of skilled, semi-skilled and unskilled workers has been declining.

10. Payment-by-results workers tend to earn more than time-workers and to work shorter hours. This difference has declined principally because the distinction between payment-by-results and time-work has become obscured.

11. Earnings averages in the industry vary between different parts of the country.

CHAPTER 3

WAGES IN AN ENGINEERING FACTORY: I

This chapter and the next are case-studies describing the pattern of wages in two large engineering factories. As such their content is largely descriptive and their conclusions are factual. It is not possible without betraying confidences to be too specific about the type of work done by these factories, or to give their location. They are both, however, in the heavier section of the engineering industry and are engaged in making producers' rather than consumers' goods. Their work is batch production or jobbing rather than mass production. They employ relatively fewer women than would be average for the industry as a whole, and have probably a higher ratio of skilled labour.

Table 8. *The composition of the labour force* in the factory, April* 1953

Adult males						Categories	Totals
Skilled		Semi-skilled		Unskilled			
Occupation	No.	Occupation	No.	Occupation	No.		
Pattern-makers	66	Machinemen	308	Storemen	82	Adult males	1956
Fitters	493	Dressers	73	Labourers	288	Females	31
Turners	188	Cranemen & Drivers	77	Others§	20	Juveniles	490
Moulders	80	Others‡	72				
Others†	209						
Total	1036	Total	530	Total	390	Factory Total	2477

* All wage-earning employees—i.e. all employees in the works below the rank of foreman.
† Includes joiners, coppersmiths, welders, platers, flame-cutters, blacksmiths, sheet-metal-workers, building trades, and inspectors.
‡ Includes progress men, furnacemen, firemen, coppersmith's helpers, strikers and asbestos workers.
§ Attendants, productive unskilled labour, and hammer drivers.

The first factory is engaged in high-quality engineering production. While there are many repetition jobs, which are handled by batch production methods, such as semi-skilled work on automatic turret-lathes; nevertheless, the flow of work is highly variable, so that jobbing is more frequent than batch production. The composition of the labour force is given in Table 8.

The firm employs all the basic engineering trades in high proportions, and

25

over half of the adult male employees of the factory are skilled. In this type of factory (and in the industry generally—except perhaps in the newer sections of it), a skilled man has almost invariably served his apprenticeship: this is the division observed in Table 8 and throughout these case-studies. Semi-skilled men have some training or expertise, but do not have the all-round knowledge of their job which the tradesman is held to acquire during his apprenticeship. In an engineering works a large number of these are machinemen, who have been trained to operate a machine, or have become expert in so doing, but are not expected to have any wider understanding. In this factory over half of the semi-skilled are machinemen. Similarly, dressers (who 'clean-up' castings which come from the foundry), cranemen, and drivers have to be expert but do not need an apprenticeship. The other occupations classified as semi-skilled in Table 8 are of a varied character, and some borderline divisions were made between them and the 'other' unskilled. Most unskilled in the factory are, however, either labourers or untrained storemen.

In order to compare the actual pattern of wages which is found to exist in an engineering factory with the formal pattern which appears in the nationally negotiated agreements of the industry, this study examines first the wage-rates actually fixed in the factory, to discover whether their operation coincides with, or conflicts with, that of the national agreements. It then looks at data on earnings of workers in the factory to discover how they are made up, how those of different occupations are related to each other, the number of hours actually worked, the importance of overtime, and so on.

The major source of this information was the wage-and-clock-cards, which are kept by and for all wage-earning employees in the factory. For each week there are well over two thousand clock-cards, and, since at one point or another in what follows, thirteen different weeks at the end of 1952 and in the early part of 1953 are mentioned, the main data analysed consisted of a collection of between twenty-six and thirty thousand wage-and-clock-cards. Needless to say, it was necessary to use sampling techniques to work with these cards. This material was supplemented by informal enquiries and discussions and by various less comprehensive records. The most important further source used was an enquiry which the management undertook in August 1951, in which they separated out the different rates payable to different groups of people in each occupation, and the numbers on each rate.

The average weekly earnings of adult males in the factory in the last week in March 1953 were £10 18s. 0d. The average weekly earnings of adult males in the engineering group of industries at April 1953, as given in the Ministry of Labour Earnings Enquiries, were £9 16s. 0d. On the other hand, hours worked in this factory were longer than those given as average by the Ministry of Labour (the factory average was 52·5 and the Ministry's figure was 48·2), so that the hourly earnings average for the factory was actually below that given by the Ministry. The average earnings of skilled men in the factory were £11 16s. 0d., whereas a similar average, based on the Engineering and Allied Employers' National Federation's enquiries for June 1953, gave the lower figure of £11 1s. 9d.; but hours were substantially higher in the factory, and hourly earnings were lower. Similar findings apply to the semi-skilled and unskilled groups. Hours worked in this factory are therefore longer than national figures would suggest to be usual (though not all sections of the industry have the same experience in these matters, and the factory does belong to a section where hours have been tending to be rather longer). If, however, these longer hours are discounted in the averages of earnings, there does not appear to be any very substantial difference between earnings in the factory and those averaged by the industry generally. This factory is therefore reasonably typical in respect of its earnings, except that the importance of overtime will be exaggerated relative to average experience. It will not provide a good measure of the extent of overtime work, but will be a good case in which to study the influence of overtime.

GENERAL DISCUSSION OF WAGE ARRANGEMENTS IN THE FACTORY

In this factory, most of the workers are on payment-by-results in order, in the management's view, to maximize output.[1] Most of the time-workers are unskilled labourers, though a number of semi-skilled ancillary workers, such as cranemen and drivers, and some maintenance tradesmen, are also on time-work.

While there are a number of systems of payment by results in use in the factory, the normal method used is based on calculations of time allowances for different jobs.[2] Particular operations can be timed by a stop watch; but usually, in this factory, they are assessed by a skilled tradesman of superior ability who estimates the time necessary—this individual is known as a rate-fixer. Times allowed for specific operations are carefully filed away in the Production Engineer's Department. The time allowed for any particular job is usually a synthesis of times allowed, and recorded in a master index, for the operations which go to make up the job. Where the job is one that is frequently repeated, then a standard 'card' showing the time allowed for it is

[1] This attitude towards output incentives in the management of this factory has to be squared with the strong emphasis on skill which has already been mentioned.

[2] A system of time allowances is used in preference to piece-work because the varying nature of the tasks falling to operatives would make it necessary to build up a list of prices for particular jobs, which might never be repeated, or, which may only be repeated after a long interval, in which changes in wage levels may require the price to be altered. In contrast, times need not be altered for changes in wage levels since a 'time' can be referred to any wage level.

prepared. Once a job has been assessed and a time placed upon it as the 'time allowed' to the worker to complete the job, 'time saved' on a job can be found by subtracting 'time taken' from 'time allowed'. A number of more or less ingenious ways of combining 'time taken', 'time saved', and 'time allowed' to give a payments system are used in industry; however, the method used is essentially simple in this factory, since 100 per cent of the time saved is paid for—'100-per-cent bonus' system. The worker is paid at a certain rate for the time he has been at work (time taken), and a bonus of so many hours (bonus hours) at a certain rate for the time he has saved. Bonus hours are equal to the actual difference between the time allowed, for all the jobs undertaken during the pay period, and the time actually taken or actually worked. Generally the individual is separately assessed, but sometimes a group may be given a job and the time saved assessed for the group.

Other systems of bonus are also used in the factory. For example, outdoor repair-workers are given bonus on what appears to be a rather arbitrary allocation of 'days' of bonus. Some groups have an indirect bonus assessed on the output of the shop in general, and are allocated bonus-hours, or given a 'bonus rate', on this basis. Indeed it is by no means necessarily the case that each man has only one bonus system applied to him, since workers may quite easily be subject to one major form of bonus, such as described here, along with several minor varieties. For example, a man could be on individual bonus, assessed as described above, but also be subject to a type of group bonus whereby, if the output of his section goes beyond a certain level, he will get an addition to his basic rate. He might also be subject to a long-term holiday bonus, which is credited to individuals week-by-week as output for large groups keeps above a certain level, and which has an increasing rate of addition for specially high output. The management have a considerable tendency to superimpose new bonus practices on top of the existing system, with the result that a very complex and rapidly changing system may readily develop.

As well as being subject to more than one bonus system, the payment-by-results worker in the factory has more than one rate. Three rates are quoted on each payment-by-results worker's wage-and-clock-card, and all are necessary to the calculation of the wage. The basic rate is used in wage calculation solely to enable the payment of bonus to be worked out (that is it is the rate which is used in association with 'bonus hours' to give the due bonus payment). A different rate is used to determine the basic payment for hours worked by payment-by-results workers, and this includes the national bonus, which is payable by the hour in addition to basic rates. The third rate which is required for wage calculation is the overtime or nightshift premium rate. National agreements specify that the premium or allowance payments (of given time) for overtime or nightshift are to be based on the time-worker's rate for the

28

appropriate grade.[1] Hence, though the man may be a payment-by-results worker, nevertheless a time-worker's rate must also be given on his wage-card. Despite this complexity, it will be generally sufficient here to consider only the basic rate, since, even though substantially different from the overtime premium rate, it differs from the basic rate, including national bonus, by a fixed and determined amount.

WAGE RATES IN THE FACTORY

The discussion that follows is concerned with payment-by-results workers' basic rates.[2] Table 9 shows the distribution of basic weekly wage-rates by

Table 9. *Distribution of basic weekly wage rates by occupation, August 1951 : payment-by-results workers*

Rates	Occupations							Unskilled
	Skilled					Semi-skilled		
	Pattern-makers	Fitters	Turners	Moulders	Others*	Machine-men	Others*	
48s. 11¾d.–52s. 11¾d.							*36‡*	
52s. 11¾d.–56s. 11¾d.							2	1
56s. 11¾d.–60s. 11¾d.						8	5	44
60s. 11¾d.–64s. 11¾d.						3	*42*	8
64s. 11¾d.–68s. 11¾d.		*216*	*14*		8	*178*	33	4
68s. 11¾d.–72s. 11¾d.		*145*	*86*		*102*	*79*	2	
72s. 11¾d.–76s. 11¾d.	*53†*	11	97	68	5	5		1
76s. 11¾d.–80s. 11¾d.	6	9	9	10	1			
80s. 11¾d.–84s. 11¾d.		3	2					
84s. 11¾d.–88s. 11¾d.			1					

* 'Others' signifies the same occupational groupings as are defined in the footnotes to Table 8, except that dressers, cranemen and drivers are included in other semi-skilled.

† In the case of all the italic figures, one-third or more of the total number employed in the occupation are paid at the same rate which falls within the appropriate range (for example one-third or more patternmakers are paid at the same rate which lies somewhere between 72s. 11¾d. and 76s. 11¾d.

‡ This low-rated group arose out of an unusual situation which has now been altered.

[1] The arrangements for the payment of premia for overtime and nightshift working in the factory are in principle the same as in the national agreements. These premia are paid at the time rate, though it may, as has been mentioned, sometimes differ from that prescribed in the agreement. One-fifth of an hour's payment is paid as premium for nightshift hours. One-third is paid for the first two hours consecutive overtime working on weekdays, and one-half for any further time spent working overtime on the same weekday occasion. Premium is paid hour for hour for Sunday work (double time). There is *no* working on Saturday, except in exceptional and unusual circumstances.

[2] No analysis of time-workers' rates is made in this chapter, since a majority of the time-workers in the factory are unskilled workers employed at a rate only slightly above that given in the national agreement. There is no clear pattern in the time rates of skilled and semi-skilled workers employed on time-work, simply because they are a very mixed group, mainly of ancillary workers, kept on time rates because they cannot be brought into any payment-by-results scheme.

occupations. It is based on an enquiry undertaken by the factory management in August 1951. The rates for each group have been arranged in distributions falling within 4s. ranges. As Footnote † to the Table indicates, certain occupations show a concentration on particular rates within these ranges.

The occupations given in the Table have been arranged (no doubt arbitrarily and roughly) in descending order of skill status from left to right. There appears to be some correlation between skill status and rates; but there is a considerable spread of rates in each occupation. In some occupations this spread is not large (for example, patternmakers are mainly at the same level with only a few superior-rated men); but in others there is quite a wide spread of rates (for example, the turners and machinemen). As a general effect, these spreads mean that while there is a descent in the level of rates as skill descends from left to right, there are many cases in which rates for people on a lower level exceed rates of some on a higher level of skill.

While there is a spread of rates in most occupations, there are nevertheless 'salient' rates in most cases (as the italics in the Table suggest). In the case of the patternmakers the salient rate (73s. 4d.) is almost the only rate. Fitters have two salient rates (69s. 8d. and 66s. 1½d.) separated by well over 3s. a week (with consequent effect on bonus earning power); but 7 per cent of the total number employed are not on either of the two salient rates. Turners also have two salient rates (73s. 4d. and 69s. 8d.) but, a large proportion (26 per cent) are on neither of these rates. Moulders have a high proportion on one salient rate—75s. 2d. Machinemen have a concentration at 66s. 1½d. but also have many other rates.

These salient rates provide useful data for comparison with national agreement arrangements for wage rates (as modified by very small district additions). The craft differential for patternmakers and moulders above the district fitters' rate of 66s. 1½d. was at this time generally recognized to be 4s. 8¼d., so that for these two groups the national arrangements suggest a rate of 70s. 9¾d.[1] In fact, both of these groups have clear salient rates, and both are above the national (but by differing amounts). The fitters have quite a large number at the agreement rate, but also have a large number above it. The turners, who are generally thought in discussions at national level to have similar rates to fitters, have very few people at the agreed fitter's rate. Labourers, who have national and district agreements which prescribed 51s. 4½d. as the district rate at this time, are well above this. The national agreements at this time had little to say about semi-skilled rates.

Wage rates are, in a sense, labels marking the status of the workers concerned. This is explicitly recognized by differentials in national agreements. Here there are three separate status ranking devices to be compared and

---

[1] Though for patternmakers on time-work, a further supplementary bonus is payable, by agreement, in addition to their rate.

discussed, the national ranking by national rates, the actual ranking by this factory's wage structure expressed by the spread of rates and the salient rates, and the ranking implicit in the ordering of Table 9.

The patternmakers have long enjoyed the title of the aristocracy of the engineering industry and have thus been accorded pride of place in Table 9: in general, this is borne out by the relative position of their wage rates. The fitters, on the other hand, are usually thought of as the typical engineering craft, and hence the best craft for national arrangements to agree upon. Thus it might be assumed that, although slightly less than those of the *élite* (the patternmakers) their rates would set the levels for other skilled rates. In fact, however, they are almost alone among the skilled trades in having a large number paid not more than the agreed rate; while the turners have very few at the basic level, have a number at the upper salient rate for fitters, and yet more at a higher salient rate. This is surprising, since fitters and turners are referred to so frequently in combination that there is little doubt that they are popularly thought to be on the same level. Indeed, any separation of them would give the turners slightly less eminence, partly because of the stigma of being a 'machine' trade instead of 'working with their hands', and partly too because it is one of the industry's beliefs that fitters can 'go places' much more readily than turners. The description 'engineer' is much more readily applied to fitters than to turners. In one sense fitters certainly have more opportunities for advancement, since their apprenticeship is a well-recognized road to the job of sea-going engineer. In this factory the 'machine stigma' does not seem to exist; or if it does, does not reflect itself in wage rates.[1]

In the case of moulders, the rates shown here and laid down in national agreements do not correspond well with the position they are generally accorded by workers in the industry. Apprentices to moulding are difficult to get since it is a 'dirty job'. They are not enthusiastic attenders at night-classes. There is evidence that the industry regards moulders as people trained to do a particular job rather than as skilled and knowledgeable. On the other hand, the unpopularity of the moulder's trade may itself necessitate the payment of a differential to secure adequate supply.

Machinemen are the only semi-skilled group separately shown in Table 9. Since they are semi-skilled they are reckoned to have less adaptability and

---

[1] A factory record which was available showed that in March 1953 turners' rates exceeded the district basic rate for two reasons: (a) a 'skilled machine-rate'—which is not an addition for individual skill, but a premium attached to certain machines and payable to any operative working these machines; and (b) an incentive bonus rate—an arrangement whereby groups of operatives working particular types of machines are able to enhance their bonus earnings by being granted an incentive bonus rate of a penny or twopence an hour. This suggests that enhanced rates for turners are due largely to their being men who work on machines.

understanding than the skilled men. Yet, in this factory's rate structure, with very few exceptions, they are given at least the nationally agreed basic skilled rate (though they have no representatives in the highest rate categories). In fact, their rate position is very similar indeed to that of the fitters. Their association with the turners, since they generally work on machines beside turners, may have allowed them to partake of the upward thrust of rates enjoyed by that group. Working on a machine may in itself have been held to be a sufficient criterion for an increase in rates. Whatever it is, these semi-skilled men have skilled rates, and there is small sign of a skill differential or reward for apprenticeship in this rate structure, particularly when machine-men are compared with fitters (the 'representative skilled group').

Table 10. *Average hours worked, average gross weekly earnings, and average 44-hour earnings by occupation in a sample of adult male workers, March* 1953

Occupations	Number in sample	Average hours worked	Average gross weekly earnings	Average 44-* hour earnings
			£ s. d.	£ s. d.
Patternmakers	13	43·9	10 2 0	10 4 0
Fitters	97	53·0	11 18 0	8 17 0
Turners	37	51·8	12 8 0	9 8 0
Moulders	16	50·2	11 5 0	9 1 0
Other skilled†	39	48·8	11 16 0	9 11 0
Total skilled	202	51·4	11 16 0	9 8 0
Machinemen	61	51·4	10 18 0	8 9 0
Other semi-skilled†	46	54·5	10 9 0	7 3 0
Total semi-skilled	107	52·7	10 14 0	7 18 0
Unskilled	73	55·0	8 10 0	5 17 0
TOTAL	382	52·5	10 18 0	7 18 0

* 'Earnings in a forty-four-hour week' was derived in each case by subtracting from the gross earnings of the worker the amount of his 'allowance time' payments (i.e.—premium payments for overtime—or possibly nightshift—hours of work), dividing the remainder by the number of hours actually worked, and multiplying the resultant hourly earnings figure by forty-four.

† As defined in previous Tables.

EARNINGS AND HOURS

The task of analysing earnings, and the associated question of hours actually worked, is undertaken in this section by means of a one-in-five sample of the wage-and-clock-cards of the wage-earning labour force of the factory (that is below foreman level) for the last week in March 1953.[1] The basic results of the sample are shown in Table 10.

Actual earnings of workers in this factory are well above those indicated by agreements. The payment-by-results worker of average ability at this time was expected to earn 147s. 2½d. if skilled, and 125s. 10d. if unskilled: the actual earnings of these men are on average well above this, whether taken gross or on a forty-four-hour basis.

The amount, which is of most importance and relevance to the individual worker, is the pay he goes home with at the end of the week. It varies according to hours worked and to effort, but it determines the individual worker's living standard. This 'take-home pay', to use an American expression, is reduced by a number of factors which are not dealt with here, for example National Insurance, Income Tax and hospital benefits, so that average gross weekly earnings as given in this Table are not a complete estimate of its average level, though they are the nearest approximation available. The averages for total skilled, semi-skilled and unskilled show a skill differential. Between unskilled and skilled, there is a fairly wide gap—wider than the 80–85 per cent figures commonly quoted as the post-war level of this differential. There is rather a small gap, however, between the skilled and semi-skilled. In their average gross weekly earnings the patternmakers have not succeeded in matching their pre-eminent skill status with an appropriate weekly income.

But the influence of hours worked and of the frequent complicating factor of overtime cannot be ignored. On the evidence of this week, those with lowest rates and least skill status work longer hours. The average hours worked of skilled are one and a half less than those of semi-skilled, and three and a half less than unskilled. In almost every case here, those groups who fare badly in their earnings in forty-four hours of work compensate by heavier overtime working. Hence the earnings pattern which appears in gross earnings is very different from that for forty-four hours of work and is subject to this compensating effort. Final judgements on the differentials established between groups cannot be formed solely on the basis of gross earnings: on the basis of the same number of hours worked, the differentials between groups are much more clearly marked. This is, in many ways, a fairer test of the way in which skill is remunerated, since it represents a comparison of remuneration for effort, which, if not the same in each case, is at least based on equal hours of work.

Most of the workers in the sample have elements of payment-by-results in their pay packet; but the unskilled are largely on time wages, and so are

[1] The details of this sample are as follows. Cards for women and juveniles, and for men who had been off for more than two days, were excluded. The remainder were arranged by occupations (which are numbered); within each occupation they were arranged by departments (which are also numbered); and, within each department, by clock numbers. A one in five sample was taken from the cards after this sorting process had been completed.

numbers of the 'other semi-skilled'. For this reason, these two groups are specially interesting. They are the lowest paid groups and they work the longest hours. The 'other semi-skilled' include several ancillary occupations working what are relatively very long hours indeed. The unskilled, on average, work the longest hours of all. The marked differentials between the unskilled group and the rest are symptomatic of the present tendency in the industry, to define as unskilled only the lowliest of occupations, and to give all others a semi-skilled rating, with the consequence that the unskilled are paid distinctly less than all others.

Table 11. *Average composition of earnings by skill category of those whose bonus is recorded on the wage-and-clock-cards of the sample**

	Skilled	Semi-skilled	Unskilled	Total
Number so remunerated in sample	136	71	17	224
Average hours worked	50·2	53·1	58·0	51·7
Amounts (to nearest shilling):	£ s. d.	£ s. d.	£ s. d.	£ s. d.
Average payment of basic rates† for hours worked	7 6 0	7 6 0	7 10 0	7 6 0
Average bonus payments	3 8 0	2 14 0	1 10 0	3 1 0
Average allowance time payments‡	1 2 0	1 4 0	1 8 0	1 3 0
Average gross earnings	11 16 0	11 4 0	10 8 0	11 10 0
As percentage of gross earnings:	%	%	%	%
Average payments of basic rates				
(a) for forty-four hours§	54·2	54·1	54·7	54·0
(b) for remaining hours	7·7	11·1	17·4	9·5
Average bonus payments				
(a) for forty-four hours§	25·2	20·0	10·9	22·6
(b) for remaining hours	3·6	4·1	3·5	3·9
Average allowance time payment	9·3	10·7	13·5	10·0
Average gross earnings	100%	100%	100%	100%

* This means, roughly speaking, all those remunerated on direct bonus. It excludes some who are on other forms of bonus. (For example, those who are given a factory average bonus, which is stable for a month or two at a time, have their bonus expressed as a rate for purposes of wage-calculation—and, hence, no bonus appears on their wage-and-clock-cards.)

† Basic rates for payment-by-results workers and national bonus addition.

‡ Premium rates for overtime or nightshift work (at one-fifth, one-third, one-half, or one times ordinary time rate). There are some nightshift elements included, but the figures refer mainly to overtime premia.

§ The amounts involved were divided to show the percentage due to 'forty-four hours' and 'other hours' as a rough indication of the additions earned in overtime working. This makes two assumptions: first, that overtime working is not combined with short-time on ordinary hours which, as later indicated, is not strictly true; and, secondly, that the rate of bonus earning is the same in overtime as in ordinary hours. (There is no evidence on this.)

The forty-four-hour earnings figures for the skilled groups yield two further points. First, the leading position of the patternmakers is clearly in evidence in forty-four-hour comparisons. Their relinquishment of the lead in gross earnings is due to the almost complete absence of overtime working. Secondly, the preferential position of the turners as against the fitters, which was noted in the examination of basic rates, is also evident in their earnings in similar numbers of hours.

Comparison of the wages of groups in the factory's labour force is handicapped by the existence of several forms of payments which go into their earnings. What is true, when comparisons are based on one set of wage payments, may no longer be true when other payments are brought in, so that the relative importance of each source of payment needs to be known. Table 11 gives the composition of earnings of each of the skilled groups.

Table 11 relates mainly to direct bonus employees, because the relevant information is not given on the wage-and-clock-cards for the others. While this means the omission of a number of workers who were included in the sample, especially unskilled who were mainly on time rates, it provides a comparison of earnings on direct bonus with the more general figures of Table 10. The earnings of semi-skilled and unskilled direct bonus employees are higher than those for all persons in the group. For the semi-skilled this may be no more than a reflection of longer hours worked; but, the few unskilled who are on direct bonus have been enabled to raise their earnings well above the level of their fellows. In the skilled group, the direct bonus employees have made the same earnings in shorter hours.

The percentages of gross earnings given in Table 11 show that basic rate payments (including the national bonus) made for the normal hours of work account for little more than half gross earnings. Bonus earned during normal hours amounts to about a quarter of gross earnings for skilled workers, rather less for semi-skilled and decisively less for unskilled workers. The effect of overtime is shown in three ways, by the increase in normal rates payable for extra hours, by the increase in opportunity to earn bonus, and by the payment of premium rates. These together range in importance from about 20 per cent of gross earnings for skilled to about 35 per cent for unskilled, with the premium rate element ranging from about half all overtime earnings, in the case of the skilled, to rather less for unskilled.

These facts suggest three important generalizations. First, in the case of these workers, only slightly over half of average gross income consisted of a sum which they could rely on without fail, provided they turned up for their normal day's work. The rest was capable of variation. While, if their bonus fell too drastically, they would revert to a time wage, nevertheless, as things stood, all, except the half or so of their income which was due to basic rates and national bonus, could be considered as uncertain and variable. Secondly, the influence of overtime and bonus earnings differs between occupations; the latter is more important for skilled and becomes least important for unskilled, while the reverse is true of overtime earnings. Thirdly, overtime is of very great importance in gross earnings, not only because it is paid at premium rates, but because it means extra hours of pay and of bonus.

Table 12. *Average hours worked, average overtime hours and average short-time hours of skilled categories in the sample*

Skill category	Number in sample	Average overtime hours worked	Average short-time hours	Average hours worked
Skilled	202	8·1	0·7	51·4
Semi-skilled	107	9·3	0·6	52·7
Unskilled	73	11·3	0·3	55·0
Total	382	9·1	0·6	52·5

Table 12 analyses the overtime and short-time working of the three skill categories.[1] Hours of overtime rise as skill declines, but in each category overtime is slightly offset by short-time during ordinary hours (on the part of other workers in the same group, or by the same workers who also do overtime). The skilled have more short-time than either semi-skilled or un-skilled. This may conceivably be due to absences which were unavoidable; but, those nearest the minimum wage may not venture to absent themselves, or be late, as much as those further up the scale.

Up till now the data on earnings and hours have been given in the form of averages, but these conceal variations between workers, arising out of the possibility of extra earnings and extra hours of work. This makes necessary distributions of hours worked and of earnings.

When the distributions of hours worked, shown in Figure 2, are examined, it must be remembered that the 'normal' or 'standard' hours of work in the engineering industry are forty four. While there was not sufficient work available to justify much overtime for some groups, this factory was, at the time of the sample, in a position to offer a total of thirteen hours of overtime a week (two evenings of three hours, and seven hours on Sunday)[2] to the majority of its workers, who could accept or reject this opportunity freely. Some workers (mainly on 'outside' jobs) had the opportunity of working exceptionally long hours, even beyond this fifty-seven hours.

[1] The use of 'short-time' here does not imply that some men were not employed for the full hours by the management, but is rather the effect of lateness and absence for short periods.

[2] The factory does not work on Saturday, and Saturday overtime is exceptional.

Forty-four hours is by no means the usual length of week actually worked by employees in this factory, when they are given the opportunity of over-time—as they have been almost constantly since the end of the war. Indeed, the 'normal' or modal hours of work are very close to fifty-seven hours. The majority of workers in the factory in this week worked between forty-eight and fifty-seven hours. Beyond this point numbers fall away steeply, as the hours of work stop referring to the general availability, and choice, of over-time and begin to refer to special chances of extra work available only to

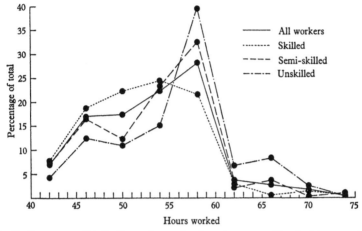

Fig. 2. Percentage distributions of sample of workers according to hours worked.

certain small groups. In all, 28 per cent of the sample worked between fifty-six and sixty hours, 22 per cent worked between fifty-two and fifty-six hours, 17 per cent between forty-eight and fifty-two hours, and only 24 per cent worked less than forty-eight hours.

The patterns of hours worked by the three categories of skill are somewhat different. The modal range for skilled workers is fifty-two to fifty-six hours (24 per cent), but a quarter of the skilled workers worked less than forty-six hours, and a quarter worked more than fifty-six hours. The modal range for semi-skilled workers is between fifty-six and sixty hours. This modal range (containing 33 per cent of the semi-skilled) is more pronounced than that of the skilled. A quarter of the semi-skilled worked less than forty-eight hours and a quarter worked fifty-seven hours or more. The unskilled distribution again has its modal range between fifty-six and sixty hours, but in this case the peak (with 40 per cent in this range) is much more pronounced, fewer workers are in the lower ranges, and the quartiles are set closer together at fifty hours and fifty-seven hours. In other words, the 'hump' in the distribution of hours worked for skilled workers is to the left of that for other groups; and, the hours worked by skilled workers are spread out rather more than those of semi-skilled and unskilled.

Some of the smaller skilled groups were at this time not able to be given the same amounts of overtime as others and were working forty-four hours only: to an extent, therefore, the different pattern of hours worked by the skilled is due to factors other than their own decisions as to overtime working. But the firm was prepared to keep the factory open and to offer overtime on two evenings and on Sunday for the majority of skilled workers, as well as for semi-skilled and unskilled, so that these distributions do broadly indicate the extent to which the different levels of skill were prepared to work long hours. The discussion of average hours worked by different groups produced the conclusion that average hours of work increased as skill declined. This happens because unskilled, and, to a lesser extent, semi-skilled, workers 'go for' the normal peak of overtime working, while skilled men are not so uniformly prepared for longer hours.

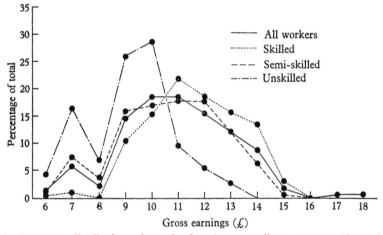

Fig. 3. Percentage distributions of sample of workers according to gross weekly earnings.

Figure 3 shows distributions of gross earnings of all workers in the sample and of each of the three skilled grades. The most striking feature of these distributions is the remarkably wide variation in earnings. Earnings vary from about £6 to about £18. There are skilled employees at all ranges. The semi-skilled range from £6 to £14. The unskilled range from £6 to £13, but are 'bunched' at about the £9–£10 level. The distribution for the skilled lies to the right of that for the semi-skilled, and that for the semi-skilled is to the right of that for the unskilled; but there is very marked overlap between the distributions of earnings for the three groups. For example, 12 per cent of the skilled and 28 per cent of the semi-skilled are below the modal range for the unskilled.

THE FITTERS

A further analysis was made, for the same week in March 1953, of the largest single occupational group in the factory—the fitters. After deduction of the wage-and-clock-cards of those fitters who were off for two or more days, four hundred and forty remained for study. Three-quarters of this number belonged to eight departments, each with more than twenty members, and about one hundred were scattered in smaller departments or in smaller groups. Table 13 contains hours and earnings averages for fitters by departments.

Table 13. *Average hours worked, average gross weekly earnings, and average forty-four-hour earnings of fitters, April* 1953, *by departments*

Department	Number	Average hours worked	Average gross weekly earnings	Average 44-hour earnings
			£ s. d.	£ s. d.
A	23	50·7	11 4 0	8 18 0
B	83	51·4	11 12 0	9 0 0
C	39	50·7	10 17 0	8 8 0
D	41	52·3	12 9 0	9 10 0
E	26	52·2	12 3 0	9 6 0
F	50	53·5	12 1 0	8 15 0
G	22	52·5	12 1 0	9 4 0
H	58	58·2	12 10 0	8 1 0
Others	98	51·4	11 12 0	9 0 0
Total Fitters	440	52·6	11 18 0	8 17 0

Earnings vary between departments to an extent which, considering that the workers are all of the same trade, must be judged to be fairly large. The gross earnings averages are affected by the amount of overtime worked; but, with the exception of Department H, the average hours worked by departments are fairly similar. Indeed, since departments with low forty-four-hour earnings tend to work longer hours, the effect of overtime is probably to narrow the differences between departments. The differences which are of most interest, and are least to be expected, are those between the forty-four-hour earnings of departments. Department H is somewhat exceptional, since it is the outside repairs department where differences in conditions are inevitable. Even excluding this department, however, there are differences in the average earnings of fitters in different departments, amounting to, at the widest, over one pound a week. The widest gap (£8 8s. 0d. for Department C to £9 10s. 0d. for Department D) is between two assembly departments both in the machine shop. There can be little doubt that bonus earnings opportunities must vary between departments even for men of similar training.[1]

The distribution of gross earnings of fitters (in Figure 4) gives an impression of a very wide spread of earnings as between members of the same occupation. Gross earnings range from £6 to £20. Certainly the individual at £6 may be subject to some short-time, since the method of excluding, from the workers studied here, those who were 'off', may still leave some who were absent for fairly short periods (e.g. a half-day) or were inclined to be bad time-keepers. Despite this qualification, however, a range of earnings where some are receiving three times as much as others strikingly demonstrates the difficulty of answering the question 'what does a fitter get?' by any other than the evasive 'it all depends'. Even if the extremes of the distribution are excluded, on the argument that they represent particular cases, it is still wide, since there are fairly substantial numbers of fitters within each of the intervals from £8 10s. 0d. to £14 10s. 0d. This demonstrates the difficulties of attaching a wage label to any one occupation or even to individuals within that occupation. It does not, however, go very far towards explanation of differences in payment. To answer the question of on what 'it all depends' requires further investigation.

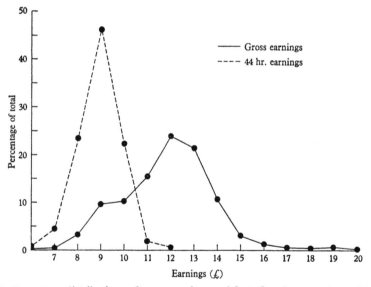

Fig. 4. Percentage distributions of gross earnings and forty-four-hour earnings of fitters.

[1] This is confirmed by a more recent difficulty experienced by this factory in the recruitment of turners and the internal adjustment of the available turners. One section of the machine shop which is now causing a bottleneck in production cannot keep its labour because its earnings potential, under the existing calculated time allowances, is relatively too low.

One possibility is the influence of differences in hours worked due to over-time and short-time. These may be eliminated by stating forty-four-hour earnings only. Figure 4 gives a percentage distribution of forty-four-hour earnings. The spread of earnings that occurs even when the effects of overtime and of short-time have been excluded is still considerable. While almost a half are in the same range (£8 10s. 0d.–£9 10s. 0d.), there are considerable numbers outside this range and differing from it by relatively large amounts. But, while there is still diversity in forty-four-hour earnings, the elimination of overtime and of short-time (especially the former) from the figures has greatly reduced the extent of earnings variation, since the effect of overtime is to extend the earnings ranges greatly and to spread out the earnings pattern of the occupation.

The continuing diversity of earnings calculated for the forty-four-hour week could be due to differences in basic rates. A previous section has discussed different wage rates, and the finding there was that all except about twenty fitters had rates which differed by not more than eight shillings. Since the forty-four-hour earnings data are presented in ranges of one pound, wage rate diversity can only account for a small proportion of the differences in forty-four-hour earnings.[1]

Payment-by-results is the only other major cause of differences in forty-four-hour earnings. It may produce earnings differences because 'prices' or 'times' are badly fixed and are not consistent from one job to another, so that the payment-by-results scheme works inaccurately and unfairly. But, the main factor, governing the shape and scope of the forty-four-hour earnings curve, is probably that of variations in payment caused by variations in the output of individual fitters in a given period of time.[2] The curve is regular in its shape. If all the workers concerned were on individual bonus, then this concentration of earnings at a peak and regular grouping of the varying earnings around the peak would imply that, though they were acting as individuals, nevertheless they had established a 'normal' rate of bonus earnings for their group as a whole (or, if the payment-by-results system is accurate, a 'normal' rate of work). In fact, a substantial proportion of the fitters are on group bonus, and to this extent the preceding cannot be verified. But there is some evidence that the working of the individual bonus scheme has produced a tendency for the workers to conform to a 'norm' in their rate of bonus earnings.

---

[1] Wage rate differences, however, affect earnings of payment-by-results workers in two ways: (a) by the direct difference in the basic rate, and (b) by the fact that bonus earnings will be calculated on a different basic rate.

[2] But, differences in hours worked may cause variations in output in a given period of time, because the spreading of work over a longer number of hours may result in a reduction of effort per hour.

The wage-and-clock-cards for the factory record, for workers who are on individual bonus on the time allowance system, the 'bonus hours' accumulated during a week. These 'bonus hours' are the 'hours saved' by individuals during the week, and can be reduced to an hourly basis by dividing by the number of hours actually worked. When this is expressed as a percentage (the bonus percentage) it provides a more accurate way of representing the rate of working of an individual than forty-four-hour earnings. The distribution of bonus percentages for the 236 fitters on individual bonus is shown in Figure 5.

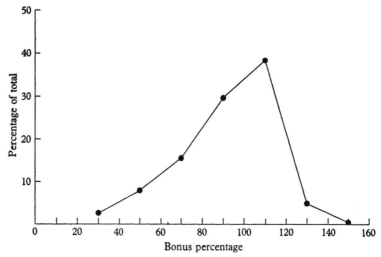

Fig. 5. Percentage distribution of bonus percentages of fitters on individual bonus.

By far the majority of fitters on individual bonus have a rate of working which yields a bonus percentage of between 60 per cent and 120 per cent above basic rates. While this is a fairly wide range of bonus earnings, which would produce at its extremes twice as much bonus for some workers as for others, the shape of the curve in Figure 5 suggests a rate of working which is adhered to, *within limits*, by the fitters as a group.[1]

Figure 6 gives a distribution of hours worked by fitters. While forty-four hours may be the negotiated hours of work in the industry, actual hours worked are generally much longer. The peak of the Figure is not at forty-four hours but between fifty-six and sixty hours. The highest concentration of hours worked is actually at fifty-seven hours (that is forty-four hours plus thirteen hours of overtime work), while, judging from more detailed figures,

[1] One further point may be taken from Figure 5. The national arrangements prescribe that piece-work prices or times must be such as to enable the worker of average ability to earn 45 per cent above his basic rate. In fact, there are very few fitters below or even around this level. This illustrates both the tendency for this 'average' to become a minimum, and the extent to which this factory diverges from national arrangements.

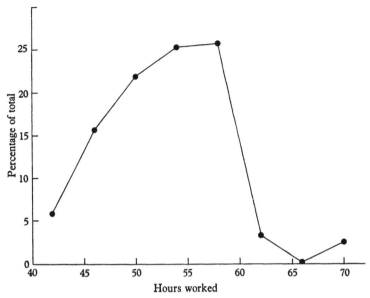

Fig. 6. Percentage distribution of hours worked by fitters.

fifty-one hours of work would have a greater claim to be regarded as 'normal' than forty-four. The 'tail' of very long hours of work beyond sixty hours is numerically rather small and represents unusual conditions applicable to a few fitters (for example those in the 'outside-repairs' department).

Overtime then appears to be the rule rather than the exception. Those workers who are able to choose whether to work overtime or not have almost invariably decided in favour of quite considerable amounts of overtime.[1] Figure 7 gives a distribution of overtime hours worked by the fitters. Over a quarter worked between twelve and fourteen hours of overtime, while slightly under a sixth worked ten to twelve hours. Half of the fitters put in more than ten hours of overtime in this week.

The arrangements for overtime work in the factory made it usually possible for a worker to build up his overtime hours on three different occasions; either for three hours on Tuesday or Thursday evening (making a total of six hours on weekdays) or for seven hours on Sunday. Work on Saturday is regarded as overtime, but is very unusual for all except people such as maintenance workers and watchmen. Workers may also have short-time by being

---

[1] The hours of overtime working by the fitters would appear to be influenced to some extent by the amount of their forty-four earnings. It was found in the general sample that the unskilled (and lower-paid for normal hours) group worked longer. This is also true within the one occupation. Those with highest forty-four-hour earnings show more tendency to vary in their choice of overtime work, while those with lower earnings tend more definitely to aim at and accept maximum overtime.

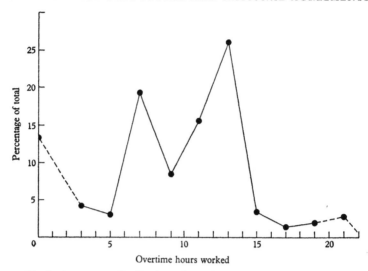

Fig. 7. Percentage distribution of overtime hours worked by fitters.

late or absent. There are thus a number of possible choices in the building up of weekly hours. The actual choices made are analysed in Table 14.[1]

Less than 8 per cent of the fitters actually worked the standard forty-four-hour week. About 87 per cent took part in overtime; but many of these

Table 14. *Fitters' hours and overtime (excluding nightshift)*

Category	Numbers	Percentages
Less than forty-four hours ordinary time and no overtime	21	5·2
Forty-four hours ordinary time	31	7·7
Less than forty-four hours ordinary time and overtime	135	33·5
Forty-four hours and overtime	216	53·6
Total	403	100·0
Overtime workers:		
Sunday and one or both weekdays*	229	65·2
One or both weekdays only	52	14·8
Sunday only*	70	20·0
Total	351	100·0

* In the case of one department, workers are paid double time for work at abnormal hours but not necessarily on Sunday. There are a few such included here as though they were Sunday workers.

[1] Nightshift workers have been excluded here, because their arrangements are of a different character.

44

had short-time as well. Among those working overtime, about two-thirds elected to work on Sundays as well as on one or other, or both, weekdays. But, of the third who did not work both on Sundays and on weekday evenings, a rather larger number elected to turn out on Sunday in preference to either of the evenings during the week. A majority of these workers were quite prepared to work on Sunday, and, where they did not choose to do maximum overtime, the attractiveness of Sunday work (at double time) was greater than that of evening work.[1]

The influence of overtime and of bonus on the final pay packet of the fitters may be most conveniently summarized by studying the average composition of the pay packet (Table 15). (Direct bonus employees and others are shown separately.)

Table 15. *Composition of earnings of fitters*

	Direct bonus	Others	Total
Number	236	204	440
Average hours worked	51·6	53·4	52·5
Amounts (to nearest shilling):	£ s. d.	£ s. d.	£ s. d.
Average payment of basic rates for hours worked	7 2 0	9 15 0	8 7 0
Average bonus payments	3 14 0	0 11 0	2 4 0
Average allowance time payments	1 1 0	1 9 0	1 5 0
Average gross earnings	11 17 0	11 15 0	11 16 0*
As percentage of gross earnings:	%	%	%
Average payment of basic rates			
(a) for forty-four hours	51·0	68·2	59·2
(b) for remaining hours	8·9	14·7	11·5
Average bonus payments			
(a) for forty-four hours	26·5	4·0	15·8
(b) for remaining hours	4·6	0·8	3·0
Average allowance time payment	9·0	12·3	10·5
Average gross earnings	100·0	100·0	100·0

* The slight discrepancy between these figures and those given in Table 13 is due to rounding-off errors.

The premium payment for overtime amounts to about 10 per cent of the average total pay of these workers; but, the effect of overtime working, once the payment for actual overtime hours worked and an estimate of bonus

[1] Some informal information acquired from the factory at a later date confirmed this impression. At this time about twice as many attended for Sunday overtime as for either of the weekdays.

earnings in the overtime period has been added, is to add to what the average fitter has earned in the forty-four hours by a third, so that overtime payments form about a quarter of total pay. This proportion is higher for those not on direct bonus than for direct bonus employees. Most of those not on direct bonus are in receipt of some form of bonus payments, but in many cases it is added on to their rate, so that bonus payments, separately shown, are of much less importance in the make-up of their pay, and their bonus can be less certainly estimated for this Table. In the case of direct bonus employees, bonus earnings amount to about 30 per cent of total pay.

EARNINGS OVER A NUMBER OF WEEKS

Up till now, this study has concentrated solely on one week; and, the question of whether this week could be described as fully typical has still to be discussed. Further, it is important to know whether individuals, who had high or low earnings or hours in one week, had also high or low earnings or hours in other weeks. These tasks were attempted by taking further samples from two other weeks. First, the week ending 5 December 1952 (fifteen weeks before that already discussed) was chosen as one that was not disturbed by holidays or other 'abnormal' features. Secondly, to see whether the original week was similar to those immediately around it, the week following it was also examined (week ending 3 April 1953). In the general discussion of the section on Earnings and Hours, pp. 32–38 above, a one-in-five sample of all employees was used. The same sample was again used but was restricted to four occupational groups—fitters, turners, machinemen and labourers. Where individuals were not found in either of the additional weeks, or had to be left out, because they had been 'absent' for a sizeable proportion of the week, they were omitted in all three weeks. The final samples of the four occupations are, therefore, somewhat smaller than those used in the above-mentioned section. Table 16 gives the averages resulting from these further samples.

The averages in each of the three weeks are similar to each other; and, the additional weeks confirm conclusions already arrived at on the basis of figures for the original week. Hours in each week are substantially in excess of forty-four; though, in the first the average hours worked by both fitters and labourers were rather lower than in the others. The average hours of labourers are considerably higher than those of the other groups in each week. There is some variation between weeks in the forty-four-hour earnings of each occupation though there is no apparent common trend. This is probably due to the influence of factors such as bonus payments, which make for irregularity in earnings. The earnings (both gross and forty-four-hour) of turners in each of the additional weeks are above those of fitters—as they were in the original week; the earnings of the semi-skilled machinemen are not far short of those of the skilled fitters; and the earnings of unskilled labourers are well below those of the other groups.

The week which has been analysed is fairly typical as to average hours and

Table 16. *Average hours worked, average gross weekly earnings, and average forty-four-hour earnings: samples of four occupations (adult male workers) for three weeks*

Occupation and number in sample	Week ending	Average hours worked	Average gross weekly earnings	Average 44-hour earnings
			£ s. d.	£ s. d.
Fitters (60)	5/12/52	51·1	11 3 7	8 14 11
	27/3/53	52·5	11 16 2	8 18 8
	3/4/53	52·1	11 17 11	9 2 2
Turners (29)	5/12/52	51·7	12 1 2	9 2 10
	27/3/53	51·5	12 11 9	9 9 3
	3/4/53	51·8	12 4 5	9 4 4
Machinemen (45)	5/12/52	51·9	11 9 8	8 10 0
	27/3/53	51·6	11 1 4	8 6 4
	3/4/53	52·2	11 6 8	8 8 2
Labourers (42)	5/12/52	56·2	9 9 6	6 8 9
	27/3/53	57·1	9 13 9	6 8 8
	3/4/53	57·3	9 12 10	6 6 8

earnings. Distributions of hours and average earnings of the sample of sixty fitters in each of the three weeks are given in Tables 17 and 18, to check the findings, which have been based on the data for fitters in the original week.

Table 17. *Percentage distribution of hours worked by a sample of fitters in three sample weeks*

Hours worked	Percentage distributions*		
	5/12/52	27/3/53	3/4/53
	%	%	%
Under 43·95	10·0	3·3	5·0
43·95–47·95	20·0	13·3	13·3
47·95–51·95	20·0	25·0	23·3
51·95–55·95	33·3	31·8	36·7
55·95–59·95	13·3	23·3	20·0
Over 59·95	3·4	3·3	1·7
Total	100·0	100·0	100·0

* These distributions and those of Table 18, should be used with care. Since only sixty persons are being studied, small variations can alter the percentage quite a lot.

The distributions of hours worked by the sample of fitters in each of the three weeks are fairly similar, apart from a somewhat larger proportion of fitters working lower hours in the first week. They all show that overtime working is more usual than the standard week. Distributions of gross weekly earnings and of forty-four-hour earnings are also fairly similar; and, despite a tendency for earnings to be somewhat lower in the first week, the modal ranges are the same in each case.

Table 18. *Percentage distributions of gross weekly earnings and forty-four-hour earnings in a sample of fitters in three sample weeks*

Earnings	Percentage distribution					
	Gross weekly earnings			Forty-hour earnings		
	9/12/52	27/3/53	3/4/53	5/12/52	27/3/53	3/4/53
	%	%	%	%	%	%
Under £7 9s. 11½d.	1·7	—	—	3·3	6·7	1·7
£7 9s. 11½d.– £8 9s. 11½d.	3·3	—	—	25·0	16·7	18·3
£8 9s. 11½d.– £9 9s. 11½d.	20·0	10·0	13·3	66·7	53·3	46·6
£9 9s. 11½d.–£10 9s. 11½d.	10·0	13·3	10·0	3·3	23·3	31·7
£10 9s. 11½d.–£11 9s. 11½d.	20·0	18·3	11·7	—	—	1·7
£11 9s. 11½d.–£12 9s. 11½d.	25·0	21·7	28·3	—	—	—
£12 9s. 11½d.–£13 9s. 11½d.	10·0	21·7	21·7	1·7	—	—
£13 9s. 11½d.–£14 9s. 11½d.	5·0	11·6	11·7	—	—	—
£14 9s. 11½d.–£15 9s. 11½d.	3·3	1·7	3·3	—	—	—
Over £15 9s. 11½d.	1·7	1·7	—	—	—	—
Total	100·0	100·0	100·0	100·0	100·0	100·0

The question of whether individuals tend to work about the same number of hours and earn about the same in different weeks can be looked at by further analysis of the hours and earnings in the three weeks of each of the sample of sixty fitters. Table 19 compares the hours worked by the sixty fitters in the earlier and later weeks with those worked in the original week. The numbers underlined in the Table show the extent to which hours worked by individuals fall into the same range in each week. Individual fitters do tend to work about the same number of hours in different weeks, and those fitters who were working long or short hours at the beginning of December were also doing so at the end of March.[1]

This may also be put by considering the extent to which hours worked by individuals differ from week to week (Table 20). One-third of the fitters did not differ in their hours of work by as much as one hour in any of the three

[1] The correlation coefficient between hours worked in the week ending 5/12/52 and hours worked in the week ending 27/3/53 is $r = 0.56$; and between 27/3/53 and 3/4/53 is $r = 0.58$. Each of these is statistically significant.

Table 19. *Comparison of hours worked by sixty fitters in each of three weeks*

Hours worked in other weeks	Hours worked in week ending 27/3/53							
	Under 48	48–50	50–52	52–54	54–56	56–58	Over 58	Total
Week ending 5/12/52								
Under 47·95	8	—	5	—	4	1	—	18
47·95–49·95	—	—	—	—	—	—	—	—
49·95–51·95	—	—	6	1	3	2	—	12
51·95–53·95	1	1	1	4	—	2	1	10
53·95–55·95	1	—	—	—	7	1	1	10
55·95–57·95	—	—	1	—	—	7	—	8
Over 57·95	—	1	—	—	—	—	1	2
Total	10	2	13	5	14	13	3	60
Week ending 3/4/53								
Under 47·95	7	—	2	—	1	—	1	11
47·95–49·95	—	—	—	—	—	1	—	1
49·95–51·95	1	—	9	—	2	1	—	13
51·95–53·95	1	1	—	2	1	3	—	8
53·95–55·95	1	1	—	—	10	2	—	14
55·95–57·95	—	—	2	3	—	6	1	12
Over 57·95	—	—	—	—	—	—	1	1
Total	10	2	13	5	14	13	3	60

weeks. This argues considerable consistency in working hours for many individuals; but, at the other extreme, there is a minority whose hours of work vary considerably from week to week; who may, for example, sometimes shun overtime and sometimes take it. While consistency in hours is most usual not all workers conform to this.

Table 20. *Hours worked by sixty fitters in three weeks: extent of differences*

Extent of difference	Weeks 27/3/53 and 5/12/52	Weeks 27/3/53 and 3/4/53	All three weeks: maximum difference
Nil	14	28	11
Under 1 hour	15	8	9
1 but less than 3	4	4	4
3 but less than 5	7	10	12
5 but less than 7	8	4	6
7 hours and over	12	6	18
	60	60	60

A similar analysis of differences in the gross earnings of the fitters is given in Table 21. A third of the sixty fitters had earnings in the week ending 5/12/52 which differed by less than ten shillings from those they had in the week ending 27/3/53; and a half had earnings which differed by less than ten shillings in the week ending 27/3/53 and that immediately following it. A third of the sixty fitters had less than £1 difference in earnings in any of these three weeks. On the other hand, quite a number had differences of over £2, which is quite a large amount in a moderate-sized pay. While for some earnings were regular, for others they varied by quite considerable amounts.

Table 21. *Gross earnings of sixty fitters in three weeks: extent of differences*

Extent of difference	Weeks 27/3/53 and 5/12/52	Weeks 27/3/53 and 3/4/53	All three weeks: maximum difference
Nil	—	12	—
10s. or under	20	18	11
10s. but less than £1	10	13	10
£1 but under £2	10	4	11
£2 but under £3	8	10	14
£3 and over	12	3	14
	60	60	60

The variation of earnings was also studied for a much smaller group more continuously and over a longer period, by examining wage-records of a small, compact, and homogeneous group of fitters in an assembly department. The average size of the department was about fourteen, and there were ten individuals whose wage-records were more or less continuous over a four-week period, followed, after a lapse of about three months, by another period of nine weeks.

In no individual case did the number of hours worked, or gross earnings, follow a completely consistent pattern. Gross earnings varied largely with variations in hours worked. There were periods of considerable regularity in hours worked, but most of the workers seemed to have one or two weeks in which earnings dived well below what they had been getting, as a result of a decline in their hours of work. These weeks of lower earnings varied from one individual to another, but in one week all showed a decline in earnings. In that week there was a one-day paid holiday but, despite the fact that it was paid, workers lost bonus earnings and had a considerable reduction in income for the week. The extent of variation in earnings altered from person to person but, in all except one of the cases, earnings in the lowest week were no more than about 60 per cent of earnings in the highest week. But, despite occasional divergencies, individuals did maintain with fair regularity their

50

relative position in the group, with regard to gross earnings and hours worked. A ranking of individual's gross earnings, and hours of work produced two individuals who had had a consistently high ranking, while two had a consistently low ranking. The others were placed round about the middle ranks.

In contrast to the occasionally erratic behaviour of hours worked and gross earnings, the variations in hourly bonus earnings were limited. There were some variations; for example, one individual's bonus earnings dropped from an hourly average of 1s. 11d. to 10d. in one week, but the chief impression was of regularity. For each individual, except one, who clearly could not make the grade, the curve showing hourly bonus earnings per week followed a similar pattern. It rose during the first four-week period, and the rise continued for the first two weeks of the second period. It then flattened out and remained steady till the last week recorded. There were two small adjustments to the basic rate, which were intended as incentives, during the period. The effect of the first of these rate adjustments was to increase hourly bonus earnings. The second rate increase, however, occurred at the point of levelling out of earnings and, indeed, earnings had levelled out before the rate became operative. The first increase in rate brought rising output, while the second coincided with a stabilizing of the group's output. There is at least a suggestion here that the group acted in unison despite the individual character of the incentive; with the result that the hourly bonus-earnings curves moved together, and remained stable together.

A DIGRESSION ON 'PAY AS YOU EARN' AND EARNINGS

Since workers' P.A.Y.E. tax code-numbers were available, these were compared with earnings and hours for fitters, in the hope that the comparison might throw some light on the extent to which earnings may be influenced by family responsibility.

Under the 'pay as you earn' system of collection of income tax, P.A.Y.E. code-numbers are used to indicate the total amount of allowances of income free of tax, which can be made to any individual. There are many possible reasons for variations in income-tax allowances. For example, a man may have an additional source of income, such as a part-time job, or an amount of interest, which has not been taxed at source, and these may bring down the size of his allowances to be set against his income from his principal source—his job. Or, a man may get an extra allowance, because of expenses incurred, or, because of life-assurance payments, or building society interest payments, or previous overpayments of tax. Though causes of variations in P.A.Y.E. numbers between one man and another can be many, the principal causes of variation in income-tax allowances, and hence in P.A.Y.E. numbers, are, in most cases, the personal and dependants' allowances.[1] As we all know, married men have an income-tax allowance which is higher than that of single men, and there are additional allowances for children and dependants. In consequence, the P.A.Y.E. numbers of a group of workpeople represent, with some certainty, the range of their family responsibilities.

The earnings of the fitter may vary because of the size of his basic rate, or because of the hours (especially overtime hours) which he works, or because of his earnings from bonus. The first of these possibilities—variation in the basic rate—may be discounted here, since the workers are all of the same occupation; and, while basic rates vary, this is unlikely to be under the worker's control, nor are the variations large. The other two possibilities—variations in hours of work or in bonus earning, are largely in the control of the worker, and are related to P.A.Y.E. numbers in Figures 8 and 9. Figure 8 gives percentage distributions of the hours of work of fitters in different groups of P.A.Y.E. numbers, which are designed to separate different family responsibilities.[2] The first group (P.A.Y.E. 20 to 50) must consist largely of single men; the second of married men without family; the third of married men with one child; and the fourth of married men with more than one child.[3] In the lower P.A.Y.E. number groups hours of work are much more varied than in the higher. The peaks of the distribution of hours worked by the lowest P.A.Y.E. group (with least responsibilities) are at forty-four to forty-six and fifty to fifty-two hours of work; and, only 36 per cent work more than fifty-two hours, as against the average of 56 per cent for all fitters. In contrast, there is a marked concentration of persons working fifty-six to fifty-eight hours in the highest P.A.Y.E. numbers group, and three-quarters of this group work more than fifty-two hours. The distributions of the other groups have an increasing tendency to concentrate at the longest hours as

[1] It seems likely that this is specially true in the case of manual workers, who are, unlikely to be men with many sources of income (in particular, unearned income) other than their job, who are unlikely to be able to claim overmuch in the way of extra expenses or heavy life-assurance payments, and who are probably unlikely to have much opportunity of getting into debit or credit with the income-tax authorities.

[2] At the date of the sample P.A.Y.E. numbers meant the following allowances in pounds and, counting only personal, marriage, or children's allowances, the following types of family responsibility fall within the various ranges.

P.A.Y.E. Number	Allowances (£)	Family Responsibility	
20– 50	£ 59–£174	Single man	(£120)
51– 80	£175–£252	Married man without children	(£210)
81–110	£253–£342	Married man with 1 child	(£295)
Over 110	£342 and upwards	Married man with 2 + children	(£380) plus
		(£85 for each additional child)	

Only 6 men had P.A.Y.E. numbers over 140, therefore only 6 had allowances of over £514 (Married man with 3 children—£465).

[3] Out of the 440 fitters, 100 were in the P.A.Y.E. 20–50 group, 135 in the 51–80 group, 102 in the 81–110 group and 103 in the over 110 group.

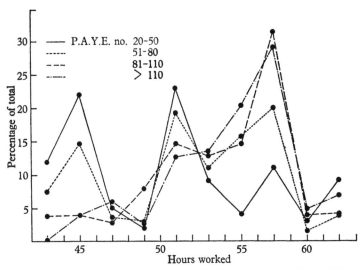

Fig. 8. Percentage distributions of hours worked by fitters: by classes of P.A.Y.E. numbers.

P.A.Y.E. numbers increase. Hours of work, therefore, tend to increase with responsibilities, at least in this case.

Bonus percentages have already been used (for direct bonus workers only) to indicate the capacity of a worker to earn bonus in a given period. Bonus percentages for direct-bonus-working fitters are classified by P.A.Y.E. numbers in Figure 9.[1] The curves for each P.A.Y.E. group are extremely similar, and there is no evidence of greater bonus effort by those with high P.A.Y.E. numbers. Indeed, if anything, the curve for the highest group has a lower modal point (though there are fewer examples of very low bonus percentages in this group).

On this evidence men seem to work longer hours when they have heavier family responsibilities, but do not work harder.[2] A qualification may, however, be necessary. Men who are married and have children tend to be older than single men. The foregoing could, therefore, be interpreted in the light of age-groups rather than family responsibility. Younger men have more spare-time activities and may have less interest in overtime work than older men, but it does seem surprising that they appear not to work harder. In any case, age and responsibility are well known to be related, and introducing this complication may add little. A point, which is not strictly rele-

---

[1] Bonus percentages are only available for the 236 fitters on direct bonus: 55 of these were in P.A.Y.E. group 20–50, 73 in group 51–80, 59 in group 81–110 and 49 in the over 110 group.

[2] A man who takes on longer hours may not, of course, also be able to work harder, in the sense of doing more work in any one hour.

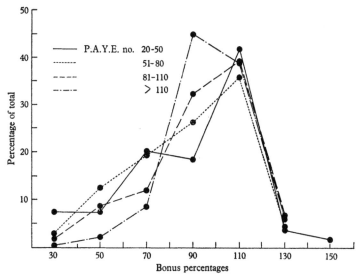

Fig. 9. Percentage distributions of bonus percentages of fitters: by classes of P.A.Y.E. numbers.

vant to the present discussion, may also be suggested. P.A.Y.E. taxation, and income tax generally, are often held to have a disincentive effect: those with higher liability for tax in this sample tend not to do as much overtime. A cautious conclusion to this analysis would be that men with family responsibilities who are usually older men, and who have more tax allowances, and so feel the disincentive effect of taxation least heavily, tend to work longer hours than others, but not to produce more in any given hour.

CONCLUSIONS

The object of this concluding section is to do no more than give again some of the main factual conclusions of the case-study. No generalizations are attempted here, and on the whole they are not attempted at all in this case-study section of the book. A few general observations on the import of the case-studies appear however at the end of Chapter 6.

1. Most occupations had a number of rates (mostly higher than the national agreements laid down). There was not usually, therefore, such a thing as 'the' rate for an occupation; but, there were 'salient' rates for most occupations.

2. There was considerable 'overlap' of rates between occupations, which caused the rates for semi-skilled and unskilled to overlap those for skilled.

3. The skilled tended to get a higher proportion of their total earnings from bonus than semi-skilled or unskilled.

4. Those groups with low averages in forty-four hours compensated by longer hours and more overtime earnings. Average hours and overtime were longer and short-time less for unskilled than for semi-skilled, and for semi-skilled than for skilled.

5. Distributions of hours worked showed wide variations between individuals. Nevertheless 'normal' hours were much more than forty-four. The unskilled group had much less variation than semi-skilled or skilled.

6. Distributions of gross earnings showed wide variations and considerable overlap between skilled, semi-skilled and unskilled.

7. Distributions of gross earnings and of hours worked for fitters showed wide variations between individuals. Distributions of their forty-four-hour earnings also showed variations between individuals; but, here there was more evidence of a regular pattern in earnings from bonus, which, when studied in relation to bonus percentages, produced a suggestion of the establishment of a group rate of bonus working. There were variations from this rate, but the variations were regularly distributed around it.

8. The hours of overtime worked by the fitters varied greatly, but extremely high proportions did work overtime. A majority of those working overtime turned out both on one or two weekday evenings and on Sundays. Of those who did not work overtime as frequently as this, a majority turned out on Sunday instead of a weekday evening.

9. The composition of earnings of fitters on direct bonus and of those who were not paid in this way showed that overtime was an important element in the payment of both, but was more important for those not on direct bonus. Direct bonus employees, on average, derived about 30 per cent of their total pay from bonus.

10. The week chosen for study appeared to be fairly typical of other weeks. Similar averages and distributions appeared in other weeks.

11. There was a marked association between hours worked by individuals in one week and those that they worked in other weeks. Some tended to work habitually long hours and overtime while others tended to work rather shorter hours. There was a similar (though not so strong) association of earnings in different weeks; the same individuals tended to have high earnings in different weeks. The rate of bonus earnings by individuals tended on the whole to be fairly constant from week to week.

12. On the basis of an analysis of earnings, hours and P.A.Y.E. numbers of fitters in the factory, it appeared that those who had heavier family responsibilities than others worked longer hours.

CHAPTER 4

WAGES IN AN ENGINEERING FACTORY: II

The second factory to be studied is a large one employing over 7000 wage-earners. Its work consists, mainly, of small-batch production, and, in consequence, workers tend to do a number of different jobs in a week (averaging about fifteen), though the same jobs are likely to recur at intervals. This tendency for jobs to vary is accentuated, because many of the employees are engaged on the production of spares, and on maintenance. The factory has a division into departments which is quite usual in engineering—the main sections being machine-shop, assembly, inspection and testing. The composition of the factory's wage-earning labour force of adult males is shown in Table 22. (Staff, charge-hands and leading-hands are excluded throughout.)

Table 22. *Composition of the adult male labour force,*
September 1953

Grade	Number	Percentage
Skilled	2879	48·0
Normally Employed	604	10·1
Dilutee	244	4·0
Semi-skilled	901	15·2
Unskilled	1370	22·7
Total	5998	100·0

Forty-eight per cent of the adult males are skilled; about 10 per cent are 'normally employed', and about 4 per cent are 'dilutees'. 'Skilled' grading, requires an engineering apprenticeship, or acceptance by the A.E.U. as skilled: it is the prerogative, very largely, of five-year time-served men. The 'normally employed' category is not usual, and refers to a particular arrangement of this firm, whereby those, who have been employed since prior to 1939 on skilled work of particular types, are regarded as equivalent to skilled. This category also includes youngsters who have not been apprenticed, but have been given a three-year training course by the firm. All 'normally employed' are paid at the full skilled rate. 'Dilutees' are not unusual in the engineering industry; they have generally entered engineering since 1939 with no previous experience, have gained experience (most frequently during the war), and have been upgraded to the skilled rate. Dilution in the factory has been mutually agreed upon, because there are, on occasion, insufficient skilled men available. The engagement of dilutees, however, only takes place where skilled labour is insufficient to meet factory requirements. Since all these grades are doing 'skilled' work and are paid the 'skilled' rate, it is apparent that about 62 per cent of the males in the factory are fulfilling a skilled function.

The semi-skilled, who comprise about 15 per cent of the male labour force' are officially defined by the firm as those 'being paid less than the skilled rate on an occupation allied to the above categories'. All machine-operators, concerned only with the actual operating of machines and working in conjunction with skilled setters, come under this category. As far as possible, operators' jobs are filled by the upgrading of suitable labourers.

The usual selection of engineering occupations appears in this factory, with the principal exceptions of patternmakers, moulders and coremakers, since no casting is undertaken. Occupations tend to be classified in considerable detail; thus, for example, machinemen are divided into many categories according to the type of machine they work. None of the wage-earning employees of the factory is paid on time-work, but on three different methods, which are all, to a greater or lesser degree, examples of payment-by-results. These are (1) 'premium' bonus—according to which the individual worker is paid a bonus, based on an assessment of the time he has taken to do a job he has been set; (2) 'pool' bonus—where groups of workers share a bonus based on the group's output; and, (3) indirect bonus or 'lieu' work—in which bonus is related to work in a number of more roundabout ways.

As in the preceding chapter, the general object here is to show how wages in the factory work out in practice. Various circumstances have combined to keep this case-study within much narrower limits than were originally planned: what follows is based exclusively on material relating to earnings and hours of the factory's wage-earning labour force in a single week—that ending 12 September 1953.[1] Because of limitations in the material available, the incidence of various special bonus schemes applicable to particular grades of workers is not analysed here; nor is the incidence of a number of special allowances payable *inter alia* for long service, quantity and quality of work, good time-keeping and minimum absenteeism. In consequence, the composition of pay packets cannot be completely stated. Moreover, overtime payments are not adequately dealt with.

---

[1] The actual material on which the case-study is based was derived from two main sources.

(i) A handbook on *Wages and Conditions* produced by the firm for the use of Superintendents and Heads of Departments. This provided 'background' and details of wage rates.

(ii) A series of figures showing numbers employed, hours worked, 'overtime extra hours', and gross earnings in the week ending 12 September 1953, for each wage-earning occupation, subdivided according to grade of labour (skilled, dilutee, etc.) and according to type of payment (premium bonus, pool bonus, and indirect or lieu work).

WAGE RATES IN THE FACTORY

National agreements current in September 1953 provided for adult male payment-by-results workers in engineering: (*a*) a basic rate of 66*s.* for skilled workers and 51*s.* for unskilled which is paid to each payment-by-results worker and from which bonus is calculated; and (*b*) a national bonus of 51*s.* 4*d.* a week for all adult male payment-by-results workers. Arrangements for wage rates in the factory differ from those laid down in national agreements in several ways. While the factory strictly adheres to the national bonus, the basic rate in the factory is higher than that laid down in the national, as supplemented by the district, agreement. (For the skilled fitter, for example, it is 67*s.* instead of 66*s.* 1½*d.*) The difference between factory and national basic rates seems to arise from two principles: first, where the national rate, or the national plus district rate, results in odd pennies, the factory rounds it off either to the nearest sixpence or the nearest shilling above (for example another occupation rated at 51*s.* 4½*d.* by agreement is rated at 51*s.* 6*d.* in the factory); and, secondly, the factory provides rates for far more grades than are specified nationally. As regards the 'minimum piece-work standard' of 45 per cent which is specified in national agreements, the factory's arrangements differ in two respects. Instead of the 'at least 45 per cent above' provision of the agreement, the factory 'Handbook' expects that, with the times instituted, an operative of average ability should earn 60 per cent bonus. Further, this 60 per cent is not calculated on the basic rate, which is used only for time purposes, but is based on an *enhanced* bonus rate, which differs from one group of specified grades to another. In the case of the skilled fitter this bonus rate is 67*s.* plus 9*s.* (76*s.*) instead of 67*s.* An example will explain the position more clearly (Table 23).

Table 23. *District and factory levels of minimum earnings of skilled fitters on payment-by-results, September* 1953

Payment	District		Factory	
		s. *d.*		*s.* *d.*
(*a*) Basic rate				
(i) Paid as time payment		66 1½		67 0
(ii) On which bonus is calculated	66*s.* 1½*d.*		67*s.* + 9*s.* = 76*s.*	
(*b*) National bonus		51 4		51 4
(*c*) 'Minimum piece-work standard'	(45% of 66*s.* 1½*d.*)		(60% of 76*s.*)	
		29 9		45 7
Total		147 2½		163 11

The last column shows the *minimum* weekly payment of a fitter in the factory. In practice, he is almost certain to earn more than a 60 per cent bonus, because, while this is the specified minimum bonus, the 'Handbook' stipulates that where any section's earnings fall consistently below 71 per cent, the job timing is to be examined with a view to raising the average earnings.

It is thus merely in respect of the national bonus that the national agreement is strictly adhered to, though the divergence in the basic rate is rather small. The main distinction between the factory's arrangements and those of the national agreements relates to practice with regard to bonus. The factory management seem to have found it necessary to replace both the level of the basic rate for calculation of bonus, and the minimum standard prescribed in the agreement. It is partly the intention of the national agreement that factories should make their own arrangements about payment-by-results, and the minimum piece-work standard is not thought of as anything more than that. It is not, however, part of the agreement that basic rates should be supplemented. The variations in the factory arrangements appear to be attempts to observe as many parts of the national agreements as possible, while giving to the bonus rate and the minimum bonus a level more in keeping with actual bonuses being earned in the factory.

A very complex occupational structure exists in the factory. The 'Handbook' sets out no fewer than 161 different occupational categories—though this includes quite a number of lower-level staff categories. Not all of these occupations are given different basic rates; but there are seventeen different rates to cover thirty-eight skilled categories, and fifteen different rates to cater for fifty-four semi-skilled and unskilled categories.

Three points must be made about this large number of basic rates. First, to a very large extent, the factory fixes its own rates without regard to national arrangements. When trade unions have a say in this, it is through local bargaining and not national bargaining. Only fitters' and labourers' rates are formally fixed by the national agreement, which is, at best, a starting point for the complex of rates in this factory, not a complete blueprint. Secondly, variations of rates within the skilled group on the one hand, and the semi-skilled on the other, are larger than the differences between the two groups. Thus, basic rates for the skilled range from 78s. 6d. to 67s., while those for the

Table 24. *Average weekly earnings of adult males by grades of skill*

Category	Average weekly earnings	Category	Average weekly earnings
	£ s. d.		£ s. d.
Skilled		Dilutee	12 4 1
Normally employed	13 3 7	Semi-skilled	12 6 5
	12 10 4	Unskilled	11 6 2

semi-skilled and unskilled range from 71s. to 51s. 6d. There are two semi-skilled rates which are higher than the bottom skilled rate (which, incidentally, is that covering the important and basic category of fitter). Thirdly, it is tempting to ask whether this complex structure of rates is really worth while. Its pattern lays down numerous distinctions between each category of skill and within each category of skill, yet all of these can be overthrown in earnings.

EARNINGS OF DIFFERENT LEVELS OF SKILL

Table 24 gives the average weekly earnings of the various grades of skill. In terms of the average amounts of pay taken home the position in the hierarchy of the different skilled groups is maintained, except that the semi-skilled average exceeds that of the dilutees who are 'standing in' for skilled labour. The range of variations of the average is not however very great: the unskilled average is 86 per cent of that of the skilled and the semi-skilled is 93 per cent of that of the skilled. These averages, are, however, in many ways, deceptive, not only in the sense that any average is deceptive in obscuring the position of individuals, but also because they are quite largely affected by the type of payment method under which the employee is remunerated, and by the hours worked, and the overtime done by people in the different skill grades.

Table 25. *Average weekly earnings of adult males by type of payment*

Type of payment	Average weekly earnings
	£ s. d.
Premium bonus workers	12 6 6
Pool bonus workers	12 8 6
Indirect or lieu workers	12 15 2

Table 25 shows the average weekly earnings obtained by those working on the different payment methods. In the week being studied lieu workers were considerably better paid than those on direct bonus, and pool bonus workers got more than premium bonus workers.

The proportions of workers employed under the different types of payment method vary with the grade of skill of the workers (Table 26). Semi-skilled workers are paid mainly by the premium bonus method; this indicates again that the semi-skilled are largely machine operators, who can be remunerated on an individual basis. Very few semi-skilled workers are on lieu payments. The normally employed and dilutee workers are also paid on an individual basis much more than on the other systems. In contrast skilled men are to a considerable extent remunerated by indirect bonus, which suggests that num-

Table 26. *Numbers and proportions of adult males by type of payment in each skill category*

Grade of skill	Numbers			Proportions		
	Premium bonus	Pool bonus	Indirect or lieu	Premium bonus	Pool bonus	Indirect or lieu
				%	%	%
Skilled	895	504	1480	31	18	51
Normally employed	385	54	165	64	9	27
Dilutee	190	25	29	78	10	12
Semi-skilled	645	156	100	72	17	11
Unskilled	108	72	1190	8	5	87

bers of them must be in the kind of jobs where bonus calculation is difficult (maintenance work for example). By far the larger proportion of unskilled workers are on lieu work; probably because their work is not part of the normal flow of the productive process.

Table 27. *Average weekly earnings of grades of skill of adult males by type of payment*

Grade of skill	Average weekly earnings		
	Premium bonus	Pool bonus	Indirect or lieu
	£ s. d.	£ s. d.	£ s. d.
Skilled	12 10 5	12 12 10	13 15 2
Normally employed	12 3 1	11 8 6	13 14 3
Dilutee	11 18 8	12 5 4	13 18 0
Semi-skilled	12 9 2	11 12 11	12 9 2
Unskilled	11 3 6	11 18 1	11 5 8

The average weekly earnings of the various skill categories, according to their type of payment, are set out in Table 27. In most cases the average level of weekly earnings obtained by lieu workers is higher than that of averages on other types of payment. This whole question of earnings under different payment systems, and indeed the whole question of earnings on different skill levels cannot, however, be divorced from the question of hours of work put in to make various levels of earnings.

Average hours are without exception considerably in excess of the 'standard' forty-four-hour week (Table 28). Longer hours are worked by those at the top and bottom ends of the skill gradation. The highest averages are those of the unskilled and skilled groups. This is quite largely a matter of the proportions on different types of payments: skilled and unskilled each have substantial proportions on lieu or indirect bonus, and average hours are longer on this type of payment. On the other hand dilutees, normally employed, and

Table 28. *Average weekly hours worked by adult males, by grade of skill and type of payment*

Grade of skill	Hours worked			
	All workers	By type of payment		
		Premium bonus	Pool bonus	Indirect or lieu
Skilled	50·8	50·5	48·9	51·7
Normally employed	49·4	49·3	46·7	50·4
Dilutee	48·8	48·5	48·6	50·8
Semi-skilled	50·5	50·8	48·0	52·1
Unskilled	54·3	50·0	50·8	54·9

semi-skilled have high proportions on premium bonus, and average hours are shorter for this type of payment. Longer average hours of work seem to be the lot of those who are maintaining and servicing the process of production rather than taking part in it.

The averages of earnings which have been given up to now have been on the basis of hours actually worked by the different groups; hourly earnings reduce these weekly earnings averages to a common basis of comparison—payment for one hour's work (Table 29).

Table 29. *Average hourly earnings of adult males by grade of skill and type of payment*

Grade of skill	Average hourly earnings			
	All workers	By type of payment		
		Premium bonus	Pool bonus	Indirect or lieu
	s. d.	*s. d.*	*s. d.*	*s. d.*
Skilled	5 2	4 11	5 2	5 4
Normally employed	5 1	4 11	4 10	5 5
Dilutee	5 0	4 11	5 0	5 6
Semi-skilled	4 11	4 11	4 10	4 9
Unskilled	4 2	4 5	4 8	4 1

The averages in the first column of Table 29, which are not differentiated by type of payment, give the general impression of smaller payment at lower grades of skill; but, except for the substantially lower average of the unskilled workers, the differences are not very great. In the case of premium bonus employees—whom we have generally assumed to be on direct production work—average hourly earnings are the same for all grades except the unskilled. When workers are in part remunerated by a bonus assessed on the individual's output, differential payments for skill grading appear to be submerged. Differentials reappear to some extent where the bonus is shared out to a group from a pool. In the case of indirect workers, there is some inversion in the levels of earnings of skilled, normally employed, and dilutee workers; but, this apart, a clear distinction emerges between the earnings of skilled, of semi-skilled and of unskilled. Evidently, indirect bonuses are generally calculated by the management to reflect relative skill gradings, whereas direct bonuses do not do so. In hourly earnings, as in weekly earnings, indirect bonus workers' averages are generally above those of direct bonus workers.[1]

These average hourly earnings will, of course, be influenced by the extent of overtime and shift-working premium payments, since some hours of work are paid for at 'premium' rates, and hence division of averages of total weekly earnings (including these premia) by average hours worked will not result in exactly comparable amounts. It would have been desirable to try to exclude overtime and shift-working premium payments from estimates of average hourly earnings; but this did not prove possible. Some help was, however, obtained by studying the amounts of 'overtime extra hours'—a concept used in the factory to assist in the calculation of overtime (and shift-work) premium payments. The result of this was to confirm generally the impression derived from Table 29. If overtime premia could have been deducted, then the average hourly earnings of different grades of skill would have been even closer together—except that the unskilled would have been even more definitely on a lower level. The 4s. 11d. level of average hourly earnings for all grades on premium bonus, would, if overtime premia had been deducted from total earnings, have been rather lower; but, the semi-skilled average would have been higher than that of skilled. In other words, figures of average hourly earnings display a strong tendency in this factory for payments for grade of skill to be submerged in earnings. In the case of direct and individual bonus operations, semi-skilled are almost certainly the higher earners: only in indirect or lieu working are skill differences maintained.

EARNINGS IN ONE OR TWO OCCUPATIONS

The three 'basic' occupational groups in most engineering works—the fitters, the turners and the machinemen—were further analysed here.

Fitters are usually regarded as the 'representative' skilled group in the

---

[1] However, there is a marked difference in the level of bonus earned by unskilled on indirect bonus and unskilled on direct bonus. Unskilled workers in this factory do well to get into the production process as direct bonus workers.

engineering labour force. If the 102 toolroom fitters in the factory (who are almost without exception on 'lieu' work, and whose earnings averages are above those of other fitters) are left out, then the average weekly earnings of the other 660 fitters, in September 1953, were £12 16s. 6d. for an average of 50·4 hours. Their hourly-earnings average was, therefore, 5s. 1d. About 60 per cent of the fitters were on pool bonus and most of the remainder were on premium bonus. Their average earnings were very similar to the average for all skilled groups, though if anything, very slightly on the low side.

Since the fitters are a uniform group with fairly clearly delineated conditions of wage payment, some approximate attempt may be made in their case to estimate the importance of different elements in their pay packet. This may only be done roughly, since it is difficult to estimate overtime payments. Table 30 gives such an estimate, assuming that everybody averaged at least forty-four hours, and giving an estimated range of overtime premium payments (and hence a range of bonus earnings).

Overtime amounts to between a fifth and a quarter of the pay packet;

Table 30. *Composition of earnings of fitters*

Type of payment	Amount	As proportion of total earnings
		%
1. *Basic Rate*		
(a) for 44 hours	67s. 0d.	26
(b) for 6·4 hours	9s. 9d.	4
(c) for total (50·4) hours	76s. 9d.	30
2. *National Bonus*		
(a) for 44 hours	51s. 4d.	20
(b) for 6·4 hours	7s. 8d.	3
(c) for total hours	59s. 0d.	23
3. *Overtime (and Shift-work) Premium Payments*	20s. 0d. to 30s. 0d.	8 to 12
4. *Bonus-Payments*		
(a) for 44 hours	79s. 3d. to 88s. 0d.	31 to 34
(b) for 6·4 hours	11s. 6d. to 12s. 9d.	4 to 5
(c) for total hours	90s. 9d. to 100s. 9d.	35 to 39
Total payments on 44 hours	197s. 7d. to 206s. 4d.	77 to 80
Total payments on overtime (and other premium payments)	50s. 2d. to 58s. 11d.	20 to 23
Total Average Earnings	256s. 6d.	100%

and, over a fifth of the total pay packet may be earned in under an eighth of the total hours. Basic rates and the national bonus account for only 53 per cent of the pay packet; while the rest arises from bonus and overtime payments, which are to a greater or lesser degree uncertain. The actual average level of the bonus percentage above the basic rate is between 118 per cent and 131 per cent, whereas the nationally agreed minimum piece-work standard is but 45 per cent. Even the factory's more generous minimum piece-work standard (such that the total payment for forty-four hours does not fall below 164s.) is, in practice, much exceeded.

Skilled turners can sometimes be confused with semi-skilled machinists, In the machine-shops in this factory, men are classified not as turners or machinists but by reference to the type of machine they operate. A man may, for example, be a grinder: if he is a skilled grinder according to his labour grade, then he is a turner to trade; if he is semi-skilled, then he is only a machinist. The average earnings of all the grades of skill working as machinists in the machine-shop are very much alike. Most of the machinists are on premium bonus (as might be expected from the nature of their work); and, in premium bonus working, the average weekly earnings of semi-skilled workers are only five shillings less than those of skilled workers, and hourly earnings of semi-skilled workers are about a penny farthing an hour lower.

EARNINGS OF WOMEN AND JUVENILES

Quite a number of the wage-earning employees of this factory are women and there are also a number of boys and girls employed. In September 1953, 792 adult females (10·4 per cent of the total labour force), 330 boys (4·3 per cent), and 377 girls (4·9 per cent) were employed.

Table 31. *Numbers, average weekly earnings, average hourly earnings, and average hours worked of adult females, and comparisons with adult males*

Category	Number	Average weekly earnings	Average hourly earnings	Average weekly hours
		£ s. d.	s. d.	
Charge-hand	3	8 5 2	3 7	46·4
Leading-hand	15	9 0 0	4 8	46·7
Adult (21 and over)	774	7 7 0	3 2	46·3
All Adult Females	792	7 7 8	3 2	46·3
All Adult Females as per cent of all Adult Males	13	59	64	90

Table 31 gives the earnings and hours of adult females and compares these with those of males. The women work rather shorter hours (though with some overtime) and average about two-thirds of men's earnings.

Table 32. *Numbers and average weekly earnings by type of payment of adult females, and comparisons with adult males*

Category	Numbers			Average weekly earnings		
	Premium bonus	Pool bonus	Indirect or lieu	Premium bonus	Pool bonus	Indirect or lieu
				£ s. d.	£ s. d.	£ s. d.
Charge-hand	2	—	1	9 0 6	—	6 14 7
Leading-hand	5	6	4	12 9 4	12 9 2	7 3 6
Adult (21 and over)	297	37	440	7 6 2	7 6 7	7 7 8
All Adult Females	304	43	445	7 8 1	8 0 11	7 7 7
All Adult Females as per cent of all Adult Males	14	5	15	60	65	58

Table 32 examines the earnings of women on different systems of payment. It appears that there is relatively little to be gained by women through being on one system of payment as against another. (Hours are also fairly similar on different payment systems.)

Table 33. *Numbers, average weekly earnings, average hourly earnings, and average hours worked of boys and girls, and comparisons with adults*

Category	Number	Average weekly earnings	Average hourly earnings	Average weekly hours
		£ s. d.	s. d.	
Boys				
Aged 18–20	152	7 17 6	3 4	47·6
Under 18	178	3 0 2	1 4	44·6
All Boys	330	5 5 0	2 3	46·0
Girls				
All Girls (18–20)	377	6 19 8	3 0	46·3
Boys as per cent of adult males	5	42	46	89
Girls as per cent of adult females	48	95	95	100

Table 33 gives the earnings and hours of juveniles and compares them with those of adults. The earnings of boys of 18 to 20 are more than those of girls in the same age group—but not by very much. Girls approximate much more closely to adult females in their earnings and hours than do boys to adult males (even if only boys in the 18 to 20 group are considered). It would appear that boys are treated much more as 'learning their job' and so either as apprentices or 'learners' are paid much less than adults. Girls are employed 'to do a job' and so earn very nearly as much as adult females.

Table 34. *Numbers and average weekly earnings by type of payment of boys and girls, and comparisons with adults*

Category	Numbers			Average weekly earnings		
	Premium bonus	Pool bonus	Indirect or lieu	Premium bonus	Pool bonus	Indirect or lieu
				£ s. d.	£ s. d.	£ s. d.
Boys						
Aged 18–20	86	4	62	8 18 1	6 10 3	6 10 9
Under 18	15	10	153	3 19 2	2 19 9	2 18 4
All Boys	101	14	215	8 3 5	3 19 11	3 19 2
Girls						
All Girls 18–20	177	10	190	6 15 6	6 14 4	7 3 10
Boys as per cent of Adult Males	5	1	10	66	32	32
Girls as per cent of Adult Females	58	23	43	92	83	97

Table 34 further confirms this impression. A greater proportion of girls than of boys are on direct and individual bonus payment. The boys are to a greater extent on indirect bonus (especially those under 18). The girls earn fairly high proportions of adult earnings on each payment system (the hours of girls on pool bonus were rather lower). It is only on premium bonus (where they are paid directly for what they do) that the boys are able to earn a fairly high proportion of adult earnings.

CONCLUSIONS

The conclusions agree broadly with those already reached in Chapter 3, and convey a similar picture of actual wages in an engineering factory.

1. Wage rates applicable in the factory differ from those laid down nationally.

2. Many more occupations than are dealt with in national agreements are separately specified in this factory and have separate rates. The rates for some groups within the semi-skilled grade are higher than those of some groups in the skilled grade.

3. The average weekly earnings of grades of skill conform broadly to their ranking in terms of skill; but the gaps between each grade are very narrow.

4. Semi-skilled workers are mainly remunerated on direct and individual (premium) bonus; unskilled are mainly on an indirect bonus; and about half of the skilled are on indirect bonus. On the whole, average earnings of workers on indirect bonus exceed those of workers on direct bonus.

5. Hours worked are much in excess of forty-four. Unskilled average longer hours than other grades. Average hours worked by indirect bonus workers (normally men not engaged on direct production), exceed hours worked by direct bonus workers.

6. Average hourly earnings figures still show some differentiation between the earnings of different grades of skill, but the differences are very small. In the case of premium bonus employees there is no difference between different grades of skill, except that the unskilled average less. The effect of the payment of 'premium' rates for overtime work is not likely to be sufficient to upset these conclusions.

7. The earnings and hours of fitters average much about the same as those for the skilled grade as a whole. Earnings of turners are also similar, but, there is no substantial difference between their earnings (or hours) and those of other machinists, who are without the 'skilled' label.

8. An estimated division of the average earnings of fitters according to type of payment shows that basic rate and national bonus payments only amount to about half of the pay packet for all hours worked. The remainder consists of bonus payments and overtime.

9. Women work rather shorter hours than men, and average about two-thirds of the men's earnings. Girls earn much the same as women; but boys earn much less than men.

CHAPTER 5

WAGES IN THE SHIPBUILDING INDUSTRY

THE SHIPBUILDING INDUSTRY IN BRITAIN

While the shipbuilding industry in Britain has a very long history, an almost complete break both in methods and location, as well as in materials, occurred when iron, and latterly steel, replaced wood as the material for ships' hulls. The present British shipbuilding industry is an offspring of the Industrial Revolution.

In the days of wooden ships, the Thames was the principal shipbuilding river of Britain. Though there are heavy concentrations of shiprepairing in the south, shipbuilding has now moved north, and the rivers of the north-east coast of England and the Clyde are now the main centres of shipbuilding activity, with rather lesser centres at Birkenhead, Belfast and Barrow. The shipbuilding and shiprepairing industry at present 'employs some 215,000 persons in Great Britain and 13,000 in Northern Ireland'.[1] There are about another 70,000 workers in marine engineering. The present output of new ships is about one and a half million tons per annum. The Clyde is on average responsible for slightly under a third of this total. The Tyne, Wear and Tees together account for rather more than another third. Single yards at Belfast, Birkenhead and Barrow between them produce about another sixth of the total output of the industry. The industry is also localized as between countries. In the latter years of the nineteenth century Britain was building three-quarters of the world's ships. In 1913–14 we were still providing over half the total tonnage launched in the world. Though this proportion has now gone down to less than a quarter, Britain still builds a sizeable proportion of world output (18 per cent in 1957), and is the second most important shipbuilding country. The other main shipbuilding countries are Japan, which is now the largest shipbuilder, W. Germany, the Scandinavian countries, the Netherlands, Italy, France and the U.S.A.

The shipbuilding industry has suffered from extreme irregularity of demand for its products. For example, the United Kingdom launched two million tons of shipping in 1920 at the height of the boom following on the First World War, while output has been running at one to one and a half million tons since the end of the Second World War; but, in 1933, total output of all

---

[1] Court of Inquiry Report (Cmnd. 160, H.M.S.O., May 1957). Members of the Shipbuilding Employers' Federation 'employ a total of 152,000, of which 91,000 are engaged on new construction and 61,000 on repairs and conversions'.

British shipyards was only 133,000 tons, and at that time about two-thirds of shipbuilding workers were unemployed. The reasons for this were many. Most importantly, a ship is a capital good of a large size; demand for which is not continuous and can be postponed. Ships need not be replaced, or replacement can be postponed when trade is poor, and new demand for ships then ceases. The size of the product makes building for stock difficult if not impossible. Moreover, sources of demand, and types of ship demanded, vary and this can cause both a variation in total demand and a variation in the demand for the product of specialized yards. Warship demand, for example, is especially variable. At present the main bulwark to demand has been the growing need for oil transportation and hence for tankers, which at present account for over a third of British launchings. The demand for passenger liners has also been fairly good in recent years, though this only affects the few yards that can build such vessels.

Because of the large size of the product and the individuality of the design of each ship, the industry has not developed 'flow' production. In recent years there has been a tendency to use prefabricating techniques which allow large segments of the ship to be built in easier conditions under cover, and only transported to the berth when completed. This development is associated with a growth in the use of welding, which is used in prefabrication, and has now become much more important than riveting as a method of joining together the component parts of the ship. It has also led to larger cranes and improved layouts of shipyards. With these exceptions, however, the industry, on the shipbuilding, as distinct from the marine-engineering, side, still uses methods which have been familiar for a long number of years.

Shipbuilding is a tradesman's industry, depending on the skill of apprenticeship-trained men. There are very few women workers in shipyards—with the exception of the two trades of french polishers and upholsterers. Unlike engineering, there has been little growth in the number of semi-skilled machinists. Semi-skilled workers in shipyards are mainly engaged in ancillary operations, such as cranemen or drivers, or are 'helpers' to skilled men. Only two semi-skilled groups have duties which are moderately independent; these are the redleaders, who give the ship plates an initial coating of red lead to avoid rust and complete all painting outwith accommodation; and the stagers, who provide various forms of access scaffolding. The majority of a shipyard's employees are skilled tradesmen.

Quite a number of trades are needed in the process of building a ship. Of them the shipwrights are probably the oldest established, but, whereas in building wooden ships the shipwright actually built the wooden hull, nowadays his duties in addition to fitting-out are associated with lining-off, erecting, and 'fairing' the steel skeleton of the ship and launching it. The metal-working trades, the platers, riveters, welders, caulkers and drillers,

70

nowadays are the people who clothe the skeleton and join all parts together. These basic shipyard trades are followed at a later stage in the building of the ship by the 'fitting-out' trades, who, unlike many of the metal-workers, can find their employment outside the industry with as much ease as inside it. The joiner, electrician and plumber are the principal such trades. In addition to the more numerous trades mentioned here, a shipyard also employs an assortment of others such as, for example, sheet-metal-workers, tinsmiths, smiths and men in the sawmill trades.

Because shipbuilding is a tradesman's industry the labour force is characterized by an emphasis on skill and on independence of mind. This latter attribute has been made manifest by the troubled history of the industry in the inter-war period with its frequent long spells of unemployment, when it was impossible to build up loyalty to the firm, and when a tough attitude was necessary for survival. It may also be due to the frequently high labour turnover in the industry. It is probably exemplified by the attitude of tradesmen to demarcation.[1]

THE WAGE RATE AND EARNINGS STRUCTURES OF THE INDUSTRY

Wage agreements in the shipbuilding industry are at present settled nationally by the Shipbuilding Employers' Federation and the Confederation of Shipbuilding and Engineering Unions, acting on behalf of the seventeen unions directly concerned with shipbuilding. Claims are raised by letter to the Secretary of the Federation or the Confederation as the case may be. Since 1930 National Uniform Plain Time Rates have been negotiated for skilled and unskilled workers, though the rates for repair work are subject to a 3s. per week addition and semi-skilled time rates are not all fixed nationally (though some, for example redleaders do have national rates).

Before and during the war these time rates were increased by bonuses which were consolidated in 1950 to produce inclusive new work plain time rates for skilled of 120s. and for unskilled of 100s. per week of forty-four hours. Since 1950 various advances have been made and incorporated in the inclusive time rates which became for skilled workers 147s. in April 1954, 158s. in March 1955, 170s. 6d. in March 1956 and 181s. 6d. in May 1957. For unskilled workers the corresponding figures are 125s., 133s., 142s. 6d., and 151s. 6d. giving differentials (unskilled as percentage of skilled) of 85, 84·2, 83·6 and 83·5 per cent. The more recent awards in the industry have broken with the war-time practice of giving flat-rate increases to all employees, so that the differential between skilled and unskilled in time rates is widening slightly. It has also become customary to insert an intermediate

---

[1] Cf. D. J. Robertson, 'Labour Turnover in the Clyde Shipbuilding Industry', *Scottish Journal*, March 1954.

increase of payment to semi-skilled workers, between skilled and unskilled increases. In March 1955, for example, this was 9s. 6d., as against 11s. for skilled and 8s. for unskilled.

While the most frequently quoted and most readily understood part of the wage agreement is that for time rates, a very substantial majority (over 80 per cent) of workers in the industry are on some form of incentive payment.[1] Piece-work is the traditional type of incentive payment, and has been the custom among members of the metal-working trades (the 'black squad') for many years. Since the beginning of the war, however, the industry has been making efforts to use other types of payment-by-results.

The methods adopted to assess piece-work prices vary from trade to trade and from place to place. For example, both the Clyde and the Tyne have published piece-work price lists applicable to riveters, and very detailed published lists also exist for drillers and caulkers on Clydeside. The platers on the other hand have not had such general lists: prices are locally determined and may vary from yard to yard. Where price lists exist they may well be very old. For example, the riveters' price list which lasted on Clydeside till 1955 dated from 1896. To use it, it had to be plussed by 7½ per cent for amendment before 1926, then plussed by 20 per cent for piece-work price percentage increases granted nationally in the inter-war period, then it had 15 per cent deducted from it since the price list was based on handwork with hammers and pneumatic riveting machines are now used, and then, finally, if Government work was involved there was a plussage of 25 per cent. There was no agreement to consolidate these percentages. In many cases, price lists, even where they exist, are not used and work is rate-fixed.

Piece-work is sometimes on an individual basis, but is probably much more frequently payable on a group basis to a squad. These piece-work arrangements were originally a contract system. For example, the riveter might accept a contract price for a certain section of the riveting on a ship. It would then be his job to collect and employ his squad (traditionally, a holder-on, heater, catcher, and rivet boy, as well as himself), agree on the basis of their payment and organize the work and the payment. Similarly a plater might contract for a section of the ship's plates or frames and then organize the employment, the work, and payment of a squad of platers and their helpers. While the pure contract system no longer applies, arrangements on the basis of division of group piece-work earnings in squads can still reflect the older system.

The shipbuilding industry has also been accustomed to use the system of 'lieu' rates. Piece-working tradesmen may from time to time be involved in work which can only be priced with extreme difficulty. In such cases the

---

[1] K. G. J. C. Knowles and D. J. Robertson, 'Earnings in Shipbuilding', *Bulletin*, November/December 1951.

practice is to pay a lieu rate—somewhat higher than the time rate—both as compensation to the piece-worker for the loss of piece-work earnings and in the expectation that the work will be carried out at 'piece-work speed'. Semi-skilled and unskilled men may also be paid a lieu rate, because they work with piece-working tradesmen and are in consequence working at piece-work speed. The platers' helpers' lieu rate is actually nationally negotiated.

Payment-by-results schemes introduced into the industry since 1940 (initially, in part under the 'encouragement' of Mr Bevin as Minister of Labour) have generally affected the fitting-out trades, and all those to whom traditional piece-work has not applied. These schemes have been applied on a yard basis and are naturally of widely varying character.

In the inter-war years the national agreements in the industry controlled piece-working wages by the device of percentage additions to, or contraction of, prices. In 1940 advances in the form of a war-bonus began. These continued at the same level for both time-workers and piece-workers up to 1950, at which time the piece-workers' war bonus was 39s. for skilled and 41s. for unskilled. The agreement of 1950 which consolidated time rates, and in the process advanced them by 11s. for skilled and 8s. for unskilled, did not alter the piece-workers' national bonus. Since then the amounts awarded on time rates have also been added to the piece-workers' bonus which reached 66s. in April 1954, 77s. in March 1955, 89s. 6d. in March 1956, and 100s. 6d. in May 1957 for skilled piece-workers. This bonus, of course, is payable in addition to piece-work earnings.

In the case of those working on some of the payments schemes now in use in the industry, neither time rates nor the national bonus are specifically used in the payment system. Agreements provide that in these cases advances, however made, shall not exceed the amount agreed to, and that in all cases workers shall receive 'only the advance appropriate to their class'.[1]

The 1950 agreement introduced a new factor into the picture. Before that date no stipulation had been made about the level of piece-work earnings. In the 1950 agreement it was laid down that piece-workers should earn not less than '17s. 6d. in the case of skilled workers and 15s. in the case of unskilled and semi-skilled workers above the new inclusive national uniform plain time rate for the class of the particular workers'.[2]

National agreements in the industry also specify arrangements for overtime payments. The time-workers receive time and a half for overtime work, except on Sundays when they get double time. The piece-workers' national bonus is similarly dealt with, and in addition average hourly piece-work earnings in the week in which the overtime occurs are increased by a third for overtime hours (and by two-thirds for Sunday overtime). An additional

[1] Agreement dated 15 March 1955.
[2] Agreement dated 13 December 1950.

third of plain time rates is paid to both time-workers and piece-workers for normal nightshift hours, and there are additional provisions for nightshift work outside normal nightshift hours.

The earnings of shipbuilding workers have tended, since the war, to be in excess of the negotiated arrangements. In September 1956, for example, skilled adult time-workers averaged 253s. 5d. for 51·8 hours while skilled adult piece-workers averaged 290s. 7d. for 47·4 hours work.[1] The agreement at that time provided for a minimum payment to piece-workers for forty-four hours' work of 170s. 6d. plus 17s. 6d. The time rate for skilled men at that date was 170s. 6d.: it is clear that actual earnings, even deducting the possible amount of overtime earnings, were much higher than this. Hours have also been somewhat longer on average than the standard forty-four week.[2] Piece-workers' earnings are not now as much in excess of those for time-workers as they used to be,[3] possibly because the genuine time-worker with no additional payments is becoming a rarity. The differential between skilled and unskilled which is laid down in time rates actually appears in earnings though it may be obscured in some cases.[4] Earnings tend to differ from region to region though this is partly due to higher earnings in shiprepairing areas.[5]

CONCLUSIONS

The following brief summary may be helpful.

1. Shipbuilding is an old-established British industry employing a high proportion of skilled workers and relatively few semi-skilled.

2. Inclusive time rates and a piece-workers' bonus are negotiated nationally. Few workers, however, are on time-work.

3. Piece-work is the most usual form of payment-by-results. It is sometimes based on a contract system and sometimes uses price lists; but both of these are now somewhat obsolescent.

4. Earnings in the industry are considerably in excess of negotiated arrangements.

[1] Information provided by the Federation to the Court of Inquiry which sat in April 1957 (Cmnd. 160). The figures for unskilled piece-workers were given as 225s. 3d. for 50·2 hours; and for time-workers 195s. 3d. for 50·9 hours.
[2] Cf. 'Earnings in Shipbuilding', op. cit., p. 361.   [3] Loc. cit., p. 359.
[4] Loc. cit., pp. 358 and 360.   [5] Loc. cit., pp. 361–5.

CHAPTER 6

WAGES IN A SHIPYARD

The shipyard, whose wage arrangements are studied here, is quite a large one with a very well-established, and well-deserved, reputation in the industry. It has a marine-engineering department and a repair department as well as a shipyard. Statistics are given in Table 35 of the numbers of workers below charge-hand level employed at the time when the wages were studied.

Table 35. *Composition of labour force* in the shipyard, February* 1955

Type of labour	Shipyard	Engine- and boiler-shops	Outside and repair	Total
Tradesmen	1058	351	185	1594
Semi-skilled†	205	159	34	398
Helpers†	259	159	30	448
Unskilled	132	16	36	184
Women	23	—	—	23
Total	1677	685	285	2647

* Any workers who was absent in the week in which wage-records were studied is omitted here—so also are those who did not put in as much as thirty hours work.

† The semi-skilled group includes cranemen, motormen, machinists, redleaders, tack-welders, stagers and a number of smaller groups. Helpers may be regarded as semi-skilled or unskilled, depending on the trade they help and the work they do. All helpers are classed together here.

This yard has the typical shipbuilding labour force structure. The majority of the labour force are tradesmen. The semi-skilled category is relatively small. The helpers are much more numerous than the labourers since the unskilled, or semi-skilled, labour tends to be attached to, and working for, tradesmen. There are very few women employed. The twenty-three women shown in the Table are french polishers. The Table does not, however, show the forty or so women who are employed in canteen and cleaning work. In addition to the numbers shown, the yard (including engine and repair departments) employs over 500 boys: most of these are apprentices, though about 100 are 'boys' and pre-apprentices.

GENERAL WAGE ARRANGEMENTS IN THE SHIPYARD

The systems of payment employed in the shipyard are complicated. In essence, however, they are either piece-work based on price lists or rate-fixing, or they are a payment-by-results scheme based on a time-study computation of hours allowed to do any particular job. Only a rather small proportion of workers are on time-work. In the main these people are unskilled workers or helpers, though occasionally skilled men may be on time-work for a short period. The 150 or so helpers in the platers' department are paid a lieu rate, and so are a number of workers in other trades. In the repair department some of the tradesmen are on time or lieu rates, because, presumably, it is difficult to work out any prices or times for operating an incentive scheme—but, on the other hand, repair-department workers are in receipt of the 3s. weekly extra repair rate and also have quite generous allowances for outside work, graduated according to distance from the yard. In other cases, including the engine- and boiler-shops, bonus schemes are in operation.[1] Piece-work is used in this yard for all trades in the 'black squad'. The determination of piece-work price in some cases is still by reference to price lists, in others it is by rate-fixing and in the case of the welders it is by time study.

At present all riveting jobs are rate-fixed, because the small number of riveters now employed, and the small tasks they undertake, do not give continuity to the work, and so each job has to be treated separately. If, however, a special job brought about something like the old continuity, then a price list might be used again. If it were, then, up until 1955, it would be basically the 1896 price list with appropriate percentage adjustments. Piece-work payments in riveting are all based on squads which at present consist of three men—a riveter, a holder-on, and a rivet boy. The riveter and holder-on each receive the same share of the bonus. The riveter determines what the rivet boy is to get and this is deducted from the squad's piece-work earnings. The yard pays the national bonus. In consequence, yard and riveter share responsibility for employment and payment of the rivet boy. If he, or the holder-on in a squad, were to leave, the riveter would be expected, with the yard's help, to get someone to replace him.

The caulkers' price list dates back to 1889. Cutting and caulking in this yard are still on these price lists. As with riveters, this means percentage adjustments to bring prices up to date—especially since the caulkers' tools are now pneumatic and the list is based on hand tools. Some jobs, however, are new and are therefore rate-fixed (making V cuts for butt-welding would be a good example). The caulker usually works on individual piece-work without a helper. Drillers also have a price list dating from the First War and now adjusted by the usual percentages. Drillers work in pairs—the driller and his mate. Prices are paid to both and halved (for both caulkers and drillers some yards operate their own price lists).

---

[1] Statistics for the repair department are not discussed in this chapter, since so many special factors operate there. Statistics for the engine shop are, however, discussed in the section on 'Earnings in the engine works', pp. 88–89, after shipyard earnings have been examined.

Platers used to be always in squads—and in some yards still are. In this particular yard, however, many of them are now on individual work which is no longer paid according to a price list, but is rate-fixed. The platers' earnings are subject to a deduction for helpers. Platers in the frame squad operate as a squad and have a price list. Calculations of prices are based on the midship frame, and prices are fixed with the squad leader. In this case, and in the foregoing, the tradesmen are consulted in the fixing of prices (Friday is 'complaints day' in the rate-fixer's office). The frame squad in this yard consists of five platers and fifteen helpers. The squad leader is expected to play a very large part in its organization and recruitment, though he gets the same return as the other tradesmen in his squad (by agreement of the association of 'framers' on Clydeside). Piece-work payments are made to the squad. A deduction of about 9d. an hour is made from this for the helpers, and the remainder is split between the platers. The wages of the helpers are made up by the yard, but there is an institution known as 'bungs' which is an extra payment made by the platers to their helpers. This is no concern of the firm at all, but is sufficiently recognized for it to be allowed for income-tax relief by the Inland Revenue. Though most of the other platers now work individually, the yard still has a platers' squad in the prefabrication department, and payment in this case is made to the squad.

Welders are on individual piece-work, but, being a comparatively new trade, they have no price list. Prices in this case have been worked out by time study. There are different prices for each type of weld and for the direction of weld (or the angle at which the welder holds his tool). Adjustments are made for 'bad fit' and for work 'on the skids' in the welding bay or out on the ship. Frequent consultations between rate-fixers and welders are necessary where 'bad fits' occur and there are large and uneven gaps between the parts to be welded.[1] Some of the shipwrights are also on piece-work but many are on small contracts for a man and his mate which are settled by bargaining.

The yard took advice from a firm of industrial consultants after the war on how best to provide incentive payments for trades which had been on time-work (principally the fitting-out trades, as has been usual in shipbuilding). A number of payment-by-results schemes were introduced—the simplest form being that applicable to joiners, plumbers and sheet-metal-workers. In each of these cases standard hours are worked out for each operation. The 'time allowed' to the worker to complete the operation is then computed —standard hours plus one-third.[2] The time allowed is compared with the

[1] It is a common characteristic of these incentive schemes that they require a staff to administer them. In this case 7 rate-fixers and 7 counters are needed to work a scheme for 130 welders.

[2] Presumably the addition of one-third to standard hours is designed to ensure that the payment-by-results scheme yielded the 33⅓ per cent bonus which industrial consultants tend to consider desirable.

77

hours actually worked ('time taken') to give 'time saved' and bonus is paid at the time rate on this time saved.

The use of the time rate in these payment-by-results schemes produces a complication which does not exist, at least in the same form, with piece-working trades, when, except for nightshift premium payments, the time rate is not used, the only time element in the piece-workers' payment being his national bonus. The standard hours were calculated with reference to the time rate in force when the schemes were introduced. Since then time rates have gone up considerably, and the firm now think it necessary, in order to relate hours to present time rates, to reduce the bonus percentage, expressed in relation to the old time rate, by a factor representing the extent to which present time rates are larger.[1] The actual standard hours used for the scheme have been arrived at in two ways. At its inception a number of jobs were time-studied and times were set up by agreement with the unions. Since that date adjustments have been made by assessments, mainly using rate-fixers though occasionally by time study, and new times have been set up. There is a payment-by-results committee elected by the men and largely composed of shop stewards, who take up complaints with foremen, and, if necessary, with the personnel manager.

Payments under this scheme are based on quite large groups and there are no schemes for individuals. The joiners and sheet-iron-workers are divided into a squad for each ship and a squad for the shop. The plumbers may have a number of squads on a ship and the work on the ship may be divided among these squads. In each case the hours allowed and taken are assessed for the squad as a whole and the bonus percentage is assessed on the squad's output. Each member of the squad, including helpers and apprentices, then gets the same bonus percentage applied to his own time rate for the number of hours he has worked.

The administration and efficiency of these schemes is much affected by the length of time required for jobs undertaken by the trades concerned. The fitting-out work which joiners or plumbers have to do on a ship may possibly take a few months to complete; and, while interim assessments of progress can be made, no final determination of the time taken is possible until the job is finished. Moreover, though the work done can be assessed in smaller sections, one job feeds into another to such an extent that it would be some-what unsatisfactory to make final payments according to the rate of comple-tion of small parts of the job. For example, plumbing work on cabins is not

---

[1] An example may be useful. Suppose an operation takes an estimated 30 standard hours, then time allowed for it would be $30 + \frac{1}{3} = 40$ hours. If hours worked on the job (time taken) $= 30$ then time saved $= 10$ and bonus percentage $= 33\frac{1}{3}$ per cent on old time rates. If time rates at present are 50 per cent greater than when standard hours were computed then bonus-payable $= \frac{2}{3} \times 33\frac{1}{3}$ per cent of present time rates, and the worker gets 122·2 per cent of present time rates for his hours of work.

likely to be done one cabin at a time, but in sequence of operations, piping first, then fixing of handbasins, etc. The result is that, despite the fact that the calculations are based on hours worked by squads so that in any one week quite a number of hours taken may be recorded, the actual jobs for which assessments have been made may run into thousands of hours and take the squad weeks or months to finish.

This situation, in which the work being timed can extend over a long period, may explain the rather late date at which incentive schemes were applied to the fitting-out trades. In the piece-working trades such as welders, caulkers, riveters and drillers, there is generally no need for any priced job to be of such a size that its completion will take more than a week. It was thus easier in the first place to adopt pricing and piece-work in such trades. On the other hand, the contract system has been very usual in the shipbuilding industry. Riveters, for example, while their work is suitable for normal piece-work pricing, used sometimes to be paid on a longer contract basis. While platers can be described as a piece-working trade, again they used to be on contract systems, whereby, for instance, the shell squad of platers might contract for all the shell plating of the ship at once. Moreover, elements of contracts still remain in these cases. The frame squad of platers, for example, are paid according to a price list but the payments may be aggregated into a contract— and certainly the element of contract and long-period settlement remain in the arrangements which the squad can make with the yard, to draw their piece-work earnings in advance, and on account, and to settle up at regular intervals. It may be, therefore, that the long-period nature of these payment-by-results schemes for fitting-out trades simply reflects the industry's predilection for contracts and their acceptability to the workers, rather than any difficulties arising out of the problem of dividing their work into small sections. Another relevant possibility is that the uncertain nature of employment in the fitting-out trades and their tendency to rapid labour turnover hindered the introduction and acceptance of incentive schemes.[1] In practice, as the squad's job proceeds from week to week, progress towards completion is assessed by the staff foreman and a bonus is paid out appropriate to the amount of progress achieved as compared with hours actually taken. When the job is completed the final bonus is used to balance the account as between the bonus due on the whole job and that actually paid out to date.

The electricians in the shipyard are paid according to yet another type of incentive scheme. While in origin this appears to have been the work of industrial consultants who did some time study of electricians' jobs, it is now a type of contract system. The electricians' payment-by-results office assesses a contract price for electrical work on a ship. This is done by aggregating

---

[1] Cf. 'Labour Turnover in the Clyde Shipbuilding Industry', op. cit.

prices, some of which appear to have been based on time study, for each type of operation (for example so much for installing so many yards of a particular type of cable). The work to be done is found from drawing-office plans of all proposed electrical work on a ship. The final contract price is for all work on a ship. Progress is assessed weekly and work completed is expressed as a percentage of the total contract, and so the amount of the contract price which has been earned to date is arrived at. This amount is compared with what has already been paid out to give the amount of payment due in the week in question. The excess of this over the value of a week's time payments gives the bonus percentage for the week, which is then paid to all electricians working on the ship. When the contract is finished a balancing payment may be made.

The hours of work done in the electricians' shop on behalf of each ship are debited against the ship's contract. Electricians in the shop are credited with the bonus percentage appropriate to the ship for the number of hours they have worked for the ship. Bonuses from each ship are pooled and paid out to electricians in the shop as a bonus percentage against total hours worked in the shop.

EARNINGS IN THE SHIPYARD

The complete Powers-Samas records of earnings in the shipyard and engine works in the week ending 18 February 1955 were provided by the management. The statistics that follow were abstracted from this material. This particular week was chosen because it was free of interruption (from holidays, etc.), and it is thought to be a reasonably typical week in the wage experience of this yard. A shipyard employs a large assortment of tradesmen

Table 36. *Numbers and average weekly earnings of some principal shipyard occupations, February 1955*

Occupations	No.	Average weekly earnings	Occupations	No.	Average weekly earnings
		s. d.			s. d.
Platers	148	278 2	Plumbers	52	253 10
Welders	130	325 7	Redleaders	37	238 6
Caulkers	47	279 7	Stagers	27	237 11
Drillers	29	324 0	Cranemen	37	205 10
Riveters & Holders-on	16	190 4	Tack-welders	59	235 4
Shipwrights	64	265 1			
Sheet-iron-workers	87	205 5	Platers' Helpers	140	196 1
Joiners	180	248 4	Other Helpers	119	211 11
Electricians	118	247 0	Labourers	108	197 5

Table 37. *Composition of average weekly earnings of some principal shipyard occupations, February 1955*

Occupation	Amounts due to:					Proportions (%) due to:				
	Time payments		Bonus		Overtime premium	Time payments		Bonus		Overtime premium
	In normal hours	In overtime hours*	In normal hours	In overtime hours*		In normal hours	In overtime hours*	In normal hours	In overtime hours*	
	s. d.	*s. d.*	*s. d.*	*s. d.*	*s. d.*					
Platers	74 5	9 0	151 1	18 4	25 4	26·7	3·3	54·3	6·6	9·1
Welders	64 9	13 5	180 4	37 7	29 6	19·9	4·1	55·4	11·5	9·1
Caulkers	82 0	19 7	120 4	28 9	28 11	29·3	7·0	43·0	10·3	10·4
Drillers	71 2	16 8	164 0	38 6	33 8	22·0	5·1	50·6	11·9	10·4
Riveters and Holders-on	100 6	—	89 10	—	—	52·8		47·2		—
Shipwrights	150 1	35 0	42 9	10 6	26 9	56·6	13·2	16·3	3·8	10·1
Sheet-iron-workers	146 2	6 5	46 1	2 0	4 9	71·2	3·1	21·6	1·8	2·3
Joiners	146 9	33 10	34 5	7 11	25 5	59·1	13·6	13·9	3·2	10·2
Electricians	145 8	27 6	42 9	8 1	23 0	59·0	11·1	17·3	3·3	9·3
Plumbers	146 3	12 5	79 4	6 9	9 1	57·6	4·9	31·3	2·6	3·6
Redleaders	126 9	31 8	44 6	11 2	24 5	53·3	13·3	18·6	4·7	10·2
Stagers	125 2	29 1	50 4	10 2	23 2	52·6	12·2	20·6	4·8	9·8
Cranemen	138 1	30 9	12 7	2 9	21 8	67·2	14·9	6·0	1·4	10·5
Tack welders	147 4	36 7	19 10	4 11	26 8	62·6	15·6	8·6	1·9	11·3
Platers' Helpers	145 2	32 4	—	—	18 7	74·7	15·8	—	—	9·5
Other Helpers	145 0	27 0	32 9	7 1	20 1	58·9	12·8	15·4	3·4	9·5
Labourers	122 9	33 7	12 8	3 6	24 11	62·2	17·0	6·4	1·8	12·6

* Time and bonus payments were allocated between normal and overtime hours in the average proportions of these hours worked. (See Table 39.)

and other workers, and some selection was necessary. Table 36 has earnings information for some principal shipyard occupations.

Average earnings of skilled groups in the shipyard varied quite a lot in this week. The welders were best paid and the riveters were the lowest-paid group. On the whole, the semi-skilled groups averaged less than the skilled groups, and the unskilled groups were lowest paid—but there were exceptions to this. The average redleader, for example, took home more pay than the average sheet-iron-worker, mainly as a result of more overtime.

The factors that determine the actual earnings positions of the various groups are bonus and overtime. This is shown clearly in Table 37.

The column of the Table which shows the total of bonus earned in normal hours indicates significant differences between trades.[1] All the piece-working trades in the 'black squad' derived a high proportion of their earnings from bonus, and a low proportion from time payments, since they have only a small national bonus as a time wage.[2] The welders had the largest bonus earnings. Since the shipyard lays much emphasis on welding as against riveting, and on prefabrication techniques, there has been considerable pressure on this trade, and higher bonus earnings is the not unexpected result. It is not, however, a result that meets with much approval among the tradesmen in the industry, since welding is quite usually regarded as an easy option among the trades, requiring less skill and knowledge than the others, and there are memories of women welders during the war. In fairness to the welders, however, it should be emphasized that welding in the shipyards requires a higher degree of perfection in workmanship than in many other industries. The point is illustrated by a pleasant story, told of two welders from a shipyard who took a job as welders in a motor car factory in the Midlands, at higher wages than they enjoyed at home. They stayed three weeks and then went back home, saying as they left, that 'yon was no' welding'. Tack welding—a job done by semi-skilled men in a shipyard—is typically the welding required in many industries.

Among the skilled trades on forms of payment-by-results other than piecework, the plumbers had the highest bonus earnings. This is a direct reflection of the difficulties of working out times or prices for payment-by-results schemes in shipyards. The plumbers were one of the trades for which industrial consultants devised a payment-by-results scheme. In practice, the times set up proved to be quite unrealistic and uneconomic in that they yielded bonuses much in excess of those obtainable by other trades without much effort on the part of the plumbers. Naturally, once the scheme was introduced

---

[1] These figures are not strictly comparable since average hours worked in normal working hours differ slightly (cf. Table 39 and footnote to Table 37); but the differences arising from this source are not of very great importance.

[2] This is less true of the riveters since some of them were on time rates—and this has affected the averages.

the workers were reluctant to accept amended times; at the date to which the wage records here apply, the yard had reduced its labour force of plumbers, especially on the jobs where times were particularly bad, and was employing an outside firm of plumbers to do much of the work. The contractors were able to quote a price lower than the cost to the yard of doing the job itself. Despite the loss of the 'best' times from their point of view the remaining plumbers still made a better than average bonus on the jobs left to them. The eventual hope of the yard management was that the policy of giving work to outside contractors would make possible a fresh start with a new plumbing labour force and new times for jobs.

On the whole the levels of bonus earned by semi-skilled and unskilled workers were less than for skilled. The redleaders and stagers have their own bonus scheme and do quite well out of bonus. The platers' helpers have no bonus being on a lieu rate, but the other helpers tend to earn quite large bonuses, since they generally share in the bonus earned by their tradesmen. The result of the combined influences of time payments and of bonus may be seen in Table 38, which gives average hourly earnings for each group (excluding overtime premium payments).

Table 38. *Average hourly earnings* (*excluding overtime premium payments*)
of some principal shipyard occupations, February 1955

Occupations	Average hourly earnings		Occupations	Average hourly earnings	
	s.	d.		s.	d.
Platers	4	2	Plumbers	5	3
Welders	6	0	Redleaders	4	1
Caulkers	4	10	Stagers	4	3
Drillers	5	6	Cranemen	3	6
Riveters & Holders-on	4	4	Tack-welders	4	0
Shipwrights	4	6	Platers' Helpers	3	5
Sheet-iron-workers	4	5	Other Helpers	3	8
Joiners	4	3			
Electricians	4	5	Labourers	3	2

The figures given in Table 37 may also be used to give an impression of the importance of overtime in the workers' pay packets. Almost a third of the average labourer's pay packet was due to overtime payments (time payments for overtime hours, bonus earned in overtime hours, and overtime premium payments). For most other groups a quarter or more of their pay was due to overtime. The riveters were the lowest-paid group because they had no overtime payments at all. Despite high bonus earnings, the plumbers' average was not among the top weekly earnings' figures because they earned less on overtime.

The average hours worked in the week being studied and the average overtime hours are shown in Table 39. Overtime was not uniformly available to all workers in the shipyard in this week. For example, no overtime was possible to riveters, and only a little for plumbers. Nevertheless, for most trades there was quite a large amount of possible overtime. In consequence, average hours worked were in excess of forty-four for all groups except riveters. Given the opportunity it seems clear that most workers in the shipyard were willing to work substantial amounts of overtime.

Table 39. *Average hours worked and average overtime hours of some principal shipyard occupations, February 1955*

Occupation	Average hours worked	Average overtime hours	Occupation	Average hours worked	Average overtime hours
Platers	48·9	5·3	Plumbers	46·4	3·6
Welders	49·8	8·6	Redleaders	52·6	10·5
Caulkers	52·2	10·1	Stagers	51·0	9·6
Drillers	52·7	10·0	Cranemen	52·6	9·6
Riveters & Holders-on	43·7	—	Tack welders	52·3	10·4
Shipwrights	53·0	10·0			
Sheet-iron-workers	45·2	1·9	Platers' Helpers	51·4	9·0
Joiners	52·3	9·8	Other helpers	52·1	9·3
Electricians	50·8	8·1	Labourers	54·0	11·6

Table 39 illustrates two other points of interest. Once again, the labourers are found to be working the longest average hours—a result which has occurred in every set of statistics of hours of work presented in this book. Secondly, Table 39 has evidence of what also appears to be a most usual result in statistics of hours of work—the combination of overtime with short-time working in normal hours. In no case in Table 39 is the average of total hours worked by a trade sufficiently large to include both forty-four hours in normal time and the overtime hours worked by that trade.[1]

The figures given up to now have all been averages; but, while this is usually the most convenient way to present such statistics, it results in much less than a complete picture. Unfortunately, however, the more detailed information provided by distributions takes up a lot of space and time. Here, the averages are expanded into distributions for only two trades—joiners and welders. Each of these is a large trade; but, while the joiners are on a payment-by-results scheme which is based on large groups, the welders are on individual piece-work. Distributions of average weekly earnings by hours worked are given for joiners and welders in Tables 40 and 41 respectively.

[1] The averages of total hours worked are in part influenced by those few workers who for one reason or another worked less than forty-four hours (but more than thirty hours, since anybody working less than thirty hours was excluded from the study). The effect of this is not, however, sufficient to negative the conclusions drawn.

Table 40. *Distribution of weekly earnings by hours worked: Joiners*

Weekly Hours	Weekly earnings												Total (hours worked)
	Under £10	£10–£10.19.11	£11–£11.19.11	£12–£12.19.11	£13–£13.19.11	£14–£14.19.11	£15–£15.19.11	£16–£16.19.11	£17–£17.19.11	£18–£18.19.11	£19–£19.19.11	£20 and over	
Under 39·9	9												9
40–41·9	1												1
42–43·9		1											2
44–45·9	16	5											21
46–47·9	3	2											5
48–49·9			2		2								4
50–51·9		7	14	5									26
52–53·9				23	3								26
54–55·9				2	3								5
56–57·9					55	6	1						62
58 and over						2	1	14	1	1			19
Total (Weekly Earnings)	29	16	16	30	63	8	2	14	1	1	—	—	180

G

Table 41. *Distribution of weekly earnings by hours worked: Welders*

Weekly hours	Weekly earnings												Total (hours worked)
	Under £10	£10–£10.19.11	£11–£11.19.11	£12–£12.19.11	£13–£13.19.11	£14–£14.19.11	£15–£15.19.11	£16–£16.19.11	£17–£17.19.11	£18–£18.19.11	£19–£19.19.11	£20 and over	
Under 39·9	4	1	2	3	3								13
40–41·9	1	2			1	1							5
42–43·9	1				1	1	1						4
44–45·9			2		2	4	3	2					13
46–47·9					1		3	1	1				6
48–49·9				1		2	1	5	3				12
50–51·9	1			1		1	1	4	9	2	1	1	21
52–53·9		1	1				1	1	1	2		2	9
54–55·9									2	2	2	4	10
56–57·9		3				1		2	3	3	4	20	36
58 and over												1	1
Total (Weekly earnings)	7	7	5	5	8	10	10	15	19	9	7	28	130

The averages of hours worked concealed quite a wide range of individual's hours of work. In each case, however, by far the majority of workers put in considerably more than a forty-four-hour week. Around six hours of over-time was usual and twelve to fourteen hours was also quite common.

The ranges of weekly earnings were also quite large—from under £10 to over £18 in the case of the joiners, and from under £10 to over £20 in the case of the welders. As might be expected for a trade whose bonus is assessed on a group basis, the principal factor in producing differences in the earnings of joiners was hours of work. The lateral spread of Table 40 for any one range of hours of work is not large, nor is the vertical spread specially marked. Joiners doing the same number of hours of work tended to get about the same payment for it. Since the welders work on individual piece-work, the spread of Table 41 is much greater. For any one range of hours of work welders get much more varied earnings. Yet, the appearance of a wide scatter of earnings for welders, and of little association between earnings and hours of work, is in part illusory. When the distribution of hourly earnings of welders is looked at a rather different picture emerges (Figure 10).

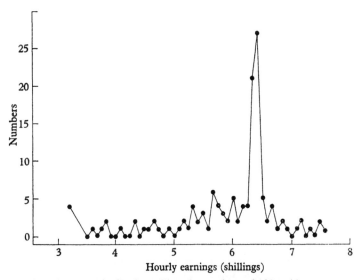

Fig. 10. Distribution of hourly earnings of 130 welders.

There is quite wide diversity of earnings among welders, even when their earnings are stripped of the complications of overtime premia and of hours worked, and presented in hourly terms. Figure 10 does, however, offer evidence of a tendency for welders to conform to a normal rate of working. Twenty men out of one hundred and thirty welders had hourly earnings of 6s. 5d. and twenty-one had hourly earnings of 6s. 4d. There is significance in

87

the 6s. 4d.–6s. 5d. level of hourly earnings of welders beyond its suggestion that despite their working individual piece-work the welders naturally tend to conform as a group to a similar rate of working. The management of this and other shipyards have the opinion that a welders' group in the Boilermakers' Society have fixed the upper level to which welders' earnings are allowed to rise, and that this 'doggie', as it is called, is enforced by a system of fines, enforced on welders whose hourly earnings exceed the stated amount. At the time to which the wage data relate the 'doggie' was supposed to be 6s. 4½d an hour. Tales are told of good welders whose rate of earnings at the beginning of the week are in excess of the 'doggie', and who therefore have to come in at the end of the week and do nothing, in order to keep their hourly average down to the approved level. There is even a tale of a welder who is in the habit of asking the management for jobs without payment, to give him something to do while he is passing the time at the end of the week. The evidence of Figure 10 supports this management belief to a certain extent, but not completely, since in this week twenty-two welders exceeded the 6s. 5d. mark in their hourly earnings—some of them by considerable amounts—and could hardly have been able to do so if rigid control of hourly earnings levels was in force. It does seem clear, however, that the convention or custom of the welders dictated about 6s. 5d. an hour as a reasonable normal rate of hourly earnings and working.

EARNINGS IN THE ENGINE WORKS

The engine works attached to this shipyard employs the usual engineering and boilermaking trades. Most of these workers are on a payment-by-results system based on time allowed to do each job with bonus payments on time saved. It is not proposed to analyse the wages of these workers in much detail. Some figures are, however, given in Table 42.

Generally speaking, the picture presented by Table 42 is not very different from that conveyed by the tables relating to the shipyard, or, indeed, to those presented in the two preceding case studies of engineering factories. Once more, overtime exercises an important effect on the relative weekly incomes of the occupations. For example, the patternmakers in this works had moderately high hourly earnings, but definitely low weekly earnings, because they were not working overtime. The differential positions of the relatively unskilled helpers, and the semi-skilled cranemen and machinists, in hourly earnings were below those of most skilled groups (though overtime alters this statement when it is put in terms of weekly earnings). The rate of earning of machinists was, however, quite clearly above that of fitters, suggesting, as was found in the other engineering factory discussed in Chapter 3, that the ease with which machinists can be put on bonus production has influenced

88

Table 42. *Earnings and hours of some principal occupations in the engine and boiler shops, February* 1955

Occupation	Number of workers	Average hours worked	Average weekly earnings	Overtime		Average hourly earnings
				Average overtime hours	Average overtime premium	
			s. d.		s. d.	s. d.
Fitters (Engine shops)	118	50·5	219 2	7·9	21 0	3 11
Turners (Engine shops)	70	51·5	262 8	8·0	21 11	5 1
Platers (Boiler shops)	44	52·7	248 10	9·7	24 11	4 9
Caulkers (Boiler shops)	19	52·4	241 9	9·0	22 6	4 7
Welders (Boiler shops)	32	52·9	264 5	10·3	26 4	5 0
Patternmakers	35	43·7	213 9	—	—	4 11
Machinists	104	52·7	240 0	9·3	21 10	4 2
Cranemen	52	53·7	200 8	10·7	22 9	3 4
Helpers	159	53·5	188 2	10·5	21 7	3 1

their earnings. The turners have the highest average hourly earnings of the skilled groups shown here—probably, once more a reflection of the operation of the bonus scheme. It is interesting finally to notice how the prospects of tradesmen vary even between departments of the same firm. The average hourly earnings of platers in the boiler shops were rather better than in the shipyard, the caulkers' were slightly poorer, and the welders' were very much poorer.

CONCLUSIONS

There is no need to present long conclusions to the essentially descriptive account given in this chapter, and a very brief summary follows.

1. In the shipyard the 'black squad' are generally on piece-work. For other trades other forms of payment-by-results are used. The contract system is still partly in use.

2. Average weekly earnings of occupations varied quite a lot in the week studied. Overtime was a principal explanation of such variation, and bonus earnings were also important, particularly for plumbers and welders, in gaining above average earnings.

3. Hours worked were generally well in excess of forty-four.

4. Distributions of hours worked and weekly earnings showed quite wide differences—especially in the earnings of welders who were on individual piece-work; but, nevertheless, analysis of hourly earnings of welders showed a strong tendency on the part of a high proportion to have about the same earning rate.

5. A brief analysis of wages in the engine works showed several points of

similarity to engineering factories studied in earlier chapters and to the shipyard.

Since this is the end of the last case-study and of the case-study section of this book, it is an appropriate place to draw impressions together. No long analysis of each point is attempted here, since this is the kind of job which the following sections tackle. It will however be useful to set down a summary of some of the most important conclusions which are indicated by the case-studies.

1. National agreements in each case do no more than provide a minimum framework for the operation of factory wages. Actual payments, even excluding overtime, are much in excess of negotiated rates.

2. While actual wage rates, or basic rates, at the factory level do in some cases differ from negotiated rates, these differences are relatively small. The bulk of the gap between the level of factory earnings and nationally negotiated arrangements has therefore to be filled by other types of payments, by bonuses or overtime rather than by wage rate increases. In this way the factories appear to be adhering, more or less, to national agreement rates, while at the same time actually paying substantially more.

3. The structure of wages dictated by actual payments differs in each case from that prescribed by national agreements. In each case relativities are altered. The major field of alteration is in the relationship between skilled and semi-skilled. Except when the semi-skilled are clearly attached to the skilled in an ancillary capacity, as in the shipbuilding case, the skilled differential, as against semi-skilled, is practically non-existent. Moreover, the effects of overlaying the negotiated rates with a number of other payments are to blur all differentials, to make their value differ according to the payments included in the calculation, and to cause many examples in which the range of payments of one group overlaps that of a more skilled group.

4. The types of payments which fill most of the gap between nationally negotiated arrangements and the actual factory payments are payment-by-results and overtime. These payments between them may amount to as much as half of total payments. Availability of a suitable bonus scheme or of overtime can be the vital factor in determining whether or not a worker is relatively well or ill paid. The type of bonus scheme may also be important.

5. Bonus percentages in each case are usually much in excess of those envisaged in agreements.

6. As a result of overtime working average hours worked in the case-studies are considerably in excess of the 'standard' forty-four-hour week. A fifty-one- or fifty-seven-hour week is more usual than a forty-four-hour week.

7. While the usual bonus percentages and overtime payments are normally obtained week by week; each is subject to some uncertainty, and some occasionally violent fluctuations, and so payment levels are somewhat uncertain.

8. On the whole, overtime appears in each case to be more associated with individual deviation in earnings than does payment-by-results. There is a tendency, for payment-by-results earnings, within very broad limits, to conform to a pattern for each group. Overtime earnings on the other hand seem to reflect individual choice, and possibly individual needs, to a greater extent. The unskilled, for example, narrow the gap between themselves and others by being much more consistent in their overtime working, and, in the one case studied in this way, family responsibilities and tax liability are associated with differences in overtime working rather than in payment-by-results earnings. Both payment-by-results and overtime produce earnings differences, but overtime seems most capable of providing individual differences which break away from a group pattern.

PART 2. FACTORY WAGE STRUCTURES

CHAPTER 7

PAYMENT-BY-RESULTS: IN PRINCIPLE

The case-studies in the preceding section emphasize the importance of payment-by-results as a major element in workers' pay packets. A method of payment cannot however simply be justified on the ground that a return is yielded to the worker: positive evidence must also be provided that it offers a more suitable way of paying wages than available alternatives. This and the following chapter are therefore concerned with discussing the justification of payment by results as a *method* of payment.

This is by no means a new method in British industry. Systems of piece-work, for example, have been traditional in many parts of the textile, printing, footwear, mining and shipbuilding industries. But general enthusiasm for payment-by-results schemes, especially the more involved varieties, seems to have grown in Britain since the war, with the post-war productivity campaign and growing interest in management training and management technique as principal contributors to increased interest.[1] This discussion is therefore conducted in an atmosphere which seems to favour progressive development of such payment methods.

In a very real sense, however, all payment is payment-by-results. The particular types of payment methods which currently come under the term 'payment-by-results' have usurped a title which might be held to be broadly synonymous with that of 'wage' itself. So, too, all payments are presumably an incentive to workers, who would otherwise in no way be held bound either to appear at a job or to work, and the description 'incentive-payment-systems' could also have a much wider meaning than that which it is usually given. While it would be simple to draw up at this point some descriptive phrases which would suffice to cover the more common types of payment-by-results, such as piece-work or premium bonus schemes, to which the term is usually held to refer, it is unwise to leave the sources of difference between the actual usage of payment-by-results *schemes* as we generally find them, and the total payment of labour, unexplained, or explained only by inclusion or

[1] According to Ministry of Labour surveys in 1938, 33 per cent of wage-earners in manufacturing industry were on payment by results, in 1949, 38 per cent were on payment-by-results, and this figure now runs at slightly over 40 per cent. On the other hand over 50 per cent of wage earners in factories employing 1000 or more are on payment-by-results.

omission from a definition. It is in this way, probably more than any other, that payment-by-results schemes are accorded properties which they do not possess, since their limits are not expressed explicitly and we are not told of the objectives they do not achieve. Some discussion of results of work is therefore a necessary preliminary. Since the results described are 'scarce', in the sense that they are not in free supply but require some effort or attribute from the worker, they are also reasons for payment.

The results of labour, or the reasons for the payment of labour, may be roughly separated into five categories, though such a classification cannot fail to be artificial, since, normally, employed labour provides its services entire, and the different aspects of its work cannot be finally separated. For example, one might reasonably claim that the harbour pilot is paid for his professional knowledge of the ways into and out of his port; but it is also reasonable to pay him only for each pilotage he carries out. These two aspects of his job, the theoretical and the practical, can be distinguished and may be paid for separately, as, for instance, by a retaining fee for placing his knowledge at the disposal of his employer, and by a fee for each pilotage he carries out. But while this practical distinction can be made, in the last analysis it is false, since the knowledge he has is based on port pilotage and each act of pilotage draws on his accumulated knowledge: the strands are interwoven. This seems true of all forms of work, though it is probably more true the more complex the work in question. For example, there are not many strands interwoven in the work carried out by a labourer though even here at least two separate, but connected, threads might be held to exist, the strength and fitness which makes the labourer an acceptable and capable candidate for the task and his actual output when set to it. The only type of result of labour (and hence type of payment) which is free of this complex nature is that which takes the form of an allowance for a specific circumstance, as for instance an instruction to a ship-repairer to do the work he usually does, with his usual insight at his usual pace etc., but to do it in a hold which unlike others has recently held molasses, or on plates which have recently been in contact with acid. In this kind of situation a specific difference is noted, and paid for. This major qualification of the inter-relatedness of different kinds of results of work reduces the possibility of separating out 'results' of work; but, if it is borne in mind, a list of 'results' may be presented.

1. Output is an obvious result of work. Work results in something being done, some article being produced or some service being rendered. This production is the output of work which can presumably be measured, at least in theory, either by counting articles produced, or by some more sophisticated measure of services. Even here, however, there is a complication since it is possible to distinguish between the output of work, the number of goods or services produced, and the output of a worker, the amount of effort or labour

he puts into producing goods. These two may diverge for all manner of reasons, which however probably divide into two, those factors which are associated with the individual worker, and those which are not. Men differ in their ability to carry out their work as well as in the rate at which they are prepared to work, and naturally such differences in ability result in corresponding differences in the number of goods produced for equivalent amounts of effort by different men. This is true not only when prolonged training is involved, so that only a craftsman baker can produce good bread, but also in the 'knack' or gift of doing certain jobs which some have and some have not, as some bakers have a deftness and a speed of production which is denied to others. On the other hand, there are the factors which are not associated with the individual worker's performance but reflect the obstacles or aids given to him in production. Even a good baker will find his speed of production of good bread handicapped by using an ancient oven, and aided by conveyer belt bread-baking equipment. If it is desired to measure the output or results of the work of men objectively, in terms of goods produced, then it is reasonable to make no allowance for differences in ability; but, if the same result is to be recorded for all those who do not differ in their individual abilities and who are putting equal effort into their tasks, all the objective factors that aid or handicap results must be allowed for in the calculation of output. In practice this can be a long list!

2. Another possible result of work is quality of product. The result of the work of a third-form schoolboy painting a picture is hardly comparable with a painting of the same subject by an acknowledged master. In some fields of activity a product or a service has no value at all unless it is of high quality. We are not all engaged on producing artistic masterpieces, but nevertheless we are bound by quality as well as quantity in the judgement accorded to our work. The minimum qualification of a baker is that he should produce bread that is palatable. The minimum requirement from a housebuilder is that his house should be wind- and water-tight and should not fall down. Sometimes, moreover, we are required to produce work that is positively 'good' and not merely negatively 'not bad'.

3. Each of these two results of work are objective in the sense that work is looked at in terms of the article produced, either its quantity or quality, and not in terms of the worker who produces. They ignore the baker and consider only his bread. As has already been suggested, in the last analysis this kind of distinction can hardly be maintained. It falls to the ground most obviously when we are considering those types of work which produce services rather than goods. Here the worker and his output can hardly be easily separated. National income analysis meets this difficulty, for example, when, faced with valuing the output of services, it has to fall back on the income of the providers of services as the measure of their output. But even where the worker is

engaged in producing a 'vendible commodity', to use Adam Smith's phrase, the distinction between work and workers can only be maintained with difficulty. To be more precise, it can only be maintained if one abstracts from the circumstance that minimum necessary abilities are needed for the production of any article, or if one looks at work produced item by item, judging it in a very short-period way, so that a long-period identification of work and workers does not take place. These two qualifications provide the third and fourth reasons for payment or results of work.

The third possible result of work or reason for payment is, then, that which relates to the ability of a worker. It is a prior condition to the successful production of either quantity or quality, that both assume the general possibility of the worker being able to make the article or do the job in question. Measurement of the output of bread by the baker has a general background assumption that the man can make bread, and payment for quality must assume that he is capable of producing good-quality bread. But ability is less specific to any one job of work than either quantity of production (the speed of carrying out the job) or quality (the way a job has been carried out or the excellence of the finished product).

'Ability' in this connection has a number of different facets, each of which is in its own way limited in supply and something we have to look for and recognize in obtaining the best results of work. Ability may be innate, or it may be the result of training, or it may take the form of an acceptance of responsibility and a willingness to take decisions. So some are fit for jobs that others cannot manage because they lack some special gift. We are not all born opera singers! Some are more able for certain jobs than others because they have been trained to do them. A joiner serves his time at his trade: a doctor qualifies for his profession. Some are prepared to take on jobs which others will not because they do not want responsibility, or are not fitted for it. Many tradesmen do not like the thought of the responsibility of being foremen: many soldiers do not want to be sergeants. But here too, apparently simple distinctions are difficult to maintain in practice, since frequently ability is improved by training and the trained man is the type who is prepared for responsibility, so all aspects of ability feed into one another. Because ability is in scarce supply and because it is required and demanded for the satisfactory performance of many jobs it is an appropriate reason for payment, and a result to be aimed at in organizing work.

4. There are some jobs in which the continued and loyal services of the same employee for a lengthy period of time are necessary to successful completion. In other cases, provided the worker has the normal abilities required by the job, it is a matter of indifference whether the same worker is on the job for a long period or is being constantly replaced. For example, it is a matter of real concern if a manager leaves his job, not merely because of the difficulty

of replacing him, but because, even if the replacement has equivalent abilities, it will be some time before he has equivalent grasp of the problems likely to arise in this new sphere of responsibility. And it is not only at the managerial level that continuity of service is needed. The same remarks apply to the building-site foreman who knows the snags of the site, or to the commercial traveller whose sales depend on acquaintance with his customers as well as selling abilities, or to the engine or lorry driver who is familiar with certain routes, or to the secretary who has a grip on the filing systems or understands her boss's peculiar methods of dictation. On the other hand a semi-skilled girl working at a belt conveyer may be readily replaced and long service may not be of relevance. This quality which arises from continued service and loyalty may also be a result of work which requires special recognition in payment.

5. Where a worker is under training it may be appropriate to remunerate him and to judge the results of his work not by his output but by the progress he has made in his training. For example, an apprentice may find that the results of his work 'for which he is paid and by which he is judged' are not the articles he has produced, but the results of his examinations and progress reports by supervisors. In another sense the work for which a trainee is paid lies in the future and his pay is, as it were, a down-payment on results which it is hoped will be delivered when he is trained.

These five subdivisions into which the results of work or reasons for payment may be classified are not by any means a complete list. They do, however, serve to demonstrate the undoubted complexity that attaches to the phrase 'the results of work'. To which of these different categories of results do the types of payment known as 'payment-by-results' refer? It is difficult even with the aid of such a subdivision to be absolutely definite in answer to this question, since payment-by-results takes so many forms and is applied in so many ways. It seems generally valid, however, to say that payment-by-results relates to the first category of results discussed here—output. On occasion, however, it may refer to the second category—quality. If, however, quality is the basis of such a payment scheme, output is usually also involved. A quantity of quality output is required. For example, the kind of payment scheme for maintenance craftsmen which is based on an inverse relation between payment and the length of time their machinery is stopped for repairs is really a payment for the quality of the craftsmens' efforts at repair, in relation to the number of machines they maintain. It is possible also to envisage schemes of payment-by-results which pay a special premium not for usual output but for the specially good effort. In general, however, the result remunerated by payment-by-results is output.[1] Moreover,

---

[1] Another possibility is that the 'result' in question will be minimization of waste. If, for example, the material being used is very valuable a scheme which is designed to ensure

while payment-by-results does not distinguish between the capabilities of workers, and is concerned only to be objective in its assessment of output, possible variations of objective factors, such as tools or materials, have to be adjusted to get the increase of output which payment-by-results seeks to remunerate.

Given that the result in question is generally output, what kind of payments legitimately come under the term 'payment-by-results'? Payments may be regular or irregular. If regular they may be at short or long intervals. They may be stable or fluctuating. Again it is difficult to generalize because of the diversity of actual payment-by-results schemes. It is generally true, however, that the type of payment to which payment-by-results schemes refer is one which fluctuates according to fluctuations in output, and there is regular provision for the assessment of possible payments. An occasional unexpected bonus, for example, may be inspired by a desire to express appreciation of, or to pass on the proceeds of, past results, but it is hardly part of a coherent payments scheme, because it lacks a direct relation of output to payment, and because, being unpredictable and uncertain, it can hardly constitute a strong incentive relation between output and reward. Finally, the payments under a payment-by-results scheme, as well as being variable with output and yielding irregular assessments of amounts due, also tend to be made at fairly short intervals, and, indeed, the current tendency seems to be to say that the more frequently output is related to remuneration and the worker gets the reward of his effort the better. At any rate, in practice, payments under such a scheme do not occur at intervals of more than a few weeks at most. The ramifications of discussion on *forms* which payment-by-results schemes may take are formidable, since limitless ingenuity has been expended on their creation. There are numerous standard varieties and large numbers of variations. A few simple points will, however, do for present purposes. Those who have the strength and desire to become masters of the detail are referred to more authoritative works.[1]

The basic need in designing a payment-by-results scheme is to find some way of measuring the output, or if by chance some other result, such as quality, is in question, of recognizing it when it appears. To this end of measuring output two usual means are employed. The first is to put a price on the constituent parts of output or to price each article produced. For

that it is not wasted would be conceivable. It is also possible to use the volume of waste as a measure of output. For example, a certain tobacco factory pays bonus to girls stripping tobacco leaves from their stalks according to the weight of the discarded stalks, with a deduction if too much leaf is left on the stalk in the stalk basket.

[1] For example—*Payment by Results*—I.L.O., Geneva, 1951; N. C. Hunt, *Methods of Wage Payment in British Industry*, Pitman, London, 1951; *Industrial Relations Handbook*, Ministry of Labour, H.M.S.O., 1953; *Employee Remuneration and Incentives*, Institute of Cost and Works Accountants, London, 1954; R. Marriott, *Incentive Payment Systems*, Staples, London, 1957.

example, a scheme may fix a price per yard of cloth produced or, in the case of a large product, it may fix prices for each sequence of operation, so that a synthesized price for the whole product can be obtained. This is a piece-work system. The alternative to pricing articles produced is to work out a time which a job should take to complete, either by special study with stop-watches or by less precise ways. Once a time is agreed, the rate of output may be measured by comparing actual times taken with the time agreed. This is a time allowance system. Payment-by-results may or may not be combined with some form of time payment (payment calculated according to time worked and not directly related to output), using such time payments either as basic rates or as guaranteed minima. Normally, time allowance systems make use of some form of time rate as the basis on which they convert bonuses calculated in terms of time into payments calculated in terms of money. Payment-by-results schemes may be related to individuals or to groups, squads etc. In time allowance schemes the worker's bonus is based on the difference between the time allowed and the time actually taken: there is quite a considerable literature on how much of the wage-value of this differ-ence, known as 'time saved', should be paid back to labour and how much retained. Various payments-by-results schemes show different divisions, the main distinctions being between those which yield a greater proportionate reward for exceptionally high output, those where the reward per unit is stable and those where it decreases. A brief, and in consequence somewhat inaccurate, definition of payment-by-results schemes might then be as follows: payment-by-results schemes are arrangements whereby the output of a group of workers, or of an individual worker, is linked to payment by a direct causal relation such that variations in output measured in single units, or over a short period of time, are reflected as quickly as possible by variations in payments.[1]

THE NECESSARY CONDITIONS FOR THE SUCCESSFUL WORKING OF PAYMENT-BY-RESULTS

The foregoing section has attempted to delimit the concept of payment-by-results, especially by indicating what types of results of work cannot be held to be reckoned by payment-by-results schemes. The upshot of this discussion is to fix on output as the principal objective of payment-by-results schemes. Of course output must be measurable before payment-by-results can be

---

[1] A useful definition is contained in W. B. Wolf, *Wage Incentives as a Managerial Tool*, Columbia University Press, New York, 1957. Payment-by-results, or 'wage incentives', are 'systems of remunerating rank-and-file workers under which the earnings of a worker, or a group of workers, are directly, promptly, and automatically related to his output by a predetermined formula relating his actual performance to a specific standard of performance'.

calculated. Further, if payment-by-results schemes are to work satisfactorily workers must be favourably disposed to them, output must be responsive to changes in labour effort, and the scheme must not be distorted by bargaining. Each of these considerations must now be discussed since each of them represents a necessary condition for the successful working of payment-by-results, and a discussion of these conditions provides the best means of studying its uses and limitations.

Output is the objective

Payment-by-results relates to output and so accents output as the result of work which above all it wishes to encourage. Before payment-by-results can be helpful it must be clear that output is indeed the principal objective in view. It may be only one among a number of possible considerations, and it is only wise for the employer to emphasize output, so far as this can be done without jeopardizing the correct emphasis on other aspects of his work and his workers. The other factors listed in the foregoing section were quality, skill, long service and loyalty, and training. This list, incomplete though it may be, provides sufficient examples of the point at issue.

Suppose, first, that an employer wants above all to ensure quality. Unless he can accent quality by some specific payment scheme then he would be wise to rely on time rates rather than on a payment-by-results scheme. It is of course possible to provide checks on quality in any payment-by-results scheme, but such checks must naturally lay down minimum standards, so that the worker would be wise to see that his work was up to standard and would be unwise to attempt to produce the very best job of which he was capable. A minimum level of quality rather than a maximum would result. Of two men, the one a fast worker with little aspiration to perfection, the other slower but more painstaking, the first would benefit most under payment-by-results, whereas the latter would produce the better quality. If maximum quality is desired, the second man is worthy of the higher remuneration and the payments system should be arranged to give that result: payment-by-results cannot do this, and so is unsuited to such a situation.

Many examples of the way in which payment-by-results may engender a clash between quantity and quality could be offered—two simple ones will suffice. In the shipyards welds must be of very high quality to withstand the pressure and strains exerted by sea and swell. Frequently more than one 'run' of welding is needed and this involves preparation of one run before another is put in. It is difficult to inspect this adequately, and yet from faulty preparation and other mistakes, a bad weld may result. (The development of X-ray inspection of welds showed that welds which looked perfect were far from being so, yet even X-ray inspection does not answer the inspection problem completely since it is a practical impossibility to inspect more than a sample of welds.) An incentive scheme geared to high output runs the risk of cutting down the care taken in preparation and so the efficiency and quality of the weld. The second example can be taken from the engineering industry. Most large engineering factories have their own toolroom. The work of the skilled men in the toolroom of necessity requires high accuracy and quality, output is much less important, and so these workers are not suited to the direct application of payment-by-results schemes. On the other hand most of the workers in comparable trades employed in other parts of the factory are likely to have their payment regulated by output and be on payment-by-results and, unless some adjustment is made, the toolroom workers, despite their skill, will be less well paid. Hence there is an agreement by which toolroom operatives receive not less than the average earnings of skilled production workers in the same establishment. Their average relative position is safeguarded but they may have fluctuating earnings if those of the production workers fluctuate.

Three points sum up the influence of the clash between quantity and quality on the possibilities of using payment-by-results.

1. If inspection of quality is difficult to arrange and if nevertheless quality is of importance then payment-by-results cannot be used unless the possibility of a sacrifice of quality is accepted.

2. If quality is more important than quantity then payment-by-results is unsuitable, or, to put it another way, pursuit of quantity is irreconcilable with pursuit of quality, unless by quality is meant a minimum and not a maximum standard and this minimum standard can be ensured by inspection. It is necessary to choose between maximum quality and maximum output.

3. Where output is the objective in one section of an establishment and quality in another, a difficult problem of relative wages will inevitably exist. This problem must be solved if those working on quality production are to be kept contented and at that type of work.

How, next, does payment-by-results fit in with the objective of obtaining a skilled labour force? The problem of the remuneration of skill is discussed more fully in Chapter 10 but the relevant points can be made here.

1. Skill, as distinct from output, is an attribute of workers rather than of work. One may regard output as variable from week to week, and payment-by-results does so; skill, on the other hand, does not vary in this way, but is rather a qualification which is acquired, and if kept in use by practice, is with the worker for his working life. In contrast to payment for output, therefore, payment for skill ought to be fixed on a more long-term basis and should be much less variable.

2. The payment which an employer decides to offer for skill is in the nature of a recruitment wage: it is the price he offers to induce skilled men to enter

his factory. In contrast, payment for output is offered once men are inside a factory to keep up their rate of working, and assumes that they have the necessary ability to do the job. It is desirable in the interests of securing good quality, skilled labour for a factory, and, in the long run, to secure good quality and quantity of skill for the economy, that the recruitment wage for skill should be adequate. Payment-by-results cannot readily form part of the recruitment wage. If it is overemphasized a decline in the attractiveness of the recruitment offer to skill seems inevitable.

3. Looked at in a broader setting, the 'reward' of the skilled man includes the status which his job possesses as well as the income he gets from it. This, of course, is a point of general validity outside, as well as within, the wage-earning community. For example, it has long been a standard remark, with considerable truth in it, that the status enjoyed by the academic man, not to mention the privilege and pleasures of the academic life, goes a long way to compensate for the loss of possibly more attractive income opportunities. But it is only where there is some obvious alternative measuring rod for status that it and income can be regarded as independent variables of 'reward' for work, and even in such cases it is doubtful whether, in the long run, status without income is a tenable position. In the case of the skilled wage earner there is some independence in the label which skill gives to the workman who can say he is a tradesman, but nevertheless income is also an important label, and the income a tradesman can lay claim to also indicates to himself and to others the status in the community which he enjoys. What is this status-income in the case of a tradesman? The answer, to the writer's way of thinking, is that wage level which the tradesman thinks of and can cite as his regular and assured weekly payment, in other words, his wage rate. In so far as payment-by-results contributes to earnings rather than to rates, it operates against the payment of a high status-rate, unless the management are prepared to go much beyond the average in the total level of their payment. Moreover, the problem of final relative wage levels has to be mentioned. If payment-by-results is being paid to semi-skilled and not to skilled, then an immediate possibility of damage to the objective of a contented skilled labour force occurs. This is the typical source of conflict between the relative wage levels of semi-skilled and skilled workers which the case-studies evidenced again and again.

Taken together these points suggest that payment-by-results is not an acceptable substitute for payments specifically designed to remunerate skill, nor was it held to be suitable where quality was the objective. Can it be fitted in with the other objectives listed—long service and loyalty and training? Moreover, can it react to special labour shortages? These can be discussed more rapidly.

Where long service and loyalty are characteristics desired by management from its labour force, then it is reasonable to suggest that payment should be designed to help in securing this. Since the worker is by definition to be with the firm a long time then the wage bargain should also be long term and should give him security. The payment should be regular and not subject to frequent fluctuations due to short-period circumstances, so as to create income security. A salary type of payment is indicated or, failing that, a time rate. 'Fringe' benefits such as pensions or sick payments (typical of salaried-class benefits) will also be helpful in engendering loyalty. Certainly payment-by-results which is neutral as between man and man and does not reflect individual circumstances hardly provides grounds for feeling that 'the firm will look after' the worker.[1] Further, payment-by-results is designed to fluctuate with short-period measurements of output and does not foster income security.

Payment-by-results can be harmful in the case of training. The ground for this view is simply that training is concerned with explanation of how and why jobs are carried out in any given way, and with practice in their performance. To superimpose an output incentive here may well cause the lesson to be half learned—unless indeed training consists only of a speeding-up process for a very simple type of job.

On occasion one type of worker may become especially scarce. Economic theory deals at length with this circumstance, around which is built the theory of relative wages designed to explain how economic forces operate to adjust the supply of a scarce type of labour to the demands for it. The situation may for example require long-term movements of the relative wage levels of industries, or regions or occupations. In the more restricted factory situation scarcity of one group will also necessitate both short-term and long-term action, and it is difficult to see how the prescription can deviate from economic theory. But payment-by-results is set up in accordance with measured rates of output, and does not ask as the primary question—will such a level for this particular group be sufficient to ensure their adequate supply. Admittedly the objective measurements may be made the subject of bargaining in which a scarce type of labour will be specially strong. But in so far as bargaining succeeds in altering objective valuations the principles of the valuer, are bent if not broken. Besides, what of the more typical short-term situation, a special shortage of a type of labour arising in a factory, where prices and times have already been agreed? There is a rigidity about such a situation, since the existing prices and times will have been defended as fair, reasonable and correct, yet the economics of labour supply may require an

[1] The shipyards typically combine their piece-working attitudes with the corresponding attitude towards their labour force, that of hiring and firing frequently. Labour-turnover records in shipyards are full of the notation P.O.J.F. (paid off, job finished)—and this persists even though a new job may be started in a few days. Cf. 'Labour Turnover in the Clyde Shipbuilding Industry', op. cit.

alteration. Payment-by-results is not helpful where the adequacy of labour supply is a frequent worry.[1]

In sum, payment-by-results requires as a condition of its success that it should be used where only output is the desired result, but with due consideration of the effect upon and by other factors. When, then, other considerations are important they require that payment-by-results should take a subordinate position, and, if used as more than a marginal payment, payment-by-results will create conflict with other objectives.

Output can be measured

The second condition necessary to the successful working of payment-by-results schemes is that variations in workers' output can be measured with accuracy. This means rather more than the existence of possible long-term checks on the productivity of large groups such as a whole factory's labour force. What is needed is an effective method of measuring the output or variations in output from week to week, or hour to hour, of the individual or group to whom a payment-by-results scheme applies. This problem exists whether we are talking of piece-work schemes and piece-work prices, where the issue is to find a satisfactory unit of output on which to put a price, or time-allowance schemes where a unit to be timed has to be found. In consequence factors which influence the ease or difficulty of measuring output on this scale automatically influence the success of a payment-by-results scheme. Such factors must now be considered.

1. Since a payment-by-results scheme tries to relate reward to output at frequent and regular intervals, it is essential that measurement of output can be carried out at such intervals. This means in effect that it must be possible to find a suitable unit of output which can be completed by the individual or group concerned in a short period. Since payment-by-results schemes generally operate on a weekly basis of remuneration, the period of completion of the measured unit should be less than a week. Preferably a number of units should normally be completed within a week, since if only one is normally completed then the earnings under the scheme will tend to be based to a large extent on an estimate of the proportion completed of a second unfinished unit. This limits the duration of a job which is being made the subject of a payment-by-results scheme unless it is possible to sectionalize it effectively. Ideally a payment-by-results scheme requires to be applied to work

---

[1] A similar point is put by Wolf, op. cit. 'The use of payment by results injects a dynamic element into the wage structure. Traditional wage differentials are often upset. From the workers' point of view such changes frequently appear illogical and unreasonable. This distortion of the wage structure is inherent in the use of payment by results in remunerating rank-and-file factory workers.' Mr Wolf's work appears to the present writer to be an excellent treatment of the whole subject of payment-by-results.

which produces quite a large number of units of output in a week. The longer the job continues the more complicated the payment-by-results scheme becomes and it can only be worked if a suitable break-up of the job is possible.

2. A payment-by-results scheme depends for its success on the presence of a precise monetary inducement made evident by a price or a time put upon the work being performed. To operate effectively this price or time has to be laid down in advance. It can be argued from this that payment-by-results operates best when output consists of the production of similar articles, and least well when only one of each type of product is produced. This conclusion follows from a number of considerations.

In order to set the price or time it is necessary for the job to be one that is already being performed or else to have a trial run. If only one is being produced, then basing prices or times on existing performance of the job is not possible and a trial run would necessitate doing each separate job twice. Of course, even where end-products are dissimilar they may be created by a series of operations which are common to a number of jobs so that a price or time can be synthesized from previously measured operations. But if the similarity breaks down, and there is surely a limit to the extent to which dissimilar end-products can be created by similar operations, then a leap in the dark is expected from those who price or time the job, which will not only be difficult to do but will again tend to mean individual consideration for each job.

The close link between output and payment which payment-by-results aims at is fostered by certainty in the mind of the operative as to the reward offered for his labour, and is damaged by any kind of arbitrariness. But a feeling of arbitrary price-fixing can hardly be avoided when the price or time for each job is fixed only as the job comes along. A long run of similar products makes for certainty about the monetary inducement offered. Moreover, it takes time to settle down to a new task, speed of work alters and ideas about the ease or difficulty of the job alter. A price or time set up for a job that has settled down has more chance of accuracy than that for a one-off job where neither job, worker, price nor time has a chance to settle down.

3. The question of providing a suitable measurement of output can of course be phrased in terms of finding a suitable way of measuring output. As well as difficulties arising out of the type of output to be measured, there may also be difficulties created by the method of measurement. Basically measurement of output must rely on either watching the process of production or estimation based on long knowledge of products and methods. It is possible to employ various different methods of fixing a price or time, of which the most obvious, though not always the most acceptable to the man, is to use a stop-watch, and varying allowances can be made for rest periods, etc.

But all methods of measurement involve a factor of human variation whether in the operative being studied or in the estimator. The method of timing test operations removes most possibility of error in the estimator, but it then becomes necessary to assume that the operatives being studied are working at their average speed unbiased by the test. This is a large assumption unless the operatives are not aware of the presence of the people carrying out the test, which is unlikely, or unless the test can be carried on over a considerable period which is costly. Indeed the question of the length of time over which average speed is to be determined represents a major difficulty in timing work. If an untimed estimation is used then most possibility of error in pricing or timing is likely. Naturally the estimator has to be someone with a very good knowledge of the type of work he is dealing with—above average knowledge. This means a risk that his ideas of how long a job ought to take will be either unduly influenced by his own superior abilities or unduly influenced by his concern for the lesser abilities of others.

4. If prices and times can be satisfactorily measured and related to suitable units of output there still remains the problem of measuring the output as it appears. On the whole it seems unlikely that this will cause many difficulties, as a simple matter of counting units of output, though it will almost certainly involve costs. A different question arises, however, over the need to ensure that the units are of the requisite quality. A satisfactory system of inspection is just as necessary as a satisfactory system of output measurement, and, as has already been argued, such a system of inspection is more necessary under a payment-by-results scheme than under other types of remuneration.

5. Once a satisfactory price or time has been arrived at it naturally relates only to the production of the unit of output to which it refers. But this comparatively simple statement holds hidden snags—producing similar units of output in this connotation means not only similar end-products but similar equipment, similar conditions of work, and similar materials available in a similar way. A whole host of special allowances can be bred by these further conditions. If a new type of machine is introduced this means a reworking of prices and times, though this view may be, and on occasions is, contested by workers or their representatives. However, subject to the possible difficulties of industrial relations, prices and times are likely to be adjusted with a major change. But what of all the minor changes in machinery that may occur— the slight modifications and improvements, breakdowns, maintenance difficulties, improved efficiency after maintenance, decreased efficiency with old age—all these possible equipment changes are relevant to correct timing or pricing of jobs. Besides variations in equipment a job may be affected by variations in work conditions. The possibilities here are limitless. The previously cited case of the welders may again be used as illustration. The angle of weld is an important variable in the speed of work and must be allowed for;

the work may have to be done in more or less awkward positions; it may have to be done outside in rain or wind, or under cover; on repair jobs there may be smell and dirt to contend with. Conditions of work may vary in both predictable and unpredictable ways. The materials with which the job is to be done may also differ from occasion to occasion. For example, a joiner's work may normally be done with soft wood with relatively few knots in it, but sometimes he may have to use hard wood, or, on other occasions, the wood may be full of knots. The time or price set by the payment-by-results scheme ought to take account of all such possibilities.

In sum, satisfactory measurements of units of output are necessary to the operation of a payment-by-results scheme. This depends in particular on the availability of a suitable unit of output, on the possibility of producing a series of units of similar type, on having satisfactory methods of measuring output and of inspection, and finally on being able to make correct allowance for variations in methods, materials and conditions of work.

Workers' attitudes are favourable

The whole idea of payment-by-results rests on the assumption that workers will react to a direct monetary incentive placed upon output by increasing their output. This is a big assumption, but one that can be accepted as broadly true. The present writer, at least, would not be prepared to contend that there is not an association between increases in pay through direct monetary incentives and increases in output. This, however, is not enough by itself to justify the use of payment-by-results. We need to know whether payment-by-results schemes are the best way of applying direct monetary incentives. We need to know the consequential effects on other types of incentive and on other characteristics of the workers' labour. We need to know the pattern of the relationship between increased output and direct monetary incentives of the payment-by-results scheme type, since while an association between payment by results and increases in output under some circumstances can readily be granted, there is a long step between this and agreement on a direct and complete correlation between the two.

This is a very large subject, going beyond the more practical question with which the preceding section has been concerned. In essence, however, it asks whether workers accept the role and attitudes for which payment-by-results casts them. In part this question has been answered in the earlier discussion of possible results of work other than output since it is there implied that if a man's efforts are directed at another objective—quality for example—then his attitude is *ipso tanto* not directed towards payment-by-results. Imposition of a payment-by-results scheme may lead to a reorientation of his attitude which will affect his other objective. Four points about workers' attitudes to

106

payment-by-results schemes, however, must still be made. In making them, and them only, the writer must plead guilty to a serious limitation of the subject, on the possibly reprehensible grounds that to proceed further is to leave economics far behind and to become involved in the mysteries of psychology.

1. Generally speaking, payment-by-results schemes may be based on three possible relationships between bonus payments and increased output: bonus increasing more than proportionately to output, proportionately to output, and less than proportionately to output.[1] Each of these anticipates different workers' attitudes to incentive payment, since while the first assumes that as the rate of output rises a further increase requires more incentive, the last appears to assume the opposite.[2] Whatever may be the assumptions behind these payment-by-results schemes, however, it is surely safe to make the assumption that there is a limit to physical effort, to which increases in rate of output of workers must tend. Moreover, as output increases is it not also reasonable to assume that effort begins to grow more than proportionately? A three-minute mile involves more than 100 per cent increase on the effort needed for a six-minute mile!

A number of points follow. First, if payments under payment-by-results are meant to reflect effort it would be sensible to adopt some system whereby payment increased more than proportionately to output. But, of course, payment is designed to produce output, and, only in consequence of output, to compensate effort. Since this is so the payment should be governed not by effort expended by workers but by workers' attitudes to the need to make special efforts to reach high outputs and to the monetary incentives offered. The second point to be made is, therefore, to relate workers' attitudes to different systems of payment. It would be folly to suggest that the worker has calculated his work accurately in terms of effort and its reward; but he can hardly fail to be aware when he is working at full pressure, and he has, one might almost say, an hereditary dislike of being cheated. If this is accepted then it seems to follow logically that workers will be averse to schemes where payment increases less than proportionately to output on the linked grounds

---

[1] Examples of these are (a) accelerating premium plans in which, after standard production has been reached, earnings increase in a greater ratio than production; (b) piece-work in which remuneration for increased output grows proportionately to output increases; and (c) premium-bonus systems (e.g. Rowan, Weir/Halsey) in which the worker 'shares' with his employer in cost reductions. For example, as in the Halsey system, a man may be paid his time rate for the hours he actually works (time taken) and bonus equivalent to his time rate for half the hours he saves, hours saved being defined as hours allowed (by time study or rate-fixing of the job) minus hours taken. There are also systems in which proportionality of output to payment is altered at specified levels of output.

[2] In practice, it may, however, be used with the idea that if output grows much above the time allowed then there must be something wrong with the times allowed, and it will be as well not to let the workers get away with too high a proportion of easily-won gains.

107

that they seem to be having to do more for less and that they are being cheated. On the other hand, schemes where proportionality of payment and output is maintained will not meet with such a pronounced reaction. As well as possessing a seeming logicality this conclusion squares also with typical trade union attitudes on this issue.

The third point which follows from this discussion is that the tendency to present payment-by-results schemes as open-ended is an illusion. The sky may be the limit, but there is no chance whatsoever of workers' earnings reaching to it. Industrial consultants sometimes suggest that the relation between output and effort is a straight-line one. This too is an illusion, since as output grows there comes a point at which effort grows more than proportionately, and indeed at some point increased effort will become a physical impossibility. Doubtless the reply would be that while theoretically, and at specially high output levels, these are illusions, nevertheless they work well enough in practice for any of the usual output variations. But these illusions are relevant to the determination of the ends of payment-by-results. If it is thought, in however vague or absent-minded a fashion, that payment-by-results opens up vistas of ever-increasing labour productivity then it is reasonable to encourage extraordinary feats of output by individuals—as showing the way to others. If, on the other hand, the attitude taken is that payment-by-results is a means of raising labour's output to a 'satisfactory' level but not as a possible means of extraordinary output, then there is much less case for encouraging the specially high productivity of the odd individual, and more reason to concentrate on group performance. This brings the discussion round to another factor of importance in considering workers' attitudes to payment by results—should these schemes be based on individuals or groups?

2. The general tendency among practitioners of payment-by-results is to say that since the monetary incentive is the thing that counts with workers it should be applied wherever possible to the individual worker. The 'economic man' hypothesis is here given absolute credence. Is complete belief in this frequently modified economic hypothesis justifiable in this case?

It is possible that employers may prefer to design incentive schemes which apply to groups of workers rather than to individuals, whether because they have realized that encouragement of the group can be more important than encouragement of the individual for the reasons discussed above, or because group schemes suit their methods of production—a point to be taken up later. Apart from these considerations, however, it is still necessary to reflect that a system of payment-by-results applied to individuals will only work on an individual basis to the extent that workers do in fact think and act individually and not as a group. Clearly the contention that workers think and act in groups rather than individually is not one that can be laid down with

108

dogmatism as applicable in all circumstances; but, on the other hand, neither can the contention that workers always do their work as individuals uninfluenced by group considerations. The theme that man is a social animal is much canvassed in social psychology and sociology[1] and its ramifications go far beyond the present subject matter, but a number of factors which qualify the individual hypothesis in favour of the group one may be put here. The extent to which any of this applies in any given circumstance will depend, of course, upon these circumstances. The strength of forces working on groups varies from case to case.

The strongest hypothesis would be that men's individual instincts and attitudes are invariably submerged in those of the more important groups in which their life is spent—the work group being possibly one of the most important of such groups. If this hypothesis is accepted then individual incentives will result in a group reaction, and a group incentive would be better. But surely this, as applied to work groups, is much too strong: there can be no doubt, for example, that individual payment-by-results schemes do not produce completely uniform results from the groups to which they are applied. What appears to be a much more reasonable hypothesis is that men do live in society and accept from the groups of which they are members limitations to their actions as individuals. This would accept the view that men are individuals but that, as individuals, they compromise with the society in which they live by accepting limitations to their individual freedom. The immediate thought that occurs is to seek the reason for the acceptance of such limitations. Four slightly different ways of putting such a reason may be suggested.

First, there is the dislike of being an outcast. Even if we fail to accept the view that man is completely a social animal there can be few to deny that he is partly a social animal and as such is not very much pleased when society casts him out. But every society or group has its rules, beliefs and customs, sometimes formal and sometimes quite informal, and membership of the group requires some measure of adherence to the rules. In the particular case of the work group, rules are likely to relate to volume of work and attitudes to work.

Secondly, there are the habit-forming results of close association. Except in the case of legal or imposed groupings, the existence of a group presumes some community of outlook, interest, attitude and purpose in its members, otherwise they are not a group. While people are thrown together in their work place much as a matter of chance, it can be reasonably argued that they do not stay there unless they find the company, if not congenial, at least bearable. It seems to follow from this that members of the work group will tend to develop, as individuals, similar attitudes to work, that these can be

[1] Not least by Elton Mayo and his associates with reference to the Hawthorne Experiments.

aggregated into a group attitude, and that they will accept limitations on their freedom arising out of their being members of a group.

Thirdly, there is the loyalty aspect. Apart from formal or informal rules of group membership which limit individual action by workers, workers will be limited in the ways in which they diverge from the expected norms or standards of group behaviour by feelings of loyalty to the group. As men work together and live together at their work their loyalty to each other grows. A work group which forms itself from common interest is welded together by loyalty.

Finally, there is likely to be actual similarity of work, of background, and of problems. The existence of a group of workmen displaying the characteristics suggested above must depend in part at least on association in the type of work each is doing. Since the problems found by men doing similar work will be similar and since, generally speaking, the men will have broadly similar social backgrounds, the emergence of groups and group attitudes seems to be a common-sense deduction.

All of the foregoing remarks may be summarized in the somewhat unhelpful statement that where workers form groups they adopt group attitudes, the inference for payment-by-results being that where a work group exists that group will prefer a group basis for payment-by-results. Two questions have been very carefully begged in this—when and how does a work group appear, and should the employer pander to these worker attitudes.

The answer to the first of these questions is not one that can be readily provided. Certain conditions are likely to need satisfying before a group of workers adopting group attitudes appears on the work floor. For example, the workers concerned must be in contact with each other. There is likely to be some resemblance in the conditions and type of work of each of them. The workers concerned will tend to have roughly the same status. If they are required to work in any way as a team then a group attitude is a probable development. This list of possibilities could be extended, but while the possibilities can be listed they cannot be turned into hard and fast rules of guidance which would allow immediate recognition of circumstances in which group attitudes will appear. It can, however, be said that normally people work together and so informal social groupings, and attitudes, are likely to be more the rule than the exception. The existence of group attitudes in workers ought probably to be assumed unless the contrary can be demonstrated.

Should employers fall in with worker group attitudes or ignore them in framing payment-by-results schemes? This is something of a side issue to the discussion of necessary conditions for successful payment-by-results schemes, but a digression should be of value. The question must obviously be answered by considering whether the same amount of monetary incentive will yield a larger return to the employer if paid individually or to groups. The fallacy of thinking that payment-by-results can make a prodigy out of every workman has already been mentioned, this suggests that group payments may suit the employer best, since in the end it is group output rather than individual output that he has to increase. Moreover, not all processes are suited to increases in the rate of work of some workers beyond others. The exceptionally quick worker could get in the way by being out of step in processes in which team-work and rhythm of work are essential.[1] In such circumstances group payments would be best. In any case, if an employer is faced with a work group with defined and strong attitudes and he attempts to apply individual incentive, one or other of two not very desirable results may occur. If the individual incentive begins to work on an individual basis then the employer will have broken up the work group, and he will then have achieved his bonus scheme at the cost of destroying the cohesion of his labour force. The workers' feelings of loyalty and 'belongingness' may then disappear and be replaced by an atmosphere which will engender higher labour turnover or more serious troubles. If, on the other hand, the work group reject the individual incentive then they may either try to manipulate it into a group payment by unofficial evening out of bonus or by limitations on individual output, or they may react more positively against the whole incentive principle. If, however, a group incentive is applied to a work group, then there is less likelihood of rejection of the incentive since the group as a whole can benefit. And also group forces which operated against incentives in the individual case now favour the employers' plans. The group's own loyalties will ensure that all pull their weight to increase output uniformly and smoothly. In other words, a group payment-by-results scheme is necessary where work groups are strongly established.[2]

3. A rather more minor point is to note the damaging effects of too many bonuses. Enthusiasm for payment-by-results could, and does in many cases,

[1] Wolf, op. cit., makes a useful distinction between maximum and optimum output, 'If the worker maximizes his output . . . the worker's rate of output will vary widely. The frequent fluctuations will tend to disrupt schedules and to necessitate excessive work-in-progress inventories. In contrast, if the worker maintains an 'optimum' rate of output, he will produce at a rate which facilitates the smooth flow of materials through the manufacturing processes.'

[2] It is sometimes said of individual payment-by-results that it sets man against man. This is a view with which the above discussion is broadly in agreement, though it tends to stress the group loyalties as being sufficiently strong in many cases to cause group cohesion to triumph over and reject the principles of individual payment. A rather different point of view criticizes payment-by-results *in toto* since it assumes different standards of loyalty from 'staff' or management, who are not on incentive or on a weekly basis of payment, and wage-earners who are. These two views may to some extent be squared. The individual incentive assumes that two workers do not have loyalty either to themselves as a group or to their employers. The group incentive assumes that group loyalty is an important part of the workers' attitudes and that this type of loyalty can be made to work, through group self-interest, in the same way as loyalty to employers. The wage payment which does not contain direct payment-by-results assumes that loyalty can be a characteristic of a group which includes both employers and workers.

111

lead to the idea that another dose can do nothing but good. One has a slightly malicious picture of managers increasing their own productivity in their own estimation by thinking out a yet more subtle scheme to add to the list already applied to their workers. But this a most doubtful piece of management economics.

This point need not be laboured since it relies only on commonsense. If, for example, a regular payment-by-results system which is based on weekly output is supplemented by a further bonus payable at holiday time according to annual output, then the one may provide some slight additional impetus to the other. But if then another bonus scheme is added, say a special addition will be made to weekly rates for each three-month average of output which tops a fixed datum line, then the worker may be forgiven if he becomes somewhat vague about the details of what he has to do about each scheme and what his various goals are. If yet another scheme is added then further confusion seems inevitable. In other words, there are diminishing returns to incentive schemes.

4. Payment-by-results produces fluctuations in earnings which reflect fluctuations in output. All of us have regular outgoings to meet and prefer regular incomes with which to meet them. Other things being equal, an income which appears regularly and with certainty is preferable to one which averages the same amount but is paid in irregular and fluctuating amounts. Workers will therefore prefer payment schemes which result in regular earnings rather than fluctuating earnings.[1]

In sum, workers are likly to be opposed to payment schemes which offer diminishing reward as output grows. Because of physical limitations on effort the idea of workers' output continuing to increase must be a myth, and a 'satisfactory' level of output may be a more sensible aim. Workers tend to form work groups and adopt group attitudes. This reduces the chances of success of individually based payment schemes, and the long-run interests of employers may be best served by group rather than individual schemes. Workers will be adversely affected by the application of too many and conflicting payment schemes. They will prefer, other things being equal, to receive their income in regular and certain payments.

Output is responsive to changes in labour effort

A somewhat obvious, but nevertheless necessary, condition for the success of payment-by-results schemes is that the rate of production is capable of being varied by the workers increasing or decreasing their expenditure of effort. For example, workers doing semi-skilled jobs to mass-production output being carried past them on a belt conveyor are in many ways suited to

---

[1] This point is discussed in the Appendix on *Variable Earnings and Wage Earners' Expenditure* at the end of this book.

payment-by-results schemes, but fail on this condition: the speed of their work is governed by the speed of the conveyor belt and so output cannot be varied by changes in their effort alone. If a payment-by-results scheme is applied to them it can only be on a group basis, and its function will not be to increase output directly, but to secure acceptance by the workers of the output dictated by a certain conveyor belt speed. Another example of the same type of situation occurs when a worker's duties are to control and inspect the running of machinery. Once again speed of output is not in the control of the worker. Yet another example occurs when workers' duties are ancillary to the main process of production. People such as storemen or cranemen have duties which require them to be at hand and ready to help production workers as required, they do not generally directly influence output, except in the sense that failure to perform their duties will undoubtedly hinder production. A direct payment-by-results scheme is of little value here.

The payment-by-results scheme is not distorted by bargaining

As a result of the growth of the machinery, atmosphere, and attitude of mind of collective bargaining in industry, there is a tendency for payment-by-results schemes to be subjected to collective bargaining processes. Unless such bargaining is confined to the very broad outlines of the scheme, it will result in hopeless distortion. No special harm, and some good, may be done to the payment-by-results schemes if bargaining takes place on, for example, whether payments by the scheme will be more or less than proportionate to output as output grows, or attempts to ascertain and then adjust the total amount that will be paid to labour as a result of a new scheme. These are matters of general importance which are proper subjects for collective bargaining. But if bargaining affects the details of prices or times, or payment, then the scheme becomes incoherent. Suppose, for example, that a time for the performance of a job is worked out carefully and is then subject to bargaining. If, as a result, the time is altered, without similar alterations being made to all times for the particular class of work or worker, then the result is likely to be that an average operative will either be paid less or more than his output merits. Some jobs will offer easier money than others. The result will be justifiable distrust and suspicion on the part of workers. Management will be able to manipulate the scheme so as to favour some employees more than others, and, if they do not, workers may well do the manipulating themselves. In consequence an arbitrary scale of (relative) earnings will grow up reflecting past bargains and adjustments of workers between easy and hard money, and not relative outputs.

It may be objected that this singles out for special condemnation the bargaining that takes place over payment-by-results schemes and fails to mention that bargaining is a very normal part of almost all decision-taking in wage agreements. It is true that bargains are commonly struck in almost every aspect of wages, but in the case of payment-by-results the effects of bargaining extend not only to the determination of general wage levels or hours, but also to the whole of a mechanism which only results in a rational division of earnings between workers if each price or time can be determined accurately, and this means without being made the subject of a bargain.

CONCLUDING REMARKS

The somewhat abstract discussion of this chapter has been aimed at establishing the nature of the results which payment-by-results systems try to achieve, and the conditions that require to be satisfied before such a system becomes a logical possibility. No attempt has been made here to discuss the actual use of payment-by-results in practice, nor to consider the extent to which actual payment schemes of this type satisfy these logically necessary conditions. It does, of course, follow from the somewhat stringent conditions postulated that, in practice, payment-by-results schemes do not always meet all of them; compromises between the logical requirements of the schemes and the needs of the actual situation inevitably follow, but this is part of the subject matter of the next chapter. Further, no attempt has been made here to illustrate from practical examples the propositions put forward, nor to consider the claims put forward for payment-by-results by practitioners. The objective has been solely to establish the logic of payment-by-results as a method of payment. This is the first step. Without doubt the question of whether or not the method results in output increase is most important, and must be discussed, but it is a step to be taken after a discussion of its principles.

Payments-by-results is concerned with output. This is the result of work which it attempts to secure. It is not, therefore, compatible with situations in which, for example, quality, or the ability of the worker, or his loyalty, are the objectives which the employer is attempting to achieve. Further, in payment-by-results schemes output is calculated regularly and payment is automatically made in relation to output at short intervals. Such a scheme requires that output can be measured satisfactorily. For this a suitable kind of output, an efficient measuring system, and a system of inspection are all needed. Moreover, it must be possible to make allowances for such changes in, for example, equipment, as may affect output. If the scheme is to work well it must depend on the workers' attitude to it being favourable. Here, in particular, the question of the group consciousness of workers is particularly relevant to the separatist effect of individually based payment schemes. Also, output must be responsive to changes in labour effort. Finally, a payment-by-results scheme must not be altered in its detailed structure by bargaining.

114

CHAPTER 8

PAYMENT-BY-RESULTS: IN PRACTICE

The effect of the discussion of payment-by-results in Chapter 7 is to set up a most formidable series of hurdles which have to be surmounted before a payment-by-results scheme can be regarded as a fully suitable method of payment. In practice, payment-by-results is not as rarely used as full satisfaction of this list of conditions would suggest. Its actual working therefore betrays many examples of conflicts of principles and of compromises. These must be illustrated in detail since to do so is to study the actual working of payment-by-results at present: this forms the subject of the next section of this chapter. Naturally, employers and others use and recommend payment-by-results because they consider that such a payment method has advantages: these advantages are discussed in the third section of this chapter, and the disadvantages to employers are also further discussed. The fourth section sums up the discussion by considering an alternative payment method.

CONFLICTS AND COMPROMISES

Two preliminary observations

Before discussion of the conflicts and compromises that result from attempts to adjust actual payment-by-results schemes to circumstances which do not favour their use, two important general points should be made.

First, it is important to notice the extent to which strong advocates of payment-by-results draw their illustrations from situations in which the conditions of Chapter 7 are largely met. It is of course also true that those who wish to criticize payment-by-results tend to draw their illustrations from situations in which these conditions are far from being fulfilled. But those who make generalized claims for a payment method are under an obligation to demonstrate their claims in the widest possible setting or they can legitimately be accused of arguing from the particular to the general. Those who criticize a payment method are, on the other hand, entitled to draw examples from the field in which the method is actually used and so to suggest by criticism that the method has been extended beyond the limits of its applicability. This is the general line of criticism adopted here. No attempt is being made to suggest that payment-by-results can never be used, but rather to suggest limits to its use.

It is instructive to consider briefly the type of work and the type of worker which are likely to satisfy the conditions set out in Chapter 7, though at this general level it is only possible to speak in very broad terms. Output must be the clear objective put in front of the workers; this tends to mean production work, or at least work where skill, or quality, or unique features in particular workers, are not specially important. There is here a strong suggestion of semi-skilled production workers. The output must be able to be readily measured and inspected and it will be better if a number of units are produced within a single payment-by-results period. This indicates that the work should produce relatively standardized articles in numbers. These two features added together infer semi-skilled workers on mass or batch production work. Since output must be variable with worker effort fully automatic mass production where the speed of work is regulated by the speed of machinery, or the rate of movement of a conveyor belt, will not be appropriate, but short of that the work should be as smooth-flowing as possible. Workers' attitudes must be favourable. This suggests that workers should agree that output is their important function and claim to payment: they must not, therefore, be especially skill- or quality-conscious. They must also be prepared to accept fluctuating earnings and, if an individual payment-by-results scheme is involved, they must not be too strong in their group consciousness. These last two points are less easy to typify in terms of workers. It seems likely, however, that young girl workers will have fewer domestic responsibilities and a more direct short-term outlook to their money and their work, and these features probably mean less antipathy to fluctuating earnings and less strong group consciousness than applies to older female workers and the average male worker. Such young female workers in industry are typically on semi-skilled machine work. In the case of males the relevant factor is probably labour mobility. If workers change their jobs frequently then they cannot readily develop either regular incomes and income security or strong group loyalties within a factory. Again the semi-skilled machine-worker tends to have relatively high labour mobility. Finally, the payment-by-results scheme must not be compromised by bargaining. This implies either weak trade unions or trade unions with long and sympathetic knowledge of these payment methods. Trade union organization in Britain is weak among women workers and in the newer mass production type of factories. Trade union understanding of payment by results is especially great in such long-established piece-work industries as textiles and boot and shoe manufacture. The picture that emerges is of semi-skilled workers, possibly especially female semi-skilled workers, engaged in routine production of a large number of standardized articles, in industries, such as textiles or light consumer goods manufacture, in which trade unions are either expert in payment-by-results work or relatively weak. This is exactly the kind of situation in which the operation of payment-by-results seems to be most often demonstrated and praised. Yet this is a much narrower range of application than exists at present,[1] and certainly does not afford support for applying payment-by-results to every worker.

The second general point that must be made here relates to the effect of payment-by-results schemes on wage structure. Most of the problems raised in Chapter 7 affect the internal consistency of payment-by-results schemes, but two of them have important consequences for relative wage levels. The condition that output must be the objective of the wage system does not only apply to the workers for whom a payments-by-results scheme is being devised; but also to other workers who are bound together with them in the same wage structure. Secondly, the working of supply and demand may at any time throw up a special scarcity of one type of worker, and it is likely to be beyond the flexibility of a payment-by-results scheme to adjust for this.

The idea of wage structure generally refers to a system of relative wage levels which are adjusted to reflect the strength of supply and demand for each group concerned, and which therefore also reflect the strength of considerations such as training, capacity, ability, age, etc., as well as social factors which influence labour supply. Payment-by-results on the other hand is not designed to fluctuate with supply and demand considerations but only with an objective measurement of output. If supply and demand factors alter, then a payment-by-results scheme offers an obstacle to appropriate adjustment of the wage structure. If a payments scheme begins to yield larger returns to the worker than were originally thought likely, then this may affect the supply of labour by altering its price. Of course it is true that the increase in reward may flow from increased effort; but if all workers subject to a scheme begin to experience earnings increases, and especially if such increases are in part due to a faulty scheme which makes extra earnings easy, then we are no longer talking of extra earnings to hard-working individuals, but of a general alteration in relative wage levels. This kind of alteration in wage structure may occur within a system in which all are on payment-by-results, if one section of the scheme begins to afford considerably better earnings opportunities than another. It may also occur in circumstances in which one section of a producing unit is subject to payment-by-results while another section is not. It is this latter case which creates an obligation on the employer who wishes to use payment-by-results, either to be satisfied that a scheme designed to emphasize output to the exclusion of other objectives is appropriate to his whole labour force, or else to find some means of insulating workers who cannot be put on an output scheme from the direct effects of the output scheme, while still maintaining their relative wage position. The

[1] It follows that payment-by-results in its widest use cannot claim to be 'scientific', as some try to call it. The use of this word suggests a system of payment which consistently follows rational, logical and objective rules. If compromise is necessary the rules must be broken and the scientific nature of payment-by-results can no longer be granted.

more important payment-by-results tends to be as a part of the pay packet, the more important will be the effects it will have on the wage structure. If these effects are to be largely avoided, payment-by-results earnings must therefore be a marginal extra and not a major part of the pay packet.

The illustrations contained in each of the case-study chapters of the kind of pay packet composition that occurs with payment-by-results show that anything from 20 to 50 per cent of the pay packet can be quite usually due to payment-by-results earnings: in other words payment-by-results would appear to be far from marginal as an element in workers' payment in these cases, and to be a major determinant of wage structure. It is difficult to say with any precision whether payment-by-results payments form a large or small part of the pay packet in the majority of cases in which workers are remunerated in this way. Piece-work systems, at least, are probably generally based in Britain on the foundation of a fairly small basic rate: in such cases payment-by-result earnings must be a substantial proportion of the pay packet. Again, industrial consultants usually work on the assumption that an increase of one-third above time rates is about the desired aim of a payment scheme, and this would mean that a quarter of the pay packet for a standard week would be due to payment-by-results earnings. Proportions of this kind must inevitably either severely hinder the flexibility of the wage structure, since a large proportion of the pay packet is due to a payment which is designed only to be flexible in relation to output and not to more long-term determinants of the labour force, or else the payments scheme must be 'bent' to conform to wage structure needs.

Three broad results may come from this confusion between payment methods and wage structure needs. To preserve wage structure requirements payment-by-results schemes may be 'adjusted' unofficially—these compromises are discussed hereafter. Secondly, attempts may be made to preserve wage structure relationships by devising payment-by-results schemes for all employees in the hope that the effects of such payment schemes on wage structures will then cancel each other out. This is probably the reason behind many of the least satisfactory examples of payment-by-results working, such as attempts to apply these payment methods to maintenance men, and may explain some of the confusions that can arise in such circumstances.[1] Thirdly, the needs of wage structure may simply not be met. In the case-studies discussed in earlier chapters, for example, the effect of payment-by-results earnings on the relative wage levels of different grades of skill was to create marked tendencies to inversions of differentials established by wage rates and to create overlaps between the ranges of skilled and semi-skilled earnings.

[1] Wolf, op. cit., pp. 33–5, has some interesting examples of the application of bonus schemes in unsuitable circumstances, due to complaints about low earnings by workers excluded from existing schemes.

Another striking example of such wage structure failures was a frequent source of worry in the shipyard discussed in Chapter 6—how to pay foremen, who were paid on time, above the level attained by the workers they were controlling, the latter being on piece-work. The management were fond of displaying a letter from a former foreman to illustrate this paradox. It explained that the writer who was a married man could not afford to be a foreman any longer, and was going back to his tools.[1]

Compromises

(a) *Compromise between output and other objectives*

It has already been suggested that different types of result require different types of payment. What happens or is likely to happen in a factory which operates a payment-by-results scheme, when it becomes clear in practice that output is not the sole criterion by which to judge a worker or on which to base his pay?

The foundry in the large engineering works discussed in Chapter 3 employed an old but extremely skilled moulder, who was not normally engaged on routine production, but was saved by the foundry superintendent for some of the tricky and unusual jobs which came along. Because of his age, he was not a fast worker, but his experience and skill could always be relied on to produce a more satisfactory job, with less likelihood of wasted materials, than some of his younger colleagues. His skill, in other words, was of considerable value to his employers. But, of course, his speed was not satisfactory in payment-by-results terms, and judged by output he was not entitled to a high wage; yet, he deserved a high wage on other grounds and it was necessary to keep his payment high in order to keep him working and contented. The management dealt with this problem by timing the jobs for which his best skill was required after he had done them; and setting a time which meant a reasonable bonus. By this simple procedure they were able to keep up his bonus earnings on the highly skilled job. For the rest of the time they kept him busy on a small routine job, which was reserved to him alone and for which the time was calculated to suit his rate of working. The management was committed to the payments scheme and so could not take the obvious step of paying the man a time rate which reflected his worth to them. They indulged in a compromise which gave the man the necessary wage—but in a roundabout, underhand and erratic way.

In the fitting-shop of the same works, there were a number of older men who had been with the firm for a long number of years and were well known to many of the managers and supervisors, who wished to reward long service

---

[1] Several similar situations are described in Wolf, op. cit., pp. 31–2. Wolf also quotes a further example from L. G. Reynolds, *The Structure of Labor Markets*, Harper, New York, 1951.

and loyalty. Because of the rules of the payments scheme it was difficult without causing trouble to do this in the obvious way of paying them more. The procedure adopted here was the somewhat dishonest one of altering these men's 'cards' on their way through the production engineer's office 'to see that they were all right'.

This type of personal adjustment is naturally only possible when the people concerned are well known and when the confidential nature of the alterations required can be guaranteed. This implies small numbers of cases and a 'blind eye' turned by shop stewards and management to this breach of the payment-by-results scheme rules. Where large numbers are involved, the same kind of action is not usually possible and both the workers concerned and, in the long run, the management, suffer. For example, in another case, rows of semi-skilled machine operatives had their machines set-up by skilled trades-men known as setters. The setters became very quick and efficient at this job and, in consequence, the wages of the operatives went up. The operatives' earnings were much above the average bonus level, since the setters' efficiency resulted in the time for the job being too generous. The setters themselves were being paid earnings which reflected the average bonus for the shop as a whole and in due time their earnings were surpassed by those of the operatives. Nothing could be done for the setters without making more favourable times throughout the whole shop since a direct production bonus was not suited to their work. The setters tried to become machine operatives.

The same problem of singling out groups for special treatment when payment-by-results rules govern the payment systems may be seen in the difficulties encountered by a shipyard management who were anxious to build up a nucleus of long-service and loyal workers and to offer appropriate monetary recognition. They found that within the piece-work system no such preferential treatment was possible since output was the sole criterion of payment.

The whole problem of payments outside the payment-by-results scheme, where one exists, is complicated by the prior acceptance by management that this is the correct basis for payment, and by the understandable reluctance of workers, other than those directly benefiting, to have other types of payment used in addition. This, for example, is the important factor in making it generally difficult to use merit money as a means of getting out of difficulties such as those described. The same cannot be said of the situations which can arise when workers gain high payment-by-results earnings, and so have more income than foremen and others of this level. In such cases the factor that counts seems to be the attitude of management to productive and unpro-ductive labour. Unlike economists who gave up fruitless controversy about productive and unproductive labour many years ago, some managers who have become thoroughly obsessed with the incentive scheme idea seem to take the line that it is sensible to pay those who produce—the production workers—as handsomely as possible, but to hold back on payments for supervisors and the like since these are unproductive workers. How else can reports of foremen persistently getting less than those they supervise be explained?

Payment-by-results rules have to be compromised to provide an acceptable system of payment for trainees. For example, a new moulder not long out of his apprenticeship was employed by the foundry of the factory discussed in Chapter 3. In his first few weeks he was unable to make the grade and achieve production levels which would entitle him to a bonus similar to that enjoyed by his mates. In order to encourage him in this initial period the superintendent of the shop adjusted his bonus week by week so as to allow him to start with a fairly good bonus and to enjoy a slowly rising bonus level. In other words, he gave the trainee a special rate and a stepped progression to the level of earnings typical of the foundry; but he did it by unofficial interference with the workings of the payments scheme; and broke its rules.

When a short- or long-period scarcity of one particular type of labour occurs in a factory in which wages are regulated by payment-by-results it is once more necessary, though not always possible, to go outside the rules to get a solution. The ease with which this can be done depends largely upon the degree of separateness of the scarce occupation. If, for example, a special shortage of patternmakers were to occur in an engineering factory, then it seems probable that a solution could be reached, without causing strong reactions from labour of other types, either by altering the bonus schemes for patternmakers, or, preferably, by some adjustment to the patternmakers' rate. Again, if it became difficult to get fitters for an independent section of the work's activity, such as a repair section, it might be possible to adjust this section's payment without causing unrest among other fitters, though, if fitters in other parts of the works heard about it, they might well take action to secure a similar adjustment. The most difficult problem of adjustment arises where one group of workers within a workshop becomes scarce and a pay adjustment has to be devised. The rigidity of the payments scheme makes alterations to the pay of one section difficult without a recalculation of times and prices. If such a recalculation is attempted then it is difficult to confine it to the section affected, since all feel entitled to the same treatment. The management's prior acceptance of the principle that output is to be the basis of payment precludes attempts to adjust by means of other types of payment, since other sections will either feel that such payments are not legitimate being based on principles other than output or, more probably, will consider that since output has ceased to be the criterion of payment they too are entitled to similar treatment. Thus, payment-by-results makes adjustments to obviate scarcities of workers in particular sections difficult, even though faulty payment-by-results can be principally responsible for earnings discrepancies that cause scarcities.

An example of this problem occurred in the machine-shop of the factory discussed in Chapter 3. A bottleneck in production took place because of a short fall in the output of a line of boring mills operated by skilled turners. This was due both to a shortage of horizontal boring mills and to a shortage of operatives for them. It was necessary to recruit more operatives both to operate the existing machines at full output and to provide workers for new machines. The shortage of workers reflected partly a general difficulty in getting turners because of high demand in the area for that occupation, and partly a disinclination of turners in the machine-shop to work on the horizontal boring mills. There were two reasons for this latter position. First, the work on which the horizontal boring mills were engaged was heavy, and cranes were required for each small adjustment in position. Secondly, possibly as a result of time lost in waiting for cranes and in setting up heavy jobs, the bonus level which horizontal boring mill turners managed to achieve was lower than that applying to other parts of the shop. The management, realizing that the most immediate help they could give to recruitment would be to reverse the differential in earnings in favour of the jobs for which there were not enough workers, tried to re-rate these jobs, but found growing signs that such action would be followed by a demand for complete re-rating throughout the machine-shop. The workers' attitude was that, if, as the management had told them, the existing payment-by-results scheme offered an equal opportunity to earn bonus, then this proposed alteration must be applied to all. Attempts to alter basic rates met similar difficulties. The management eventually produced a new and additive bonus scheme which applied to the whole machine-shop. By getting more workers into the machine-shop and by increasing output from existing workers it was hoped that eventually there would be enough workers for, and enough output from, the horizontal boring mills section. In other words, the management were defeated by their own payments scheme!

(b) *Compromises resulting from inadequate measurement of output*

The first essential in measuring output is to have a suitable unit of output which is both small enough to be completed within the time span of the period for which payment-by-results output is measured, and which is sufficiently standardized to be repeated a number of times so that a price or time can be worked out by study of a number of units in production. Many parts of the work of the shipbuilding industry fail to meet either of these requirements, yet payment-by-results is quite usual in the industry. Examples of the consequences can be drawn from a shipyard.

The electricians are paid as a group according to a scheme which has as its unit of output all the electrical work of a ship. After assessment, a grand total price for the work on the ship is laid down. In each week the percentage of the total job completed is estimated, and compared with the amount completed at the end of the preceding week and with the amount paid out in time wages (excluding overtime premium) to the squad of electricians. This comparison yields the percentage of time wages declared as bonus for the week.

It would appear from this description that a decline or increase in the rate of work by the squad in any one week would lead to a variation in earnings, and also that the total earnings for electrical work on the ship would be governed by the prior calculation of the price for the total job. In practice neither of these things is true. The management appear to be aware of the large possibility of error in their total estimate for electrical work on the ship,[1] and also in their weekly assessment of progress. In consequence they are not prepared to take drastic action when calculations show that rate of output has fluctuated markedly. They prefer to take the view that the calculations are faulty and that no doubt rate of work has been much the same as usual. Even when the conclusion that rate of output has altered becomes inescapable, management feel sufficiently doubtful about the scheme to be unprepared to take the appropriate action. One result of all this is that it is highly improbable that the amounts paid out to the men will balance with the contract price. Another result is that the designed incentive is replaced by a management compromise. Two examples will suffice. One week immediately after a holiday the men did not work too well and calculations suggested that no bonus above the time rate was payable. The men were paid a 25-per-cent bonus against an average of about 30 per cent in the weeks preceding the holiday. A few weeks later a 90-per-cent bonus became payable according to calculations; the bonus-percentage declared was 35·6 per cent. (The decimal point was apparently introduced since it gave an impression of accuracy!)

The difficulties of measuring output when the unit of production is not standardized may be illustrated by a bonus scheme for shipyard welders. Since some standardization is possible in welding work this is not an example of the problem at its worst, which occurs when one only of a particular job is undertaken and it is necessary to try and price or time it for payment purposes.

Prices or times can be set up for each of the standard types of weld—butt, fillet, etc.—after this has been done, however, standard corrections may be required for (a) direction of weld, since a downward weld, for example, is easier than one for which the electrode is angled upwards; (b) thickness of plates to be welded; (c) size and type of electrode; (d) number of runs of weld

---

[1] One indication of this is their practice of retaining some part of the original contract price 'up their sleeve'. All calculations and payments are made on the basis of a total contract price which excludes this amount, which is never mentioned if things go well but is brought in whenever things go wrong.

required; and (e) type of plate (armoured, etc.). The existence of such a number of possible standard variations already complicates the pricing of the work and introduces possible disagreements as to which type of situation the welder has to deal with at any given time, and, of course, wherever debate becomes possible the simplicity of the concept of payment-by-results gives way to suspicion and bargaining. This, however, is not the end of complication in this case. Welders often have to work outside and in awkward corners. Moreover, slight discrepancies in measurement and fitting of the plates and bars that make up the ship cumulate at the joins which the welder has to secure: he is often required to make a good weld with a 'bad fit'. Further discussion is inevitable. Complaints to the foreman and to the rate-fixer are regular occurrences. Friday, as well as being pay day, is also complaints day. Lack of a standard unit of output destroys the precision and ease of the scheme and causes wasted time and dissatisfaction.

This same example also illustrates the practical problems of allowing for alterations in factors outside the worker's control but influencing his earnings. Small variations in the material he is supplied with, such as a faulty electrode, or in the conditions under which he works—it might be raining heavily—affect his output but cannot be readily allowed for. The difficulties of finding a good means of actually measuring output in such circumstances as these make it necessary to rely on subjective judgements from rate-fixers, which are not always acceptable to the men. In such conditions bargaining about details of payments schemes can hardly be avoided.

The traditional piece-work basis of the shipbuilding industry shows all the marks of an incentive scheme which has been bargained rather than designed in accordance with some principle. The original piece-work price lists were in themselves negotiated by employers and unions and were no doubt the subject of hard bargaining, especially since they ante-date the introduction of accurate time study. But whatever merit they may have possessed has long since been lost by changes in technique which have occurred over the fifty years or more since some were introduced. The only major concession made to changes in technique appears to have been the corrections applied to prices for caulkers, drillers and riveters when hand tools were replaced by pneumatic tools. This correction consists in each case of a percentage deduction from the prices agreed for work with hand tools. This percentage was the result of bargaining. The whole procedure is based on the heroic assumption that every aspect of these trades' work was proportionately affected by the change-over to pneumatic tools.[1]

[1] The deleterious consequences to the efficiency and accuracy of payment-by-results schemes of variations in conditions of work and of bargaining about the scheme, have their place in the literature on this subject. For example, both are commented upon in Tom Lupton and Sheila Cunnison, 'The Cash Reward for an Hour's Work under Three Piece-work Incentive Schemes', *Manchester School*, September 1957.

(c) *Compromise with workers' attitudes*

Payment-by-results schemes in operation display a number of signs of compromise with workers' preferences for regularity of income and for group working.

Workers try to obtain their income in regular weekly amounts and endeavour to defeat a payment-by-results scheme which is likely to make for irregular earnings. To this end attempts are often made to adjust payment-by-results schemes unofficially by 'banking' bonuses. A system which operated in the factory described in Chapter 3 was based on job cards. When the worker took on a new job he collected a job card with it, and bonus was credited according to the job cards, turned in by the worker and initialled by a supervisor, indicating that the job was finished. It was possible for the worker to keep finished job cards in his pocket for a few days while continuing on new jobs. The practice was to hold back job cards towards the end of the week when it seemed that bonus had reached about its average level. These cards were put back in circulation in the following week and replaced by others at the end of that week. When the 'bank' of cards showed signs of growing consistently week by week, the weekly bonus level was allowed to rise to bring the 'bank' back to manageable proportions. 'Banks' were run by individuals and by groups—sometimes one man with a head for such matters was entrusted with the job of 'banker' on behalf of individuals or a group. The effect of this system was to replace fluctuating bonus earnings with a regular weekly amount which altered only at intervals and then adjusted itself to a new regular level.[1]

Collective restrictions on output which enjoy names such as 'stints' or 'doggies' have both formal and informal existence when payment-by-results schemes operate. Formally workers' associations may 'suggest' or dictate what workers are to regard as the maximum weekly bonus level. The welders' agreement mentioned in Chapter 6 seems to be of this sort. Informally men may agree among themselves about an acceptable level of bonus earnings. Less formally still men who work together may arrive at a general opinion as to what is a 'decent' level of output in a week.[2]

Such collective limitations on output seem in part to reflect a desire to obtain regularity in earnings. In the study in Chapter 5 the suggested maximum imposed by the welders on individual earnings turned out to be the modal level. It appears to have reflected with some accuracy both a possible level to which most welders could reach and a comfortable level at which they were prepared to stay. In Chapter 3, analysis of hourly earnings of fitters

---

[1] Similar systems are described in Lupton and Cunnison, op. cit., and Wolf, op. cit.

[2] Such output limitations are also discussed in Marriott, op. cit., pp. 138–53, and Wolf, op. cit., pp. 40–5.

again showed a strong tendency to concentration at about the same level—which may once more suggest a comfortable point at which to hold bonus earnings week by week.

Evidence of collective limitations on output, whether formal or informal, as well as suggesting a desire for regularity in earnings also indicates acceptance by the workers of group attitudes. Distribution curves of hourly earnings of workers on individual payment-by-results do not show a cluster of workers at one end who do not react to the incentive at all, and a cluster at the other end of those whose reaction is very marked. The typical curve approximates to a normal distribution.

ADVANTAGES AND DISADVANTAGES OF PAYMENT-BY-RESULTS FOR EMPLOYERS

Advantages

Despite all that has been said in the foregoing about the extremely difficult conditions needed before payment-by-results can be operated in a factory, despite the inference that it should not be used as often as it is at present, and despite the examples of compromise and inaccuracies which arise through its use, one inescapable fact remains—employers use payment-by-results and are frequently enthusiastic about it. They obviously think it is of benefit to them. These benefits must now be examined.

The principal benefit claimed for payment-by-results is, of course, increase in output. An increase in the output of labour, or more strictly, the productivity of labour, its rate of output in a stated time period, has the major advantage for employers of reducing production costs. Under most of the methods of payment currently used an increased rate of output, even accompanied by increased bonus earnings to the worker, results in a reduction of the labour cost per unit.[1] However, even if this reduction in unit labour cost were not present, there would still be a reduction in the total cost of each unit due to a reduction in the incidence of fixed overhead costs which can now be spread over a larger output. Such costs as maintaining a factory and

---

[1] The only exceptions here are (a) piece-work, when unaccompanied by a basic rate payment, (b) time allowance systems when one hundred per cent of time saved is payable, and also when there is no basic rate payment, and (c) systems in which earnings vary more than proportionately to output changes. The basic rate element in the pay packet is usually present when (a) and (b) are used. As output increases, the cost of the fixed basic rate element in payment is spread over a larger output, so giving decreasing labour costs per unit to the employer. There is no direct evidence on how frequently systems of the (c) type are used, but the generally accepted impression would appear to be that they are somewhat rare, at least in Britain. Moreover, even when they are used, increasing unit labour cost cannot be taken for granted, since, if there is also a basic rate element in the workers' pay-packet, increasing unit labour cost will only occur when, as output increases, the amount by which bonus increases beyond one-hundred-per-cent bonus is greater than the decrease in the amount of the basic rate attributable to each unit produced.

its machinery are incurred no matter what the level of labour productivity may be, and the greater the output with given equipment and administration the less heavily such costs weigh upon each item produced.

It seems probable that some incentive element in payment, or some relation between output and payment, is responsible for an increase in output as compared with unadorned time rate systems. But this does not mean that all payment-by-results schemes result in output increase, or that a payments scheme of the type of which we have been talking is the only monetary method of increasing output. When we attempt to quantify this increase in output with more precision, it is difficult to get any reliable estimates. A recent, and most valuable detailed survey of research and opinion on incentive payment systems records that 'one of the surprising features of the literature on the subject is the infrequency with which their success or failure has been demonstrated in unequivocal and reliable quantitative terms'.[1] Dr Hilde Behrend has recently conducted a set of sixty interviews with representatives of management and trade unionists. She states that 'the first point that emerged from these interviews was that it is virtually impossible to obtain a definite answer to the seemingly straightforward question of whether the introduction of piece-rates results in increased effort and thus raises output'.[2] The main reason for these doubts may be that incentive schemes are rarely instituted without parallel changes in methods and technical equipment, and such changes in method and equipment, as well as personnel are continually in operation. It is however of major importance to realize that it is not usually possible to assess the productivity effects of incentive payments with any degree of certainty, since this tends to take incentive payment systems out of the category of managerial tools which are so obviously useful that their character and usefulness need not be discussed, and to justify, and indeed require, that their fundamental assumptions should be investigated. Since the increase in output which is due purely to incentive scheme operation is not something that can be stated with dogmatism, managerial acceptance of incentive schemes reduces to a widely held, and possibly justifiable, belief that an incentive element in payment is useful in obtaining productivity increases and cost reductions. Further, one of the major detailed questions of incentive scheme working is similarly not readily susceptible to proof. 'There are unfortunately no research studies directly comparing the effects of individual and group payment methods.'[3]

There are a number of other advantages which are claimed to accrue to

---

[1] Marriott, op. cit.

[2] Hilde Behrend, 'The Effort Bargain', *Industrial and Labour Relations Review*, July 1957. Dr Behrend goes on to claim that a further two hundred interviews still left the question of the effectiveness of incentives in doubt.

[3] Marriott, op. cit.

employers as a result of payment-by-results. It is a frequent management claim that payment-by-results reduces the need for direct supervision, since the incentive acts as a stimulant to work unaided by the presence of a foreman. This seems a reasonable claim, subject to three comments. First, it is doubtful if such incentive need take the form of a regular payment-by-results scheme. Secondly, it may be fortunate if payment-by-results does lead to less supervision, since in many cases, in practice, one of its side effects is to make supervisors relatively poorly paid and therefore difficult to come by. Thirdly, while direct supervision may be reduced this has to be offset by an increase in the number of people of supervisory grade required to set times and prices, and to check and inspect output.

Payment-by-results provides a lot of direct information on the wage costs of specific units of output, and this information can be held to be of considerable value to the accountant. This is an attractive notion in theory, if one assumes an accountant whose figures are based on detailed calculations of the precise cost of each particular operation. Unfortunately, in practice, accountants seem to find the information provided by payment-by-results working to be too detailed for their requirements, and they tend to revert to an average wage cost per occupation as the most convenient measure for use in giving labour cost estimates. In each of the three cases considered in detail in earlier chapters this was the position. If payment-by-results provides an invaluable store of data for the accountant, up till now it has not always been opened.

A less obvious way in which payment-by-results may be of benefit to the management is by taking their wage structure out of the hands of their employers' associations. When standard rates are laid down by an association payment-by-results gives the employer freedom to fix earnings to suit himself. This point and its consequences are discussed more fully in later chapters.

The most subtle benefit claimed for payment-by-results schemes is that without them managements would lose the benefits conferred on them by time study and work study experts and industrial consultants. Time study men are at present closely associated with the process of timing jobs for time allowance systems of payment-by-results, while there can be few industrial consultants who do not leave a brand new incentive scheme behind them in each factory they have visited as their equivalent of the doctor's prescription. To the extent that either time study men or industrial consultants feel that payment-by-results schemes are essential to their continued existence they do themselves an injustice. Time study men look at jobs to see how they are being done and how long they take to do. The term 'work study' is also used and by implying this wider function is much more sensible. In studying work being done they see new and better ways of doing it. In timing jobs they are also comparing alternative ways of doing the work. In studying men at work on machinery they are evaluating the design of the machine relative to operative efficiency. Indeed, a time for a payment-by-results scheme is quite as much a by-product as an end-product of their activities. It is, moreover, arguable that if the relation between their activities and an incentive scheme were removed it would be easier to persuade workers to co-operate with them and their other activities might then have a more fruitful yield. It is no doubt comforting to the industrial consultant to leave something behind him in return for his fee, and for firms to get something for their money. But unless we are prepared to accept the view that firms are like patients who always want a bottle of coloured water from their doctor, it by no means follows that a consultant must do this to be successful. The consultant entering a factory has a number of jobs before him. His main assets are that he is fresh to the problems of the factory and that he is an expert. He sees what is wrong with procedures that are accepted by the factory's management for no better reason than that they have always been that way. He examines the layout of the factory; he examines methods of supplying raw materials, of keeping stocks and of issuing stores; he examines methods of progressing; he examines the numbers and types of machines and their relative capacities; he studies the distribution of the factory's labour force and its capacity; he studies particular jobs to criticize the design of the material and its passing to the next process; he examines despatch from the factory; and, after this and probably much more, he puts in new incentive schemes. Would not all the rest be just as important without the incentive scheme?

Disadvantages

The major disadvantages of payment-by-results for employers are its tendency to play down all worker objectives other than output, and in the longer run, its tendency to destroy or distort the wage structure. Both of these points have already been discussed. Moreover, payment-by-results may have the effect of creating opposition and competition between worker and worker in the work group and between workers and management in the factory—a point which is mentioned in Chapter 7. Other disadvantages, however, still require specific mention.

The direct cost to the employer of a payment-by-results scheme is that of running it. Broadly, it can be said that such costs grow strongly when the conditions suggested in Chapter 7 as logically necessary for a payment-by-results scheme are lacking. They arise out of the need to price or time output, to inspect and count it, and to work out the appropriate wage payment. The need to price or time units of output is fundamental to a payment-by-results scheme. Where output is standardized and easily measured this may not involve much expense. But there will be a substantial increase in expense if output is varied and difficult to measure, both since pricing or timing will have to be done more frequently, and since, if output is difficult to assess, more time will be spent in settling disputes arising out of prices or times which can only be roughly estimated. In those cases where jobs are timed, the work of the time study man has its importance beyond the actual calculation of times for payment systems, and therefore additional costs here should not be put wholly to the charge of payment-by-results. Rate-fixers too may be said to have wider responsibilities in examining and studying jobs for pricing, since they also, as experienced tradesmen, lay out a method of doing the job and avoiding snags. But, while in both cases other justification for their presence can be found, nevertheless a major cost of running payment-by-results schemes may lie in the need to employ large numbers of such people. Inspection of output is specially necessary under payment-by-results because of the risk that speeding up the work and accenting output will cause a decline in quality. It may also be that an increased wastage rate should be held to be a cost of payment-by-results. Actually counting the units of output as they are produced is unlikely to be a major cost where units of output are easily identified and recorded. It can, however, be high where the work is very varied and not easily counted, or where, as in the case of ship welding, the counter has to go over the job *in situ* reckoning output. The more complicated the payment-by-results scheme, again probably a factor related to the suitability of the work for payment-by-results, the more duties will fall on the wage office both in designing the records of work done and in calculating weekly payment. This office work is a direct oncost of payment-by-results.[1]

If an individual payment-by-results scheme is in use, the employer may suffer an increase in costs because of irregular rates of working by his labour force. If a workshop is one in which production is supposed to proceed smoothly, the products passing from stage to stage in a predetermined sequence of operations, and if an individual payment-by-results scheme is imposed, then rates of working may alter and spread out, and alternate gluts and shortages of material at each stage become likely, with consequent troubles and cost increases. To take another example, if production is in part dependent upon the use of a machine by each worker in turn, and if one worker begins to work at a faster rate than others, he will be using the machine when others want it. While one worker's production goes up it may be at the expense of lower output from his mates. In other words, 'Stakhanovites' have costs as well as benefits.

ALTERNATIVES TO PAYMENT-BY-RESULTS SCHEMES

The general conclusion of all the foregoing is that payment-by-results schemes, which relate payment to output in a very short period and in a mechanical way on an individual or very small group basis, are not as generally applicable

[1] An example mentioned in passing in Chapter 6 is relevant here. The shipyard discussed there employed seven rate-fixers, seven counters, and two wage clerks on the payment-by-results scheme for 130 welders.

as their exponents have suggested. The conditions necessary to their success are not by any means to be found in every job. Payment-by-results earnings can contort and destroy wage structures based on more long-period evaluations of the relative worth of occupational groups. The use of such schemes in inappropriate circumstances can cause both trouble and costs to the employer and dissatisfaction to the worker.

Such a far-reaching criticism of payment-by-results naturally involves the obligation to make some constructive suggestions about alternatives. In some situations where it is wise not to over-emphasize output as the sole criterion of worth, for example where high quality workmanship or loyalty are the most important characteristics looked for from a labour force, a time rate, or a payment as near to a salary as possible, can be the most satisfactory form of payment. Nevertheless, high output, which is so much emphasized by the exponents of payment-by-results schemes, is not a consideration which can be ignored, and, while precision and proof are largely lacking, it seems reasonable to suppose that the wide support given to payment-by-results schemes indicates that output is encouraged by some closer relationship between output and payment than that implied by a plain time wage. Any system of payment proposed as an alternative to payment-by-results should also ensure that due attention is paid to the need to secure high output, and must make some provision for the incentive relationship of payment with output, though not necessarily in the form of a payment-by-results scheme.

Most of the criticisms levelled against payment-by-results in the preceding pages refer to the way in which it is immediately related to small units of output, either for individuals or small groups, and for small periods of time. If, then, it is possible to secure regularity of earnings over considerable periods, to take a much less atomistic view of output, to preserve the differentials thought appropriate to a wage structure, and to encourage and sustain group and other loyalties, and at the same time to make payment relate to output, this would be the desired answer. The high time rate system is a formal attempt to do this.

In a high time rate system of payment workers are paid a high level of time rate (equivalent to the kind of level that might be expected from a basic rate plus payment-by-result earnings). The high time rates are appropriately structured for different levels of skills and other elements in wage structure. In return the workers are expected to give a high level of output. Output by fairly large groups of workers is measured in periods of (say) three or six months. This measurement can be done on a much more general method of assessment and with less detail than is required for payment-by-results schemes, and can indeed be an offshoot of general management collection of cost and output data.

A formal agreement is made with the workers to review and adjust time rates according to output movements at regular intervals of (say) three or six months. The relation of output to payment ensures an incentive to output; but, at the same time, stability of earnings is ensured. Work groups are not broken up, and the onus of disciplining the lazy worker is, in part at least, shifted to his mate who will eventually suffer from his lack of effort. Short-period variations in output are ignored. Differentials and the wage structure are maintained. The high time rate idea meets the objections to payment-by-results schemes of the more usual variety while retaining in a more long-period way the long-period relation between payment and output.

This formal high time rate framework derives its formality from an agreement specifying a regular periodic review of payment and output. It will be obvious that an understanding that management will be prepared to offer more wages as output goes up would be a possible informal alternative, provided workers were prepared to believe in management's intention to share the proceeds of extra output. Payment-by-results schemes are quite largely an admission of the failure of management to get loyalty and good work out of their labour force. Managements have been unable to persuade their workers of their good intentions without a formally detailed scheme. This implies both a lack of a positive approach to employing labour and a lack of leadership from management. One clear aspect of positive management is a willingness to discuss payment of increased wages without being pushed. In other words a successful informal high time rate method of payment implies supposedly old-fashioned advice to management. It implies that management has been able to gain the trust of workers and that it leads instead of following.

It is commonly said that American society reckons status in terms of income and values the symbols of wealth more than our own society. It is to be hoped that our society does not simply equate status and income, and that it will continue to be slow to do so. Nevertheless, it is true that much incentive to good work comes from the desire to have the income which brings about a satisfactory standard of life. In the past the working class in Britain seems to have envied the middle class for its security and the income which makes middle-class living possible. Security is partly a question of being able to get and keep a job. As long as full employment continues we all have this in some measure. It is also a question of having a secure income, which in turn depends on having a job and on the method of payment of income. Examination of income statistics in present-day Britain forces the conclusion that there is little to choose in quantity of income now between many lower-middle-class people and many of the better-off working class. Working class desires to be level with the middle class are, for many of them, therefore largely satisfied as far as job security and level of income are concerned. Yet lack of income security—fluctuating payments especially associated with payment-by-results—prevents adoption of middle-class standards and ways of living, and may be a major remaining difference and ground of distinction between the classes. It could therefore be argued that, if income security were also granted, more working-class people could and would adopt middle-class standards and aims, and that therefore regular, not fluctuating, payments by opening a new avenue of incentive towards a new pattern of life, would be the better incentive to output.

APPENDIX TO CHAPTER 8
ILLUSTRATIONS FROM TWO STRIKES

The general line of argument and discussion being put forward in this chapter and in Chapter 7 can be illustrated with some effectiveness from two strikes which occurred in the Clyde area during the broad period to which the data of this book refer. Short descriptions and discussions of these strikes therefore form a useful appendix to the chapter.

The Man Who Worked Too Hard

A large engineering works in the area got itself into the national press over a strike which developed among fitters in a section of its machine-shop, spread over most of its employees, and seemed capable at one point of involving the whole engineering industry on Clydeside in a dispute about the closed shop. A cartoonist in one of the popular daily papers characterized the strike, from the incident which started it, as the case of the man who worked too hard.

A new employee was introduced into a small and rather isolated section of the machine-shop, a section which was regarded as on the whole being a not very desirable place to work, in respect of the type of work, its isolation (social rather than physical) and its relatively low bonus earnings. The man was, at his own wish, put on nightshift and began to turn out work which passed the inspectors at a much higher rate than that of the other workers in the section. Since he was on nightshift, most of these other workers had not met him, but those who had found him awkward, unsociable, and not prepared to take any cognisance of group attitudes, or of the need, where other men are working, to co-operate with them. Moreover, the man had been employed in the factory during the war—a fact of which the management were unaware though the men remembered. Long memories among the men spoke of him in his previous employment as being a rate-fixer and demonstrator who had taken a delight in fixing prices which were too low for the average man to make an average bonus. Those who knew his private life said that he had a small business of his own which had run into debt, and that he was working by day at it, and attempting to earn enough on the nightshift to pay his debts. He had been a union member but his membership had lapsed since he owed a number of subscriptions. Trouble grew in the section and there were a number of petty incidents involving the man and the other workers. The issue was finally taken by shop stewards to the management who were asked to discharge the man since he was not a union member. The management, who knew nothing about the man except that his output was exceptional, declined to yield to pressure, especially on the grounds that they had not conceded the principle of a closed shop. A strike began and grew, ostensibly on this closed-shop issue, and only finally ended when more and more information got through to each side from the other, and the man, having been the subject of a number of compromise suggestions from management, finally left.

There are a great many points of interest about this strike, the closed shop, the attitude of management, the lack of effective communication, the tendency to reduce a complex story to a single issue in dispute, the longer memory of men as against management, and so on. Most of this is irrelevant to the present discussion but some points of importance for payment-by-results emerge.

(i) It became apparent that the man was breaking rules which were very real to his workmates though they had no formal statement. His rate of output was quite outside the level acceptable to the group. This did not appear to mean that the group took consistent objection to rates of output above a pre-determined level, since other members of the group were earning substantially above the group norm. The reaction was rather a social objection—'a fellow like this cannot be one of our mates and cannot be allowed to make a mockery of our level of output'. He reacted to incentive as an individualist, the others as a group, though substantial variations in rate of output were permitted to those who were part of the group. A group attitude to incentive was more meaningful to the average worker than purely individual incentive.

(ii) One standard objection to 'the man that worked too hard' was that his short-period effort was compared with the rate of work which others were prepared to keep up for a lifetime. Knowledge of the man's background made the workers certain that he regarded his job as a few weeks of back-breaking work to get together as much money as possible as quickly as possible. Most of the men who found his output a subject for anger were long-service employees who had settled down to a rate of output which they could sustain over the months and years. The younger men earned a bit over the group norm; some of the older men were below it. All, however, interpreted effort and incentive in a long-period way. They were concerned to achieve a rate of work which would yield a reasonable wage with considerable regularity over the years. It was, therefore, the management who took a short-period view of work, both in their emphasis on individual payment-by-results and in their admiration for short-period effort. It might then be argued that the generality of the workers regarded a long-period view of output as preferable to short-period fluctuations. They were predisposed to a high time rate system if management had offered it, and attached values other than output to their work in the factory.

(iii) The man's work passed the inspectors, but others at the same job regarded it as not quite up to their own painstaking standard. It is of course true that if the work met the management's minimum standards it did all that was required. Nevertheless, high output was achieved at the expense of high quality and the incentive scheme penalized those who thought more in terms of quality.

(iv) Much of the reason for the exceptionally high output of this man was due to his being on nightshift. There were very few other workers about to get in his way. Those who were found him difficult to work with, since he would not wait his turn at the machines, and he did not clean up his place of work and equipment for others coming behind him. This was one very real sense in which he was unco-operative. Where a number of men are working together, even though they have separate jobs, all work is co-operative, since they must at least keep out of each other's way. The individualist, especially if encouraged by individual incentive, may do his job at the expense of the output of others, and at the expense of rhythm of work and team-consciousness on the work floor.

Clyde Shipyards' Strike—Autumn 1956

During August 1956 platers, caulkers and burners, and welders in shipyards on Clydeside were involved in mounting disputes with the employers over demands by the workers for a guaranteed minimum rate. The dispute had already been the subject of unsuccessful local and national negotiations, and at the end of August a strike started, which ended in a somewhat vague compromise some three weeks later.

The workers' claim was for guaranteed district rates at levels rather similar to prevailing earnings in the trades in question. For example, the welders' claim was for a guaranteed minimum rate of 6s. 3d. per hour. This claim followed upon the concession of such a guaranteed minimum rate to riveters, given on the grounds that they were now small in numbers and engaged on special tasks, and that the application of a piece-work basis of payment to them was no longer appropriate.

The workers based their claim partly on the precedent of the riveters and partly on expressions of dissatisfaction with the existing system of piece-work, which worked faultily and produced arbitrary fluctuations in payment. They took the attitude that their earnings should be more regular and should be protected from the arbitrary element of faulty piece-work systems. It was fairly widely conceded by the workers, however, that in practice fluctuations in earnings which might arise from faulty piece-work were settled by protest to, or negotiation with, yard managements, and that the arbitrariness of the situation lay in being dependent on the discretionary powers of managements as a protection against downward fluctuations in earnings. Obviously, too, the claim by the workers reflected a long-term desire to protect earnings against a change in the demand for their services as well as against short-period insecurity of earnings.

The managements' attitudes to this emphasized the point that this proposal was for a very high rate which was unrelated to any conditions regarding maintenance of output levels. The rates asked for were much above time rates ruling in the industry or outside it. Management statements on the cost of conceding the claim varied according to how much account was taken of possible falls in output caused by a system of payment which offered high wages without output guarantees. There was, however, some fair measure of agreement with the proposition that if output was maintained at existing levels the rates claimed would not involve much increase in wage outlay. Management also emphasized the long-period significance of the claim and the extent to which it would fix labour costs even for possible future recession periods. The nub of managements' attitudes was, however, to emphasize the long-standing piece-work basis of payment and the correctness and wisdom of relating payment to output in such a way. They were however prepared, and in some cases eager, to revise and adjust piece-work prices by negotiation.

The whole detail of the dispute and its settlement need not be gone into here. Some points of importance for payment-by-results should be brought out.

(i) The men expressed a strong preference for regularity in earnings, and were prepared to suffer the hardship of strike action to obtain such security. The claim was not basically for more money.

(ii) The men disliked and distrusted a system of payment which at times left secure earnings to the discretion of management or to a bargain with management. Their reaction to the irrationality of existing piece-work was to try to get rid of it.

(iii) Managements were placed in the awkward position of having the anomalies of their payment scheme attacked by workers and of having workers initiate demands for its improvement. They were forced to defend a situation, though they were prepared to agree it had anomalies and were prepared to alter it. They had lost the initiative in the control of their wage expenditure.

(iv) Managements were undoubtedly right to show the failure of the workers' proposals to guarantee output as well as wages. But, faced with a clear expression of the preference of workers for regular payments they insisted in following the piece-work ideal. Yet a possible, and fairly obvious, compromise position might have been to relate output to guaranteed payments in a high time rate system or some variation of it. It was not apparently part of managements' objective, other things being equal, to pay wages in the form in which workers wanted them.

(v) Despite the general premise of a piece-work system that payment should relate to output, the suggestion was little disputed by either side that it was general practice to make-up wages when the system recorded an apparent fall in output and hence indicated lower earnings. Compromise had a daily place in a supposedly objective system of payment.

CHAPTER 9

OVERTIME

Since the end of the Second World War the economy of Britain has been in an almost constant condition of inflationary excess demand. Excess of demand over supply of final products has caused labour also to be subject to excess demand. Unemployment rates have been extremely low and generally much lower than the levels which have been suggested as appropriate to full-employment conditions. The search for new sources of labour supply has brought about an increase in the proportion of married women at work and a new solicitude on the part of Government and employers for the welfare of the children of potential working mothers, exemplified by the provision of nursery schools and the like. Attempts to increase labour supply have also resulted in attempts to get increased output from the existing labour force: payment-by-results is one such attempt and regular overtime working is another.

Thus post-war overtime can be deduced directly from the circumstances of labour demand and supply as an attempt to increase the supply of labour by increasing the length of time worked by the existing labour force. It is also possible to deduce overtime payment from the effects on the price of labour where demand for it exceeds its supply. In such circumstances, the normal reaction is for the price to rise. If the negotiated price of labour—the wage rate—is slow to move, or does not sufficiently reflect the variations in intensity of demand from area to area or employer to employer, then the price will rise in less obvious ways, by enhanced factory wage rates, by generous bonus schemes, and by overtime payments being offered as a regular source of income to attract labour. It may, therefore, be said of overtime that it is needed to maximize output in conditions of labour shortage, or that overtime payments are needed in the peculiar circumstances of national collective bargaining to produce an equilibrium price for labour. Overtime has to be thought of as a method of increasing output and of increasing payment, and from the outset it has to be noted that its influences are complex.

That overtime has been an important factor in the British economy throughout the post-war period cannot be denied, though large-scale information on overtime in any precise form is difficult to come by. Ministry of Labour statistics of overtime are not too helpful since they give only the proportion of the labour force working overtime and do not give the quantities of overtime involved. Moreover, they do not specify the type, age or sex of labour concerned, and this can make considerable differences. The

138

scale of overtime working in Britain can be judged most readily and generally by simply looking at the average hours worked in industry—statistics which are given by the six-monthly 'earnings and hours' enquiries of the Ministry. In October 1955 average hours worked by men over twenty-one were greater than they had been in 1938, notwithstanding the reduction in standard hours in the intervening period. Moreover, at 48·9, average hours were much in excess of the usual forty-four-hour standard week in 1955, whereas, at 47·7, hours in 1938 were lower than the then usual standard forty-eight-hour week. As a generalization, however, it can be said that overtime is of much more importance for men than women. Hours for women over 18 in 1955 were lower than in 1938. At neither date was the average of women's hours of work as great as the standard week. In 1938 the average was 43·5 and in 1955 it was 41·8. The data on overtime given in the case-studies support the contention that overtime has been important, at least for men. The case-studies showed large proportions of the workers doing long overtime hours, and deriving much of their income from overtime working.

THE OVERTIME PREMIUM

The basic idea of 'overtime' is simply that some hours of work are less suitable and cause the worker more inconvenience than others. For the majority of workers who are on day-work this means hours outside the span of the normal day's work, or on days outside the normal working week—work in the evenings, or on Saturday, or Sunday, or public holidays. For shift workers, overtime means work outside the regular shift hours. Overtime may also be translated literally to mean extra hours beyond the covenanted length of the standard working week. Undoubtedly the word has this meaning too, but less precisely. For example, a man who had put in less than the standard number of hours in a week might nevertheless be regarded as having worked overtime, if some of the hours he worked were at times of day or on days of the week outside normal working hours. For a man who has worked the full standard working week, overtime will have the same meaning whether it is taken to refer to 'extra' work or to work at hours outside periods of normal work. But, since it is not a necessary condition for the recognition of overtime that total hours worked in a week should exceed the standard number, while it is necessary that the work in question should be done outside the normally accepted periods of work, the latter is the more essential feature of overtime.

A premium payment for overtime work is customary for wage earners though notably less so for those who are paid by salary. It reflects the idea of hours that are awkward or inconvenient as well as extra by varying in amount according to the time of day or week in question. Thus, for example, the overtime premium in engineering grows larger as work in the evening becomes

139

more prolonged, and is especially high for Sunday work or work on public holidays. The notion that the proper time to work is during the day and that other times are less suitable and convenient also seems to determine the payment of premia for shift work, whether nightshift or some other type. Normally overtime premia are based on the time rate and expressed as a proportion of that rate. Thus they generally leave the method of calculating bonus unaffected. It seems logical, if the premium is regarded as reflecting the inconvenience of being at work at such a time, that it should be paid on a time rate basis.

Explanations or justifications of the overtime premium may be phrased to describe it as a deterrent or as an incentive. There seems little doubt that it originated in a desire to discourage employers from thoughtlessly keeping their labour at work when they should have been enjoying rest and leisure. Overtime premia were therefore thought of as penalties to be paid by employers who were inclined to expect workers to do more than their day's work, the penalties in consequence reflecting the seriousness of the infringement of leisure involved.[1] The assumptions involved in this way of looking at the premia are that employers will not regard overtime working as a normal occurrence and will be deterred from using overtime, unless in specially urgent circumstances, by the penalties involved; that those few employers who have been in the habit of using overtime working as a regular production period will be suitably penalized and deterred; that the workers will not want to work beyond their usual weekly times; and, that if, by virtue of the superior authority which the employer has, the workers have to turn out for extra and inconvenient times of work, they will be to some extent compensated for their trouble by the premium.

If overtime premia are regarded as incentive payments then a change of atmosphere and emphasis occurs. It is no longer necessary to infer that workers are so disinclined for overtime work that it should be heavily discouraged and that the payment of a premium, while the least that the employer can do to compensate for loss of leisure, is not an adequate compensation and cannot be encouraged as a long-term substitute for leisure. Nor need the inference be made that only bad employers will make much use of overtime. The whole atmosphere changes from a studied attempt to ensure a specific way of life for workers—the way of regular hours of work and regular and adequate leisure—to the atmosphere of a simple commercial bargain. The overtime premia now become incentive payments designed to be

---

[1] Good examples of overtime provisions which are specially designed as deterrents and penalties are to be found in some Wages Council Orders relating to retail trades. It is possible to visualize an employer wanting his shop to be opened for a short time on a holiday or a Sunday. The Orders provide that a worker called on for work of this kind must be paid for at least four hours at double time.

attractive to workers and to produce the necessary amount of overtime working, employers paying them as and when they feel the desire to increase production by overtime working.

Opinions vary as to which of the two interpretations of overtime suggested above should now be applied. There is some strong tendency for trade unionists at the official level, in accordance with the historical position of their movement, to suggest that the first interpretation is the correct one. In doing so they are automatically forced to discount the evidence of prolonged and regular overtime working in post-war years and to designate this as a temporary situation, even though it contributes a large, and not unwelcome, proportion of current wage earnings. Employers would appear generally unwilling to accept the full implications of the first view, since it involves them in a moral obligation not to make much use of overtime working, and so they emphasize the commercial nature of the transaction and draw attention to the fact that their production needs may require overtime working, and that in some industries such overtime may be frequently necessary. There have been disputes in industries in which overtime can become an important feature of the employer's ability to meet his production demands, such as the docks or transport industries, over the issue of compulsory overtime imposed by employers on reluctant workers. Such employers have tended to shy clear of the description 'compulsory overtime' with its various ethical implications but have, nevertheless, been forced by the nature of their production commitments to maintain strongly their right to use overtime as and when it may be needed, provided they offer the appropriate reward—the overtime premium. The opinions of employees, as distinct from their trade unions, are not capable of being simply formulated, since there are so many individuals involved and since they are most frequently represented by trade union leaders, while the independent views of union members are less formally expressed. Two points should be made. The attitude to overtime which says that it is an unwarranted intrusion into leisure which should be deterred as far as possible seems to come to the fore when issues such as 'compulsory overtime' indicate that overtime has become very great and has gone beyond free choice. In other words this seems to be an attitude for the extreme case. On the other hand the foregoing case-studies and statistics suggest that when faced with the choice of working or not working overtime, employees choose extra money rather than extra leisure and regard overtime premia as incentive payments designed to give them adequate recompense for this decision.

In the face of the prolonged and regular overtime which has been a feature of the post-war period in many industries, and is exemplified by the case-studies, the attitudes of employers and employees to overtime have, it may be suggested, undergone a change. This change is more than simply a change of degree or of emphasis, but, since it substitutes for overtime as an occasional and irregular means of adjusting production problems, the use of overtime as a regular period of production, it is a change in the nature of overtime. The trade unions, as an earlier remark indicates, have tended to write this problem down, and to regard it as a temporary, and somewhat unfortunate, divergence which should not alter their general policy or attitude. Employers and employees, being rather more closely affected by the advent of regular overtime can hardly adopt this distant attitude.

In each of the foregoing case-studies overtime was found to be a substantial and moderately regular part of the pay packet. In statistics relating to the engineering industry and to industry generally it becomes clear that, for men at least, hours longer than the standard week are a normal occurrence. In such circumstances, overtime working can come to be regarded as a normal part of the working week or, more accurately, overtime working can be regarded as something which is regularly available to employers as a supplementation of productive time and is made equally regularly available to employees as a means of supplementing earnings. In consequence, overtime wage rates including the overtime premia become regular supplements to wages due for the standard week. The incentive which must now be attributed to wage rates earned on overtime and to overtime premia becomes more than simply a means of getting men out to work occasional extra and awkward hours of work. They are working such hours regularly and the supplementation of their pay is also reasonably regular and certain. The incentive effect of the extra payment is, therefore, translated into an effect parallel to, and reinforcing, that of the usual wage rate payment, though, due to some uncertainty, not having quite as strong an effect. The form of incentive which a wage rate offers is an incentive to recruitment. If payment offered is attractive a man will take a job. Regular offers of overtime, regularly taken up by workers, result in an increase in the incentive to recruitment.

In recent years the advertisement columns of newspapers have had long lists of situations vacant. A study of these will show a strong tendency to include regular overtime as part of the recruitment inducement. It is a well-recognized feature of present-day labour problems in shipyards, for example, that, especially in the case of fitting-out trades, where the irregular nature of the demand for their services means high labour turnover and fewer long-service employees, it is necessary to offer plenty of overtime when trying to recruit more labour. In these changed post-war conditions, therefore, men tend to expect overtime to be available and look for it as an incentive to take a job. Employers must, for their part, use overtime as a production period with fair regularity and offer overtime regularly whether or not there are special circumstances to warrant it.[1]

---

[1] The personnel director of a very large concern has described this type of overtime to the writer as 'policy overtime'.

Persistent overtime working in the post-war years has therefore been used by employers partly as a means of recruiting and keeping labour, so that overtime payments become a disguised, and in some ways unsatisfactory, wage rate increase. Such a situation can only arise where actual wage rates are inadequate. National wage rates are negotiated at industry level between national trade unions and employers' associations. The latter then attempt to have their members adhere to the agreed rates. Such national rates cannot possibly reflect every employers' position and must reflect in their level the position of the poorest employers. An employer who needs labour, who is bound through his employers' association to adhere to national rates, but who can nevertheless make a better offer to labour and needs to do so to get labour, must resort to less obvious devices. Overtime, regarded as a means to recruitment, is such a device. Thus the origin of the inference that overtime is used as a means of getting labour and of paying it more, as well as a means to extra output, can be traced directly back to the system of national rates, and overtime rates and overtime premia become substitutes for negotiated wage rates.

ADVANTAGES AND DISADVANTAGES OF OVERTIME TO EMPLOYERS

The possible benefits which employers may attribute to overtime can be discussed under four headings. These are (*a*) increases in output, (*b*) shortening of delivery dates, (*c*) increases in recruitment power, and (*d*) reduction in overhead costs per unit of output. There are a number of snags qualifying the possible benefit from each of these. However, in order to get the conceivable advantages clearly established, the snags may, for the present, be set aside, and attention given to the advantages. The discussion is intended to refer primarily to circumstances in which regular overtime is customary (the post-war case) rather than to sporadic use of overtime as an emergency relief for an overloaded production process.

(*a*) If one assumes that no deleterious effects on the output of either labour or capital in the standard working week are created by regular overtime working, then any output which takes place in overtime hours will result in a net increase in total output from the factory. Given that demand for the final product is in excess of supply or is at least adequate, a condition that seems generally reasonable under the conditions of strong demand for labour which make regular overtime likely, then an increase in saleable output will result.

(*b*) Under conditions of high or excessive demand in the economy, the possibility of getting a product, or the question of when a product can be delivered, may be more important, within limits, than the price that is charged. If inflationary excess demand is much in evidence there may be a shortage of a product which leads to doubt about whether any one customer can expect to get it at all, and, even if prospects are not as bad as this, certainly delivery is a likely problem. In both cases the problem reduces from the producer's point of view to concern over delivery dates. Increased output in overtime working may make a shortening of delivery dates possible.

(c) If the preceding analysis of the partial transference of regular overtime earnings from being an incentive to overtime to being an incentive to recruitment is granted, then the employer will find overtime payments a useful method of recruiting and keeping his labour force. If he is restricted by the agreements and rules of his employers' association then he will not be able to increase wage rates overtly. The offer of unlimited overtime gives him a useful means of achieving a somewhat similar effect.

(d) Any process of production involves both capital and labour. It is to the interest of the owner of capital to spread its use over the largest possible number of units of production so as to reduce fixed costs per unit. This increases the rate at which the capital wears out but reduces the overall actual or imputed costs of interest and the risks of obsolescence and other standing risks (rust, for example). In any given production period there are limits to the extent to which this can be done, limits set by the maximum capacity of the capital and the reduction in the output per unit of labour if too much labour is used in conjunction with too little capital. If the production period is extended then more output becomes possible, unless output in the standard hours is thereby reduced, and a reduction in fixed costs of capital per unit of output is achieved. Overtime working is one way of doing this. It should be noted, however, that shift working may also achieve the same result, with fewer consequential problems.

These are the major advantages to employers of using overtime working, uncorrected by several necessary qualifications which now appear as part of a somewhat longer list of disadvantages.

(a) Output goes up under overtime conditions if a simple addition of overtime output to unchanged output in normal hours can be recorded. This, however, is not a permissible sequence of thought. Two points have to be mentioned. (1) There may be a reduction in hourly output both in normal and overtime hours as hours of work increase. (2) There may be a loss in hours of work through sickness and absenteeism occurring in normal hours, and associated in their intensity with the volume of overtime hours.

There is quite a considerable body of literature[1] on the subject of the

---

[1] Useful references are: Industrial Fatigue Research Board Reports (especially, 1, 19 and 23); Industrial Health Research Board, Emergency Reports 1 (1940) and 2 (1942). P. Sargeant Florence, *Economics of Fatigue and Unrest*; H. M. Vernon, *Industrial Fatigue and Efficiency*.

relation of hours of work to output and to absence, mainly derived from the work of the Industrial Fatigue (later Industrial Health) Research Board, especially during and just after the First World War. Its relevance is limited, however, since the research work on which it is based refers to the special circumstances of wartime and to hours substantially longer than those generally fashionable in peacetime. As far as the first point raised above is concerned, the general impression is that overtime on top of a forty-four-hour standard week does not generally get up to and beyond the point at which these studies suggest that output in any given hour is substantially reduced to compensate for longer hours of work. On the other hand, the point of numbers of hours worked at which an individual's output per hour declines may be different in peacetime when the compulsive pressure of war is removed, and, in any case such an effect is influenced by attitude of mind as well as direct physical fatigue. If the general attitude of society is that, in the normal way, forty-four hours of work is enough in a week, then consistent overtime may be reducing output per hour below the level which might otherwise be achieved. Unfortunately, precise evidence on this point is not available. All that can be said is that the increased output secured by overtime may be less than is apparent because of possible reduced output per hour throughout the week.

The proposition that an increase in the number of hours of work produces increased absence is enunciated many times in the I.H.R.B.'s work and seems to be proved. They were not, however, dealing with the contrast between a shortened working week and longer overtime hours. The overtime premium has an important role here since it is an incentive to transfer work from the normal working week to overtime hours. In the case studies in earlier chapters it is evident that short-time is associated with overtime, and that, where overtime periods are freely available, while most workers take overtime work not all do, and the extent of overtime working differs from case to case. It has been part of the post-war management problem that overtime has not been carried through with a full attendance of the labour force, nor, where overtime is being worked, have the normal hours secured a full turnout. It has been a most usual occurrence to hear managers refer to the forenoons after overtime work on the previous evening as bad mornings for labour attendance. In other words, to an extent at least, overtime, and the overtime premium, result in a transference of work periods to overtime, and a tendency for the labour in a works to spread its effort and attendance more thinly over a larger than normal range of hours. In such circumstances a reduction in the apparent contribution of overtime to output must be recorded. The extent to which production with less than a full labour force will cause a fall in output will depend on the type of production. In jobbing production the loss may be proportionate to the proportion of absentees. In an integrated line production system a few missing workers may greatly reduce output.[1]

The increase in output which comes from overtime working is therefore subject to doubt as to its effect on output per hour. Moreover, the apparent increase in output through longer working is partly controverted by overtime and short-time appearing together. In consequence shortening delivery dates through overtime working is in some respects less certain than it appears to be. Further, this argument proceeds on the assumption that management really require the overtime working, have concerned themselves with the issue of what work is to be done on overtime, and have succeeded in conveying an atmosphere of urgency to their workers. If, however, overtime is being offered as an instrument of wage or recruitment policy rather than as a production policy, management, while doubtless seeking increased output and providing work, may find difficulty in avoiding the impression that overtime working is an opportunity for extra earnings rather than extra output and so may not get high output during overtime working.[2]

(b) It was claimed as a benefit from overtime working that fixed costs per unit of output will be reduced as output increases. This naturally assumes that output is in fact increased by overtime working. In any case, fixed costs of machinery are only one of the costs of production.

If a works is open for production at any time, there are a number of costs which immediately arise and which are, within limits, unvaried by the volume of production actually achieved. The works will require to be lit and heated, and routine ancillary personnel, firemen, gatemen and the like, will have to be present. It will not be necessary that the hours of attendance of the administrative staff should coincide with the hours at which the works are open, but a certain proportion of the administrative and supervisory staff will have to be there. Power will have to be laid on to the machines and it may be necessary for all machinery to be operating. In other words, there are a number of running costs which are fixed overheads for any given production period, in that they are incurred whenever production is undertaken but do not reflect variation in the volume of output actually achieved. If output during overtime hours is low, or if the general effect of prolonged overtime is to spread

---

[1] This point may also be put in terms of bottlenecks in production. An integrated production process carrying out repetitive work on a mass produced article depends for its rate of total output upon dovetailing the outputs of all its subsidiary production lines and the efforts of each successive production worker. If such a system is in use an uneven incidence of overtime working or of absenteeism can mean excess production in some sections and bottlenecks in the supply from other sections, with consequent production delays and losses. In jobbing work on the other hand variations in product mean that the output plan must always be flexible. Irregularity in the turnout of workers simply adds another variable which, though awkward and time-wasting, is only one among the many planning complications.

[2] This point is again referred to in the third group of disadvantages discussed below under (d).

out the attendance of workers over all the alternative periods of work offered, so that attendance (and output) is not full at any one period, then costs of this type will bear more heavily on each unit produced.

Overtime working can provide the benefit of being able to use machinery more intensively, thus getting in a larger number of productive hours per machine in a year and reducing the burden of fixed costs per unit of output. This, however, assumes that output is indeed increased by overtime working, otherwise the idea is not valid. The actual circumstances of working machinery on an overtime basis may cause difficulties in the way of output increase. Little is gained if as a result of persistent overtime working proper maintenance of machinery is not carried out, or if maintenance work is done during production time and cuts down the efficiency of production. With a factory organized on a day-work basis without much overtime, maintenance can be carried out using overtime working by maintenance engineers. If overtime is already being persistently worked then maintenance may intrude into the day. Of course it may be possible to get night-work from maintenance men. This depends on the attitude of the factory generally and of the maintenance staff. If day-work is usual it may be far from easy to persuade maintenance men into night-work. A factory working a regular shift system does not have these difficulties: shift work is a regular feature of work in the factory and a maintenance shift can be organized. Bad maintenance, or breakdowns in maintenance during production, will disrupt the flow of output and put up costs per unit of output.

The obvious increase in unit cost through using overtime is increase in labour cost. Even if it cannot be finally established that there is a reduction in output per hour when consistent overtime is worked, which would naturally increase labour cost per unit of output, nevertheless labour cost will go up in any case because of the additional overtime premia payments. As against production during the standard weekly hours only, overtime working is expensive in labour cost.

In balance, then, cost per unit of output will be favourably affected by more intensive use of machinery, but will be unfavourably affected by incurring fixed running costs for less than a full labour force, by production difficulties engendered by working short-handed, by possible reductions in rate of output, by machinery maintenance difficulties, and by the increase in labour cost which overtime premia create.

(c) It may possibly be said again at this point that if producers are operating under conditions of inflationary excess demand then the important thing to consider is total output or delivery dates rather than costs. There is truth in this idea, and under ideal conditions the use of overtime working does provide the benefit (listed as such above) of enabling delivery dates to be shortened. It is hardly beneficial, however, to substitute for long delivery dates which are relatively certain, uncertain dates even though these may be shorter. If, as has been argued, overtime working induces absenteeism then production will be subject to arbitrary variations and delivery dates will be difficult to foretell. With overtime working the proportion of the labour force turning out is somewhat uncertain. The carry-over of this attendance uncertainty into normal hours accentuates management difficulties and the whole problem of controlling the labour force to secure a steady flow of production. Besides, there are, from the long-term viewpoint of the community, if not the industrialist, strong reasons for doubting the philosophy that high cost is less important than output. Even in the short period, and with excess demand, inflation of costs cannot be achieved without displeasure on the part of buyers and a tendency to resolve to seek other sources of supply wherever possible.

(d) The final set of disadvantages to the employer[1] of prolonged overtime working arise out of the obligations which are placed upon him to use overtime even when he is not needing to do so. Regular overtime payments are a substantial inducement to recruitment, but if all employers go in for regular overtime the recruitment pull of any one employer tends to be lost in its general use. Moreover to continue to hold labour it is necessary to continue overtime working.

If it is granted that an employer is bound by national agreements and so is somewhat restricted in his adjustments to basic rates, then if he is prospering and short of labour he will use some other means to recruit labour. The offer of regular overtime is one way of doing this. In the first instance, with shortage of labour, overtime will probably be justified by the production needs of the employer. As time goes on occasions may well arise in which the demand for the services of one particular group within the labour force, or the labour force as a whole, may temporarily slacken, but in order to keep the labour force against competition from other employers similarly offering the overtime inducement, an employer may have to continue to offer overtime.

The consequences of this are three-fold. In the first place, if the overtime is being used as a recruitment wage then it is not quite as effective for this purpose as a straight time rate. Even if the strongest guarantees are offered, prospective employees may regard their chances of making overtime earnings as probable but not fully certain, and so discount the attractiveness of the offer, which therefore loses some of its effect without losing any of its cost. Besides the offer does involve overtime working and so is less attractive than an offer of the same money without overtime. Secondly, the obligation on the

---

[1] Another disadvantage of regular overtime might be mentioned though it is of lesser importance. If overtime is only used occasionally and for special reasons then it is possible to account for it to the customer involved. If overtime is used regularly then the accountant cannot attribute it to any one order. Its cost is averaged out over all orders and not specifically costed. All prices rise.

employer to provide regular overtime is likely to involve periods of overtime working undertaken to satisfy this obligation rather than for production purposes. Undoubtedly, some production will be achieved at such times but a feeling of lack of urgency can be infectious. Jobs thought up to keep workers busy tend to look just like that and to be treated as such by workers who keep themselves only moderately busy. Hearsay evidence suggests that Sunday work has tended to be institutionalized as the period in which this attitude is most fully reflected. 'Real' overtime as it were is carried on during week-day evenings while Sunday overtime is offered (at double time) as the period when wages are made up and the workers are kept contented[1] though output is low. Thirdly, the presence of consistent overtime working causes a fundamental alteration to wage structures. Overtime working which is used by an employer to lever up his wage structure to stave off competition for labour, or to adjust to prior action by his competitors, becomes a built-in feature of his wage structure and has three effects. (i) It actually adjusts the employers' wage structure level relative to that of his competitors, though perhaps not in the best possible way. (ii) It directs his internal wage structure towards emphasis on overtime working. (iii) It penalizes those of his labour force who are not, for some reason or other, disposed to work overtime. This penalty may act in conformity with the employer's general wage structure requirements but it need not do so.[2]

ADVANTAGES AND DISADVANTAGES OF OVERTIME TO WORKERS

The major benefit of overtime working to workers requires little explanation: overtime offers an increase in income from work which is not at present offered in any other form, and with the increase in income comes a new range of possible expenditures which cannot otherwise be undertaken. The costs of it derive from the obligation to do more work: this again is quite simple and obvious at first sight, but requires some further exposition. Before going on

---

[1] No more than hearsay evidence can be offered here—impressions derived from conversations with employers and workers. The point should therefore be accepted with caution. It should be noted that if one accepts the notion that Sunday work is regarded, as far as effort is concerned, somewhat more light-heartedly than work on other days, 'double time' makes it easy to get up to the usual day's earnings with less effort. An amusing illustration of this may be offered. Blacksmiths employed in a small shop in a very large Scottish works suddenly developed pronounced Sabbatarian principles—not against Sunday work, but against Sunday *bonus* working. Investigation showed an economic motivation. Given that they had no intention of working hard on a Sunday, they had found that they would do better on time rates and 'double time' than on 'double time' and bonus, and they were not then 'fussed' by bonus working on the Sabbath.

[2] In practice unskilled workers seem to be specially disposed to work overtime and record longer average hours than skilled or semi-skilled (cf. evidence presented in Chapters 2, 3, 4 and 6). One wage structure effect of consistent overtime is therefore to narrow the gap between unskilled and skilled. It is to be doubted if this effect is intentional.

L 149

to this however, it should be noted that it is possible to exaggerate the benefits of the increased income which accrues to the worker from overtime working. The point may be put very briefly, since it is the subject of expanded treatment in Appendix 1 of this book. Despite the regularity with which overtime is generally forthcoming, income from it nevertheless cannot be counted on with as much certainty as basic payments for the standard week. In consequence the worker is limited in the types of expenditure to which overtime payments may be devoted. Especially he will tend to avoid permanently committed lines of expenditure and spend overtime payments on items which can be cut out if overtime should disappear. In this way overtime payments are somewhat restricted in their value to the worker.

One other benefit to the worker of the provision of overtime opportunities is the scope which this gives for varying earnings according to individual needs and desires. The average wage earner is not generally in a position to increase his payment by promotion, or, at any rate, the number who can be promoted is limited. His wage rate is fixed nationally and, while local variations are quite usual these tend to be for the group rather than the individual. His opportunities of varying his earnings to suit his needs therefore depend either upon taking a second job, or working specially hard at his present job, if an individual bonus scheme operates, or extra hours, if overtime is available. The practice of holding two jobs certainly appears to be quite usual in the United States where standard hours are generally shorter than here. In Britain, however, it seems unlikely that holding two jobs is, as yet, a major factor in the determination of wage earners' income.[1] While individual bonus schemes appear to offer excellent opportunities for extra earnings, and, in fact, wide variations in individual rewards do occur in this way, nevertheless earnings from this source seem to group themselves around a norm and complete adaptation to individual circumstances does not appear to occur. For example, the analysis in Chapter 3 of fitters' bonus earnings by categories of P.A.Y.E. numbers, which imply family responsibilities, did not disclose marked differences corresponding to differences in family responsibilities.[2] Overtime opportunities on the other hand seem to offer a specially unhampered chance for individuals to build up their pay packets as their needs require. For example, unskilled workers quite generally appear to restore some of the gap in their relative earnings levels as against more skilled groups by working longer hours.[3] Indeed, variations in hours worked seem generally to be more marked and to have a less conformist pattern than varia-

---

[1] Possibly, however, the presence of two wages, the second coming from a working wife, has been the major source of extra earnings in the incomes of wage earning *families*.

[2] Cf. Figure 9 and the discussion about it in Chapter 3, also Figure 5 in Chapter 3, and Chapter 8 *passim*.

[3] This point occurs in most relevant wage statistics. It appears, for example, in Chapters 2, 3, 4 and 6.

tions in bonus earnings, and thus to reflect more readily differences in individual needs.[1] This ability to adjust hours of work and earnings to individual circumstances is therefore a considerable benefit which the provision of overtime working in plenty confers on workers. It should perhaps also be emphasized, however, that from the point of view of the employer irregular attendance by workers for overtime hours, which is implied by the above, is by no means a benefit.

The principal cost of overtime to the worker is that it involves additional work, or, to use the traditional expression, it involves the sacrifice of leisure. Work may have two aspects in this connection: it may mean effort or time spent. The sacrifice of leisure may mean the using up of energies that could be conserved by rest or devoted to leisure-time pursuits, or it may mean the sacrifice of the time in which to pursue leisure. Both effects occur at the same time.

The man who works consistent overtime is more tired by his work than if he does not do so. This seems true even if we evade the question whether he works more or less hard when he is doing overtime: a 'long day' is tiring in itself. Moreover, the actual timing of overtime seems calculated to have the maximum tiring effect: it generally puts two specially long days into the working week and takes one day out of the weekend rest period. No attempt is made to spread overtime thinly over the working week, and the recuperative effect of the weekend is sadly disturbed. Relating tiredness to effort, we can say that overtime reduces leisure by expending more effort on work or creating more tiredness from work.

In another sense overtime reduces leisure by simply substituting time at work for leisure time: workers cannot pursue leisure because they are working. Week-day overtime is likely to reduce by two-fifths the opportunities for leisure activities on weekday evenings. How this affects behaviour on the other three evenings depends upon the type of person the worker is. Some may redouble their efforts to seek enjoyment, having lost two evenings out of five. Others may find that having been out two evenings already, they want to stay at home on the other evenings, so that the overtime may cut out evening activities outside the home. In any event, some form of evening leisure activity must fall a casualty to the overtime. One suspects that the type of activities which reformers would like to see more frequently pursued by the working class, educational or semi-educational activities, hobbies or any aspect of 'creative leisure', trade union branch activities, etc., are sufficiently far below entertainment in the list of priorities for available evenings, that they suffer most heavily. In any event, all leisure activities stand to suffer from the reduction of opportunity.

[1] The discussion on the relations between P.A.Y.E. numbers and overtime hours in Chapter 3 showed that longer overtime and high P.A.Y.E. numbers (indicating family responsibilities) went together (Figure 8, Chapter 3).

Generally similar remarks on the effect of overtime in curbing leisure activities may be applied to Sunday work. Since organized entertainment[1] and organized meetings, other than religious meetings, are not generally available on a Sunday, the chief sufferers from Sunday overtime among leisure activities are the Church and leisure activities associated with the home and family life. Both losses are held to be serious by the protagonists of Church and family life. Even though they can hardly fail to recognize the value of extra earnings to the worker, churchmen have deplored the effects of Sunday work on religious duties (using this term to encompass church attendance, Sunday religious activities of all kinds and simply Sabbath observance).[2] In consequence they have been anxious to press for alternative arrangements in industry which do not involve Sunday overtime. Sociologists and social workers tend to stress the importance of the family as the basic social unit. Men who are out at work during the week and out at organized entertainment on Saturday do not see much of their family. Sunday could be described as the day on which the father of a family takes his proper place, being with his wife, getting to know his children, going for family outings and family visits. If the head of a family works on a Sunday then the thread binding him to family life may be very thin.

One should however be wary of making Sunday work the scapegoat for lack of male interest in the Church and for a decline in the bonds of family life. The relationship may not be causal. After all, the choice of weekend overtime could theoretically fall on Saturday rather than Sunday. It does not do so. Saturday overtime is not usual, though Sunday overtime is. It seems that collectively workers prefer their day off to be one on which they can go to organized entertainment rather than one on which they go to Church, or visit relations, or stay at home with the family. It may be doubted whether restoring Sunday as a day of rest would immediately and in large measure increase workers' interest in the Church, or cause an immense strengthening of family life. It is a pity that Sunday work should make the attempt to do these things so difficult.

The influence of the overtime premium is important in this issue. Sunday work carries the heaviest overtime premium (double time). Presumably it was put so high in order to penalize employers who expected workers to turn out on Sunday and to prevent this from becoming a widespread practice. On the other hand, in the prevailing social climate it seems reasonable to suppose that the worker is equally reluctant to work on Saturday, and especially on Saturday afternoons. It would therefore appear sensible to suggest that the

[1] Other than television. It might be interesting to speculate on the effect of the growing popularity and availability of this entertainment medium, on willingness to work on Sundays.

[2] Cf. for example, articles in *Life and Work: the Record of the Church of Scotland*, for October and November 1956.

premium for Saturday afternoon work should be the same as the Sunday premium. Looked at the other way round the present premium for Sunday work acts as a strong incentive to take Sunday work, a stronger incentive than usually exists for Saturday afternoon work. Even if we remain impartial on the wisdom of preferring leisure on a Saturday to leisure on a Sunday, we can still suggest that it is unreasonable to provide a stronger incentive to one than to the other. The premium for Saturday work regarded as an incentive should be the same as that for Sunday work. But if, on social grounds, we regret the existence of any incentive towards weekend work, then it would also be reasonable to suggest that neither the premium for Saturday work nor that for Sunday work should be high enough to act as an incentive, and that the way to discourage employers from indulging in excessive weekend work should not be by means of penalties in the form of premia but by direct limitations on the permissible quantity of weekend working and special rates, negotiated for each case as the circumstances warrant.

A SHORTER WORKING WEEK?

This discussion of the workings of overtime in present circumstances is obviously relevant to claims for a shorter working week, such as the claim which has recently been advanced by the engineering unions for a reduction in standard hours from forty-four to forty. The issue of a shorter working week must be looked at both in the long term and in the short. A shorter week is an understandable part of the improvement in our standards of life and conditions of work which is the natural long-run hope of us all. In consequence, we ought to expect to find claims for reductions in standard hours as part of a trade union's armoury and of its attempts to improve the conditions of working life. In the long run it seems highly probable, if not inevitable, that such claims will be granted, and that both actual and standard hours of work in industry will be shorter. In the short period, however, full account must be taken of immediate practical difficulties. It is curious, therefore, to find such claims being pressed when hours have been consistently higher than the present-day standard week. A harsh judgement would be that trade union leaders, being aware of the situation as it is, have put forward the claim for shorter hours so as to obtain for their members the same pay for a shorter standard week plus more pay for overtime, hoping that employers in the heat of negotiation will not notice that this is just the same old wages claim with a new twist to it. This is hardly a fair judgement. Probably the truth is that trade union leaders in advocating the shorter working week hope for both results, shorter hours (especially in the long run) and larger pay packets (especially in the short run).

Three possible results might arise from a successful claim for a shorter

153

working week under present conditions. Actual hours would be unaffected so that more overtime would be worked and more pay earned. Actual hours might go down by the amount of the reduction in the standard week, so that shorter hours would be worked, but overtime and pay would continue as before. Results outside these limits, such as the third possibility that hours will reduce to the level of the new standard week, seem improbable. Indeed the most probable result is that hours would settle at some point below the present actual level, but would not fall by as much as the reduction in the standard week; so that hours would be lower and pay higher. In any of these probable results the difficulties of persistent overtime, as described in the foregoing would continue. Would it not then be a more sensible course of action at present, to attempt to weed out of overtime working that part which is designed simply to raise wages and then to transfer the pay for these hours to the wage rate. This would reduce hours nearer to the standard week without reducing the pay packet. If this could be done successfully it would then become possible to consider a further reduction in the standard working week in more realistic terms. If this cannot be done, and it probably depends on a shift of emphasis from national to local negotiation, it would be to everybody's interest that employers should grant equivalent wage increases rather than be pressed into agreeing to a shorter working week which may well involve them in an increase in the proportion of overtime working in their week's production.

CONCLUSION

This chapter has really been concerned with two rather different types of overtime working. The first is occasional overtime undertaken to meet some special emergency situation and specially remunerated by an extra payment which is intended to reflect roughly the degree of inconvenience to which the worker has been put. The benefits and disadvantages of this type of overtime to the employer rest mainly on the special circumstances of the particular case, or the urgency of his need and his success in dealing with it, and on the inconvenience and cost of meeting the need. To the worker the benefit is the extra payment earned and the disadvantage is the inconvenience of the work. This was the usual meaning of overtime before the Second World War, and thus the type of situation to which our thoughts go when overtime is mentioned.

Another type of overtime is, however, the most important for post-war discussion and is the type which occupies the attention of most of this chapter. It is persistent overtime working, organized on a regular basis, and continuing over long periods of time. This type of overtime can be regarded as a natural reflection of excess demand in the post-war economy, which has caused managements to be almost always engaged on 'rush jobs' trying to meet potentially over-large orders or imminent (or missed) delivery dates, and so has created excess demand for labour alleviated by consistent overtime working. On this way of thinking the overtime premium payment becomes an incentive extra to the normal level of payment to keep workers turning out for overtime work.

As well, however, as being regarded as a natural response to excess demand by providing the possibility of extra output, persistent overtime provision by factories in post-war years can also be regarded as a natural response to excess demand for labour in a situation dominated by too-rigid national negotiations and national agreements. This aspect may be thought of as reflecting standard weeks which are too short for actual requirements under excess demand, and here demands for shorter standard weeks while regular overtime continues are indicators of the gulf between national arrangements and particular local needs. Alternatively, it can be regarded as reflecting the inadequacies or rigidities of national wage rates which are conformed to by employers, but which require to be supplemented by local additional payments, of which regular overtime is one. In this latter case overtime payments are being used as supplements to wages and as a recruitment inducement. In such circumstances overtime work becomes something of a by-product of 'policy' overtime designed to meet the needs of the labour market.

In any actual situation it is difficult to separate out these distinct types. It seems certain that managements have fitted overtime output into their attempts to meet delivery dates and demands in the post-war period, and that this pressing need was in large part the origin of the overtime boom. It seems also certain that the needs of wages and the labour market have served to keep managements tied to overtime work, and that the reflection of this wages situation conditions management's expectations of output from overtime work. It is also true that the older picture of overtime as an unfortunate and occasional necessity has its part to play. Managements faced with a persistent lack of work to justify overtime would certainly cut it out, and so they regard it as a temporary situation and a temporary payment, which has nevertheless made its strong mark upon wage structure and upon the way of life of wage earners. The air of uncertainty which is provided by this reference back to overtime as occasional extra time prevents workers who depend on large overtime payments from enjoying security in this part of their income.

Discussion of the benefits of overtime to employers rests on the prospect of an output increase, which has to be qualified especially by erratic turnout of workers, and of the prospect of cost reductions in the spreading of overhead costs. These advantages have to be offset by the costs of spreading running costs over a longer period and a less full attendance of labour, of disorganization of production and of the premium payment to labour. In addition, the diversion of the factory wage structure, which persistent over-time creates, has to be reckoned with. From the men's point of view the benefits of extra income have to be set against the social disadvantages of longer and more awkward hours of work.

All in all the benefits of overtime, other than the occasional type, are much cast into the shade by its disadvantages. If long-term extra output is its reason, an adjustment of standard hours and payment could be a much better solution. If overtime is created by the need to adjust labour's remuneration then it is a bad way to do so and has deleterious effects on wage structure.

CHAPTER 10

REWARDS FOR SKILL

The study of relative wages may be conducted in terms of the determinants of the wages of individual workers of given characteristics and in given economic circumstances. If a somewhat more distant view is taken then individuals of given characteristics are aggregated into groups and the study of relative wages becomes a study of the determinants of relative wage levels of groups of workers defined by given characteristics—the study of wage structure. There are various obvious characteristics which may be used to separate workers into groups, such as industry, occupation, location, sex or age. In a study of factory wages not all of these attract attention: in the cases studied here, where little has been made of sex or age differentials, the occupational differential is most important, and is therefore the differential selected for study in this chapter.[1]

Occupations may be distinguished from each other by quite a number of features; some may involve more danger than others or less comfortable working conditions, they may carry less social repute, and so on. The most striking distinguishing feature of an occupation, however, tends to be the skill or training which distinguishes those who undertake it. For this reason occupational distinctions, and differences in occupational payments, especially in the long run when mobility problems are overcome, tend to be thought of as skill differences and skill differentials.

It is important to be aware of what is meant by skill here, and generally in this type of discussion. There is a possible distinction between skill which results from training and that which results from innate ability. In practice the two are frequently mixed. In the arts it is possible that a 'flair' or gift for some type of activity is a complete substitute for trained expertness. In industry most forms of activity require training as well as ability, so that differences in natural ability are overlaid by differences in training. When exceptional ability shines through it is likely to be reflected in promotion or in a higher rate of output for given effort. At any rate, skill means the possession of qualifications to do a job resulting from training and ability.

Skill could refer to simple manipulative dexterity of the kind which untrained labour can pick up by doing the same limited sequence of operations

---

[1] Since it is considered important to establish the principles involved in discussion of this differential before looking at detailed illustrations, the procedure adopted here is to do this first and then go on to the actual movement of the differential in post-war Britain and to the import of the case-studies.

over and over again. It may also refer to the ability required to do jobs involving wider knowledge and understanding. It is wise, however, to give the former the appellation of semi-skilled, indicating only a limited range of skill. The latter, wider, type of occupational ability, whether acquired through formal apprenticeship or other lengthy period of training, involves more than dexterity but also understanding of a wide range of jobs and an appreciation of the way in which one operation fits into a complete series of operations. It is necessary to make this distinction so as to clarify the difference between payments for skill and payments for output. In the case of semi-skilled work of the simplest repetitive type there is little gap between the two types of payments since greater repetitive skill means greater output. In more skilled work, skill lies in the ability to do the job fully, while output refers to rate of performance. Moreover, if the wider type of skill is given due prominence then the gap between skill and responsibility narrows. If we ignore the passive type of responsibility which does not require action, such as rests on the engine-driver of a passenger train, and would be with him even if his actual duties were reasonably simple, then responsibility means a willingness to take decisions and implies an ability to weigh alternatives and consequences. Skill in its widest sense involves knowledge and understanding of difficulties of the type which leads to the ability to take responsible decisions. In this sense the difference between the skilled wage earner and the staff employee with a heavy load of responsibility is only one of degree.

The inference of any discussion of rewards for skill is that there are, or should be, differences in the payments made to wage earners. Thus some reference must be made to the age-old controversy of inequality of earned incomes. The issue of equality versus inequality is frequently political, and has to be judged according to the current, and usually varying, conceptions of what constitutes a 'good society'. There are those who 'believe in' economic equality as the only way in which man may attain a proper dignity in society. Others tell us that it is only if economic rewards are available to give a stimulus to effort that we develop our powers to the full, and that, besides, an undifferentiated society can in no sense be desirable or interesting.

Considered at their widest, the conflicting principles of equality and of inequality must inevitably bring us into the realms of political controversy. It is doubtful, however, if political considerations should bulk large in discussions of the income differences to be found between members of the industrial labour force, the chief representative of these being the differential payment to skilled men.

It is necessary, to justify this remark, to consider the various types of income inequality which arise in our society. Two broad distinctions may be made, between types of income which create the inequality and in the scale of inequality which is experienced.

158

Sources of income may conveniently be divided into two types, 'earned' incomes and 'unearned' incomes. The former type, as of course its name suggests, is made up of the various forms of income from work—wages, salaries, fees, earnings of self-employed persons, etc.; while the latter consists of all other sources of income—rent, interest, profits, etc. It is dangerous to seek simple statements on such a complex issue, but it does seem permissible to say that on the whole much more of the weight of controversy about the appropriateness of these various sources of income, and of the social wisdom of their continuance, rests on unearned incomes than on earned. It is possible to come across many people who are prepared to contend that, for example, profits of any kind should not be paid. There can be very few who would deny that work must be paid for and thus provide a source of income.

If substantial agreement can be assumed on the principle that work deserves payment, and that therefore 'earned' income is politically and generally justifiable, then political controversy about earned incomes must rest on the size of incomes involved. There are, as we are all aware, considerable differences in earned incomes in Britain between, for example, the managing director's salary and the wage of the cleaner. Such extensive differences undoubtedly lead to controversy which must be described as political. But before these political arguments can be properly applied to differentials in wages two further points must be made. In the first place the political remedy normally applied to inequalities in earned income is redistributive taxation, especially graduated income taxes. Such taxes operate on incomes after they have been determined and therefore should not affect discussion about the relative sizes of gross incomes before tax. Secondly, the scale of inequalities which forms the basis of political discussions is wider and larger than that which is being discussed when differentials in wages are at issue.

It may be thought that a difference of degree does not constitute a permissible argument for a difference in kind, and that it is not valid to argue that, because wage differentials are much smaller than the differentials which exist in the wider setting of all earned income, they should, therefore, be separately treated. There is some truth in such a contention, but two lines of thought suggest that political considerations should be set aside in discussion of wage differentials. First, if it is right to argue that political discussion on inequalities is concerned with the *scale* of these inequalities, then it is *ipso facto* permissible to conclude that if differences are small—as they undoubtedly are in the case of wage differentials—then these differences raise much less in the way of political discussion than do wider differences. Secondly, it is also possible that those who argue for equal incomes and those who defend inequality, faced with the considerable inequalities which exist in Britain even in earned incomes, can afford, as it were, to use blunt instruments. If the issue of equality versus inequality were ever to be reduced to a stage where only inequalities of the order of those found in wages existed, then it would be necessary to agree that these inequalities were live political issues. For the present, surely differentials in wages can be treated on their merits and as matters for economic rather than political discussion. At any rate, this will be done here.[1]

THE DEMAND FOR SKILLED LABOUR

The most useful framework in which to study the reward for skill is that of the market forces of demand for and supply of skilled labour. It must be admitted that, in the short period, wages may be influenced by institutional pressures, and, especially during inflation, there may be marked short-term movements of the relative reward for skill which might appear to be solely due to institutional causes. In the long run, however, a wage is a price, and the relative wages which may be secured by skilled workers depend on demand and supply.

Skill in British industry has traditionally been associated with apprenticeship training. The apprenticeship system is to be found in many of the older industries, where the status of skilled tradesmen is only conferred on those who have been apprentice-trained. On the other hand, it is possible to exaggerate and pretend that the apprenticeship system has been universal in British industries. This is not true; industries such as textiles, iron and steel and coal-mining have not generally used this system. The correct point to make is that, for many years, the apprentice-trained skilled man was the symbol of skill in British industry.

The division of the labour force into craftsmen and labourers had the advantage of being tidy. It also reflected the status divisions of those whose work was not on the land and in the country districts from which so many new industrial workers had come. The building trades had, and still have, a craftsman and labourer system of organization: craftsmen such as blacksmiths, harness-makers, cobblers, saddlers and the like were the normal representatives of industry in settled communities. The new engineering works and shipbuilding adopted the same system. We became conditioned to regarding skill in the industrial labour force as being represented by the distinction between craftsmen and labourers.

Two consequences followed from this. First, it was difficult to see any

---

[1] It may be felt that rather too much is made of this discussion about the political implications of equality or inequality in wages. It arises, frankly, from a reaction to Lady Wootton who in her book *Social Foundations of Wage Policy* (London, 1955), not only dismisses economic argument on wage differentials, but seems to argue for equality in wages by drawing examples indiscriminately from the whole range of earned incomes.

gradation in skill—a man was either skilled or unskilled. Especially in those industries where the apprenticeship idea was most firmly held to, groups occupying positions intermediate to the skilled and labouring grades were regarded as rather unusual exceptions. Moreover there was no obvious place in the structure for wage earning groups with a status higher than that of tradesmen. Secondly, the interchangeability of words such as 'tradesman' and 'craftsman' with 'skilled' made it clear that the skilled man was somebody who was engaged in production. Skill implied ability to carry out all aspects of the trade's work as well as understanding whatever technical principles were involved. In other words this way of classifying automatically shifts those whose job consists of being knowledgeable and does not involve production work out of the category of workers and into the 'staff'.

It is now no longer possible to get an accurate picture from the simple distinction between craftsmen and labourers, however useful it may have been at one time, and it never covered the whole industrial labour force, since textiles especially had different skill ladders. In consequence the demand for skill cannot simply be translated as the demand for apprentices and journeymen.

Three important reasons can be given for the decline in the primacy of the labourer-journeyman relation. First increased use of machinery has at times caused a complete abandonment of some former craftsman's job. It has generally resulted in craftsmen working machines and in the advent of semi-skilled machine operators. Thus machinery has produced a semi-skilled group of workers to be inserted between the craftsmen and the labourers. Secondly, industries developed in this century have not been rigidly attached to the apprenticeship tradition. They have grown in areas away from the strongly traditional industrial centres and with less trade-union control. They have tended to favour mass-production techniques and increased intensity of machine use. Where they have required skill and expertness they have got it by training courses specifically designed to their requirements. Such courses have varied from very brief periods of indoctrination for routine semi-skilled operators to long courses of study. They do not yield clear divisions into skilled and unskilled. Finally, modern technology has been responsible for extending the range of technical knowledge required by the most skilled workers in industry. For them an apprenticeship carried out by the old method of helping an established journeyman is no longer enough, and an apprenticeship is not the key to skill. For these reasons if we wish to assess the demand for skill we should be thinking of the varying demands for a range of jobs of differing degrees of skill, and not simply of the demand for apprentice-trained men.

What factors then have been building up or diminishing demands for different skill levels in British industry? Such a wide general question can only be answered in general terms, but the general picture is interesting.

1. Machinery is reducing the demand for the services of skilled tradesmen in routine production. The old-fashioned craftsman made the goods in which he specialized, using machinery as ancillary to his task. To an increasing extent the machine now does the work more efficiently than a tradesman, and with more simple controls. In consequence, there is a tendency to find tradesmen reduced to the status of machine minders. In engineering, for example, turners may often find that their machine tools are so designed that skill of their level is not really required. Thus turners work side by side with semi-skilled machinemen.

2. The use of batch- or mass-production techniques has led to standardization of products and to the design of more specialized machinery which requires less skill in its operation. If a number of products of the same kind are to be produced from the same machine, it can be designed specifically to that purpose and requires little skill in its supervision. Thus all a turner's skill may be required to set up a machine for a one-off job, but if the machine is pre-set for routine production a tradesman is not required to operate it. These two points are essentially combined: more machinery has encouraged standardization of production and standardization has led to more opportunities to use machinery. A race of machinists has replaced tradesmen. Where standardization is difficult, as in printing, or where machinery cannot readily be used, as in building, craftsman operators remain. In the bulk of manufacturing industry machinemen have become more usual.

3. The old style tradesman was able to turn his hand to any aspect of his trade. Even where skill of a high order is still required in modern industrial production, with more specialized units of production, what is required is not somebody generally aware of the problems involved in any branch of industry, but one who is trained in a specific type of industry and method of production. A specific course of training can be more suitable than a general apprenticeship. A 'typewriter engineer' specifically trained is of more value to a typewriter firm than a fitter qualified by apprenticeship.

4. These three points suggest a relative decline in demand for skill of the general types in production work, accompanied by some increase in specific skilled jobs particularized to one industry or factory. If we look away from the production side to maintenance and control of production a rather different picture emerges. As machinery goes into increased use in a production process it frequently happens that the skill of its operative declines, but it always happens that the skill and knowledge of those who create it go up. So, too, does the problem facing those who maintain more complex machinery become more difficult. In other words, the developing use of machines may cause less skill to be needed in the operation of machinery but it involves more skill and understanding on the part of those who build and maintain machines, or of those who superintend new and complex processes.

162

It is now possible to sum up these rather general pointers to future demand for skill. The suggestions made seem to indicate that an alteration is in progress in the demand for skilled tradesmen in routine production associated with the increasing use of machinery and machinists. In some trades, where new techniques are at present less possible, the old type of tradesman seem to be continuing. In many cases skill now has a much more restricted field of operation and is much more specific. At the stages where new machinery and processes are brought into being and maintenance is necessary, however, skill and knowledge of a high order is still likely to be needed. Three points can thus be made.

1. Quantitatively, a decline in the demand for skill seems likely.

2. Qualitatively, the demand for skill in future is likely to be less for one uniform skilled level—the apprentice-trained—and more for a range of skills from specific machine skills to technicians with expert knowledge as well as manual skill.

3. A simple classification of skilled and unskilled is no longer appropriate. A semi-skilled group have to be recognized. In consequence of their appearance it has become unfashionable to designate many jobs as unskilled: since most jobs involve some element of skill, however small, the unskilled have lost ground to semi-skilled. The term unskilled now has less meaning and the term semi-skilled includes a wide variation in the degree of difficulty of jobs. Moreover, the skilled group includes at its lower end men whose job is not much different from that of semi-skilled, and men whose job is, in difficulty and knowledge, that of a technician. Yet all bear the same label, though there is an immense difference in the demands made upon the knowledge of the electrician who is engaged on a routine replacement of electric light bulbs as against the electrician in charge of electronic computing equipment. The skilled group is in process of being split up: some are becoming semi-skilled; some stay where they are; and others are becoming technicians. All these features suggest that the idea of a range of skilled grades should replace that of a simple contrast between apprentice-trained and unskilled.

GENERAL FEATURES OF SKILLED LABOUR SUPPLY

The most fundamental points to be made in any discussion of the supply of skilled labour relate to the supply of ability in the community and to the supply of training. On each of these matters it is possible to enter into prolonged discussion. This is not the intention here, however, since sufficient can be said quite generally.

In the first place, while people differ in their views about the abilities of a community, four statements can be made without much controversy arising. These are (1) that different levels of ability exist in any community; (2) that abilities are not all of the same type; (3) that not all members of the working population have the ability to take skilled work; and (4) that the more difficult and skilled the job the smaller the proportion of the population able to undertake it. These propositions lead us to the somewhat obvious conclusion that the possible supply of workers to any one job other than, or possibly even including, the most unskilled, is less than the total labour force and that the more difficult the job the more restricted potential labour supply will be.

The availability of education has been much increased in recent years, both because its cost has borne less hard on the individual concerned, however much it may cost the community in total, and because of increased provision of educational institutions. The consequences of this may be regarded as two-fold: it has raised the general average educational standard of the community, and it has increased the number of those with the requisite education to undertake tasks at the upper level of the occupational ladder.[1]

The combination of these two forces of ability and of education results in two clear conclusions. These are (a) that the quantity of workers able to take on skilled work at differing levels of skill declines as the difficulty of the job increases; and (b), that nevertheless the supply of such skill relative to the total of the working population has tended to increase in consequence of more adequate education.

THE BALANCE OF DEMAND AND SUPPLY

Out of the above remarks on supply of skilled labour and on demand for it may also be deduced the general conclusion that a decline in the relative remuneration of skilled workers, occurring in the present period and over the last few decades, can be theoretically justified. Our conclusions as to demand for skill suggested that there is likely to be a quantitative decline in it. Quantitatively, supply and demand for skill have therefore tended to move in such a way that a fall in the price of skill is a likely result. Neither what has been said about demand nor about supply however, offers any evidence on the extent of the fall in skilled remuneration needed to achieve balance in demand and supply. The evidence is not in fact available to allow such a calculation to be made. Two further points help to clarify the situation but still obscure the answer.

In the first place, while the foregoing statements on supply may be applied quite generally over the whole range of remunerative activity, the remarks on demand relate much more specifically to skilled wage earners. Outside the wage earning group there seems little doubt that the growth in professions, in administration, and in the technical nature of all our activities has caused an

[1] Cf. A. G. B. Fisher, 'Education and Relative Wage Rates', *International Labour Review* xxv, June 1932.

increase in the demand placed on the ability and knowledge of our working population. Thus the increased supply of educated labour in part results in a procession of trained men by-passing the industrial wage earning labour force entirely and filling professional and equivalent jobs. Indeed, whatever may be said of the wage earning skilled, a shortage of ability at this higher level seems likely to occur in the near future. Thus the price for skilled wage earning labour may be somewhat upheld by pressure from this competing demand. This point should not, however, be exaggerated: there are a great many factors both economic and social that limit transference between the wage earning and professional groups of society.

Secondly, one of the difficulties involved in any assessment of the rightness of a given wage level in balancing the demand and supply of skilled labour is the slow reaction to change which characterizes the supply of skilled labour. A training course, or apprenticeship, or any form of educational preparation for an occupation, is normally carried through in youth. Once the training period is over a skilled or trained man becomes extremely unwilling to suffer a loss of that skill, and so tends to be recruited for a lifetime into the occupation he chose as a young man. It is natural that this should be so since a qualification resulting from training is in the nature of a capital asset to its holder. It cost time and money to acquire (either in premia or through low wages under training), it distinguishes its holder from other workers and, provided it can be put to use, it provides a lifetime of income. Thus the bulk of the supply of labour to any one skill, or to skilled work in general, is relatively fixed for a long number of years. In consequence reaction to short-period influences can be slight, and is normally confined to the marginal intake of new entrants. Here a further complicating factor may be mentioned —the supply of skilled labour is dependent on recruitment in youth and will be specially influenced by recruitment conditions offered to youth, and these may show different trends from those of a skill as a whole. For example, wages of apprentices relative to wages for other work available to young men may be rising while those for tradesmen may be showing a relative decline; or immediate promotion prospects may be good but be followed by a life-time's stagnation. Undoubtedly such circumstances may keep up the flow of recruits unless they are endowed with commendably long sight, and this situation may continue unless, or until, the general dissatisfaction of trades-men conveys itself to those contemplating taking up the trade.

Despite these added points we are still left without adequate grounds for constructing a pattern of the fall in the price of skilled labour necessary to equilibrate potentially rising supply and a tendency to a falling demand. One possibility which must occur here is that equilibrium will only be reached when the wage level of skilled workers has sunk to that of unskilled work or to below the unskilled level. This possibility has been canvassed by writers on the effects of education in improving the potential supply of skilled workers.[1] The argument is based on the assumption that education releases a flood of potential applicants for occupations requiring educational attainment and that in consequence scarcity of ability or of training is no longer a sufficient factor limiting supply relative to demand to necessitate a differential payment for such qualities. In such a situation the dominant factor determining levels of relative wages for different jobs becomes their attractiveness to workers. It is therefore argued that the dirty, unpleasant heavy manual jobs, in short the whole range of unskilled manual labour, will be inadequately supplied with workers and will command a premium over the pleasant and comfortable and well-regarded skilled jobs which confer the status in the community which the 'hewers of wood' do not get.

The practical answer to this is either to doubt whether the fall in demand for ability is as great as is suggested (what fall has been mentioned in the foregoing can hardly be of this dimension), and, besides, it has been suggested that there will be an increase in demand for the highest levels of ability, or to doubt whether the innate ability of the population justifies the contention that education can accomplish, or has accomplished, an easy increase in the supply of educated labour, and here extreme doubt must be recorded on the potential supply of the highest levels of educated personnel. But the practical critics are at a disadvantage since it can hardly be denied that education has increased and has had some effect, and that as a consequence, even if professions and administrators are left out, for skilled wage earners at least there has been a tendency to lack of balance in supply and demand and to a fall in price. The extreme position is one point to which the fall might go. Are there any factors that exclude this possibility and make it clear that, however small differential payments for skill become, they must continue to exist and must be positive, if a satisfactory and adequate supply of skilled labour is to be available? Two such factors can be put forward. These relate to the influence of considerations of status and of quality.

Status

In the minds of those who see the possibility of attractiveness or unpleasantness or other such criteria being the basis of differential payments, skilled work will be at a discount in payment since it is manifestly pleasant and attractive. There is, however, always an important difficulty in the use of words such as pleasant and attractive; they get their meaning both from the viewpoint of the participant and from that of the observer. To say that a job is satisfying means not only that it gives pleasure to the performer but also that others are prepared to endorse the satisfaction. It is a strange and lonely man who does not look to others to set the seal of approval on his work, be

[1] Cf. A. G. B. Fisher, op. cit.

166

he artist or tradesman. Thus we have to measure the attraction of skilled work both from inside and outside, and the satisfaction of the worker is conditioned by and reflected in the opinion of others.

The aspects of skilled work, or indeed of any work above that of straight manual labour, which are likely to cause it to be favoured by prospective workers at it, may be roughly classified as physical conditions of work, conditions of work resulting in remuneration or equivalent benefits, the satisfaction of a job which is intrinsically worth doing, and the satisfaction of being responsible or respected at work, of having a 'say' in decisions which matter.

The physical conditions under which work is carried out can vary enormously. Some jobs require little or no manual labour and are carried out in pleasant surroundings seated in a comfortable chair in a comfortable room. Other jobs require that they should be carried through outdoors in all weather conditions, or are subject to heat, noise, dirt, smell or other unpleasantness, and involve hard physical labour. It may be doubted whether the division here is clearly according to the skill or knowledge required of the worker. The civil engineer working on an outdoor site has not noticeably more pleasant conditions than the workers at the site; and certainly the building tradesman suffers the same conditions as his labourer. The marine engineer has precisely the same conditions to put up with in his period on duty as has his oiler. And so through many possible examples. It would, however, be futile to pretend that *in general*, though subject to many exceptions, skill and responsibility do not confer improved conditions of work.

Remuneration from work hardly requires explanation except to say that it is reasonable to regard those fringe benefits such as hours of work, length of holidays, holiday payments, free lunch etc. as equivalent to remuneration or as capable of being converted into remuneration. At present the general position is that both remuneration and these variants of it increase as the ladder of skill and knowledge and responsibility in work is mounted.

The satisfaction of doing a job which is well worth doing derives from an ability to see the significance of your work in relation to the wider achievements of your industry or the wider purposes of society; or, alternatively, from the simple artistic pleasure of creation of something of beauty or significance. There can be little doubt that in general this is a benefit of work which accrues more heavily to those whose work is skilled than to unskilled. Yet, in large measure this satisfaction is externally imposed. The artistic sense may flourish without approval but surely it depends in part on support from others. For most of us it is surely true that the feeling of a job well done depends a lot on how much emphasis society places on the job's being well worth doing.

The satisfaction which can be derived from being a responsible or respected member of a working unit is to be found in all forms and at all levels of work above that of the unskilled wage earner without supervisory duties. It may simply take the form of a skilled tradesman being left to himself to get on with a job which he knows best so that he is responsible for the job and has full control in his own limited sphere. It may be the direct supervisory responsibility of the foreman, or indeed, of the managing director. It may be the much less formal but no less real sense of responsibility felt by the much-trusted senior employee of long service. This responsibility refers almost exclusively to those above the base level of 'common labour'; it is an attribute of the skilled level or above, though extending 'skill' in this sense to cover the case of those whose job is not in itself very difficult but involves burdens of care and duty. Since responsibility normally refers to a relationship with other people or to the attitude of other people to you and your work it depends in part on others. Some will seek responsibility out of some form of power ambition, but most will want it for the esteem it carries with it.

This doubtless incomplete and certainly scrappy listing of the supposed advantages of skill and of higher level jobs generally has the essential feature of insisting that the attractiveness of skill, apart from its remuneration and by no means invariably better physical conditions of work, depends on opinion outside the job as well as direct personal satisfaction. The status or standing of a job with the community in general, as well as reflecting the attractiveness with which its practitioners and everybody else regard it, also conditions that attractiveness. Removal of the status of the job in the eyes of the community is not only a loss of position in the community but may make the job intrinsically less attractive as well.

The most convenient symbol of status of productive work in an economic world is the payment which it receives. It is not precise, especially there need not be a precise proportional relation between status and remuneration. Further, it may sometimes occur that high payment may, in a given social climate, reflect lack of status. The best current example here is that of the miners, since miners in Britain have had to be recruited from outside the traditional mining areas, where they have had little status, and it is at least partly true that the high relative wage level of miners reflect this. Then too there are some jobs where status is maintained despite low remuneration, since status is by no means purely a monetary concept and may involve other valuation processes entirely. Professional men such as doctors and teachers, and especially ministers, can enjoy this kind of status. Nevertheless it remains true that level of remuneration is a frequent first approximation to status.

What happens to the attractiveness of occupations if we proceed to remove the benefit of enhanced remuneration from them? This means that the obvious symbol of status is no longer there. It is no longer apparent that the community thinks highly of the occupation, its attractiveness promptly declines for those who attend to the community's feelings. For those less interested in the community's point of view, those who feel an artistic or vocational urge to some form of skill or responsibility, the only point that matters will be the feeling that the job is worth doing. For this they will depend on their own judgement much more than on that of the community, but even here a general trend of community opinion away from the type of work will in the end diminish in number those who feel a vocation for it. For those whose status does not depend basically on their money valuation no immediate loss of status occurs if the money symbol of status is withdrawn; but they are not immune from another important aspect of the general relationship between money, status and the attractiveness of occupations which affects all types of status. We have been arguing that the attractiveness of jobs depends on their status and that this status is reflected by the money valuation of the job; but it is also true that the status of an occupation is conditioned by the general status of its representatives in the community. This point can be simply met by saying that if the appropriate type of people take jobs then they will also have the appropriate status in the community. Unfortunately, however, status in the community depends in part on having the income to keep it up. It is permissible to say that a minister or doctor has a status independent of income, but as his income falls it becomes difficult for him to keep up any appearances of separate status or afford the necessary symbols of it. Very equal money incomes make for an undifferentiated community in which status is difficult to maintain.

This discussion has put the negative effect on the status of skilled men which equal remuneration, or special payments for 'unpleasant' jobs, would produce. The negative effect would be to reduce the attractiveness of skill on all counts. But a positive effect of this situation must also be recorded. If extra payments are made for 'unpleasant' jobs then they acquire a symbol of status through increased money income. At first this may be thought of as compensating rather than status giving, but the increase in income will enable its recipients to acquire the outward symbols of increased income and a possible positive change in their status may occur. A new set of values may affect a society which aggrandizes unskilled labour, and the community's view of what is the manly and sensible job to go for may alter over a period of time. Status considerations can give even neighbouring communities quite distinct cultures as, for example, in the case of Athens and Sparta. This is especially important since in all this discussion we are really thinking of effects on new entrants into skilled jobs, and these are young men who will be most subject to new values. If unskilled manual work is presented to them as the best-paid work it may well become manly to go to such work. Moreover, all forms of skilled work require training and effort in their acquisition, and yet could be no longer attractive. This last is a most important issue. It is difficult to see how young men can be persuaded to undertake the effort required to get a job which has low status.

The argument that it is possible to visualize a future reversal of the present differential remuneration of skilled work over 'common labour' is based on the assumption that the skilled work will continue to be attractive and will get enough recruits without special payment. The counter argument here is that attractiveness of work is related to status and in turn status is partly related to income. If the income of an occupation falls to the general level its attractiveness will fall not only on account of the fall in income but also through lost status. It is thus not permissible to assume that an occupation will remain attractive without income differentials which give status. Further, a reversal of income differentials *ipso facto* implies long-run transference of status to the gaining occupations which may then become attractive for reasons wider than simple income increase. Finally, the young workers at whom all recruitment policy aims will be asked to accept as attractive skilled work, which has lost income and status, and which always involves more mental effort and a longer training period than unskilled work. It seems improbable that they will be attracted or be willing to undertake the necessary effort in training.[1] On all these grounds the status argument results in a recommendation for positive differentials in payment in favour of skilled work.

Quality

Even if we feel satisfied that an adequate supply of suitably qualified recruits will come forward for skilled work at any given relative payment level, we must still ensure that the highest quality of recruits become available for skilled work. The foregoing has argued that, where there is no differential, considerations of status will stem the flow of recruits; but, even if this were not so it would still be necessary to ascertain, for the sake of the community's wellbeing, that the best recruits presented themselves, and that competition in quality would be as great as possible for the more difficult jobs. Even if it could be proved that the supply of recruits for jobs above the 'common labour' or semi-skilled levels can become more than adequate to the demand, it would not necessarily be proved that there should be no differential in rewards in favour of skilled and responsible work. It would still require to be proved that the best recruits were taking the skilled work so that it would, in the community's interest, be performed as well as possible. This is a most vital consideration in the life of a healthy economy, and is precisely what

---

[1] Loss of status may be more important than simple loss of income in cutting off the flow of youthful recruits. Recruitment of young people to skilled work may lay stress on the non-monetary aspects of position in the community more highly than the monetary, and pressure by parents and friends is likely to be towards the socially accepted superior jobs.

cannot be guaranteed if no reward is offered to stimulate competition.[1] Is it not likely that in such circumstances those with most energy and ability will seek the jobs where differential rewards are offered? There is at least this risk, and therefore in order to ensure selection from quality it is necessary to provide a ladder of differentials corresponding to the ladder of skill and responsibility.

Thus for two reasons—of status and quality—positive differentials to skill can be affirmed as necessary. Nothing however is said here about the actual extent of such differentials which need be maintained. It is impossible to be dogmatic on this. For one thing the slow change in occupational supply, which has to wait for one generation to be replaced by another with different ideas, means that here we are in a market with a very long-run equilibrium. Besides, the extent of reward needed to make a salary or wage appear attractive can differ from time to time for social reasons and from habit. It seems fairly clear that the post-war generation of professional people have settled down to accept a lower real value of differential than was customary before the war. There are complaints about it and there are very pronounced complaints when post-war relative standards are disrupted or a professional group are found to be falling to wage earner status; but, meanwhile, habits and standards have altered and the level of living corresponding to professional status has altered. As time passes habit makes an altered differential acceptable. All that can be said firmly is that some differential is required to separate each occupation on the ladder. Something more definite can be said about the type of differential required: since recruitment supply takes a long time, and since status is important in the attractiveness of skilled work, the differential must be clearly seen to exist and to have some permanence. It is not enough to provide that the occasional extra earnings of skill should average out at more than those of unskilled. If an enhanced wage is to confer status and still more if it is to give an appreciable upward lift to living standards it must be a regular and permanent extra not a casual one.

---

[1] A circularity seems frequently to appear in current reasoning about the relationship between quality and remuneration in particular occupations. We begin with a reduction in relative reward. This in due course causes a fall in the quality of recruits and a tendency for their concept of the job to narrow. Hence the actual work they carry out becomes less significant and important than it was. The public's estimation of the job and of the people who do it also declines. When the differential payment for the occupation comes up for discussion it is then argued that the work being done, and the people doing it, are not worth a larger differential payment. But the occupation and the people as currently exemplified cannot be taken as measures of the job that should be done, since it has been debased. It is quite possible that the original concept of the occupation's importance was the correct one, and that wider differentials and increased status are needed to restore that concept. This point is particularly relevant if the job is such that the scope of the work can be altered according to the attitude adopted by those doing it, and the intensity of effort and experience which they bring to their task, and if it is both difficult to carry out properly, and pleasant if lesser effort is put into it. The recent controversy about school teachers seems to fall neatly into this pattern.

The conclusions of this discussion of the basic questions relative to the reward for skill can now be summed up, before the present practical situation is considered. Four conclusions may be drawn.

1. A ladder of skill and responsibility is now a more appropriate concept than that of a simple journeyman/labourer relation.

2. It is necessary, and will continue to be necessary, to denote differences in skill by differences in payment.

3. No precise estimate can be placed on what actual size of such differences is needed.

4. The differentials must however be clearly visible and relatively permanent.

A COMMENTARY ON ACTUAL MOVEMENTS OF SKILLED WAGES

The foregoing sections have provided an attitude to skilled payments which must now be applied to the trends in these in post-war Britain. At the most general level, however, an immediate basic difficulty occurs since official statistics are largely silent on this point: the source of general data has therefore to be private research.

The bulk of private research in Britain on the relation between skilled and unskilled wage-rates in different industries is to be found in various articles which have been appearing since 1951 in the *Bulletin* of the University of Oxford Institute of Statistics by Mr K. G. J. C. Knowles and the author and by Mr Knowles and others.[1] It would be wearisome to repeat here all the detail derived from such studies, especially since the inferences of their general conclusions can be put most simply.

The main observed tendency in relative occupational wage rates was for the skill differential to grow smaller during the First and Second World Wars. After the end of the First World War and in the ensuing depression relative wages opened out again somewhat, but not to the pre-1914 extent. They then remained generally stable in the inter-war years. In the Second War wage rate differentials again narrowed and continued to do so in the post-war years, though after about 1953 negotiations and settlements in many cases began to reflect a desire to stop narrowing differentials and a reversion to percentage increases instead of flat rate money increases. In the years before 1914 the usual level of unskilled wage rates as a percentage of skilled wage

[1] Most of these articles have already been mentioned at various points in the foregoing. The most relevant ones here are 'Differences between the Wages of Skilled and Unskilled Workers, 1880–1950' (April 1951); 'Earnings in Engineering 1926–1948' (June 1951); and 'Earnings in Shipbuilding' (November/December 1951)—all by Knowles and Robertson: 'Rates and Earnings in London Transport' (August 1953), by Knowles and H. J. D. Cole; and 'Earnings in the Boot and Shoe Industry' (February/March 1954) by Knowles and Monica Verry.

rates was somewhere about 60 per cent. In the inter-war years this figure had become 70 to 75 per cent and since the last war 80 to 85 per cent has been usual.

Data on differentials in average earnings between unskilled and skilled may also be derived for a number of industries. They suggest that differentials in average earnings tend to be slightly wider than differentials in negotiated wage rates, but to have been subject to very similar trends. In a number of cases average earnings of semi-skilled grades may also be adduced. They fit in between those of skilled and unskilled but tend to come fairly close to skilled workers' averages. There has been a fairly general tendency in British industry to up-grade occupations from unskilled to semi-skilled, since it is in any case always difficult to say that a job has no skill content whatsoever. It is therefore not specially surprising that, despite longer average hours, those occupations left under the unskilled label should lag in earnings. A consequence of this, however, is that for purposes of comparison the semi-skilled average earnings figure probably has more relevance than that for unskilled workers.

The general tendency towards a narrowing gap between skilled workers' remuneration and that of other workers is by no means out of line with the argument of the preceding section, the rapid movement of the differential in the war periods and since the last war and its stability at other times suggest the presence of short-period forces. What special short-period forces were operating on relative wages at this general level in recent years?

There are those who regard the tendency since 1939 for differentials to narrow as mainly a function of prevailing institutional practices and attitudes. Two ideas are involved here, that the type of wage settlement achieved by collective bargaining is conditioned by the argument which is most convenient to the wage claimant, and that the trade union's attitude and problems condition the wage claim it puts in and accepts. In wartime and the early post-war years, when prices were rising and the atmosphere of sacrifice and sharing burdens was usual, the most natural argument with which to put forward a wage claim was a rise in the cost of living and the most natural result was a flat-rate cost of living bonus which maintained money differentials and narrowed percentage and real differentials. Mr H. A. Turner[1] has pointed out, however, that the typical narrowing in differentials in negotiated wage rates which resulted from the application of flat-rate cost of living bonuses did not occur in all industries. For example, it did not occur in coal, steel and textiles. In these industries, Mr Turner points out, the unions include both skilled and unskilled but owe much of their strength to the skilled workers. Moreover, the skilled workers are recruited from the unskilled so

[1] H. A. Turner, 'Trade Unions, Differentials, and the Levelling of Wages', *Manchester School*, September 1952.

that, because of a promotional ladder between them, there is less conflict of interest between skilled and unskilled. Mr Turner suggests that because the unions' attitude and those of their members did not favour narrowing differentials, they did not narrow.

An alternative suggestion is that narrowing differentials between skilled and unskilled workers has been possible because of narrowing differentials between apprentices and skilled workers and between apprentice and other juvenile labour. The tendency for differentials in wage rates to narrow in the years since 1939 has not been confined to the relative wage rates of skilled and unskilled workers. It has also been true of a good number of other differentials, for example that between men and women. Among the differentials which have narrowed have been those relating apprentices and journeyman, and those relating boys to adult unskilled workers, while the gap between the unskilled boys' wages and the somewhat lower wages of apprentices has also closed. Thus it has now generally become possible for an apprentice on time rates to be earning more than youths of the same age working as juvenile unskilled labour before the end of his apprenticeship. If the contrast is between apprentices on time rates and boys on semi-skilled work under payment-by-results, the foregoing relationship is not so certain; but on the other hand apprentices too are sometimes put on payment-by-results.[1] In general, therefore, while the reward for acquiring skill may not be as good as it has been, the monetary sacrifice involved during its acquisition is now frequently much reduced. Since youth probably tends to discount the future handsomely, and since recruitment to a skill is from youth, this change may have been an important counter to reduced skill remuneration.

An argument on the short-term causes of narrowing skill differentials which owes little to institutional factors is that advanced by M. W. Reder.[2] His argument, reduced to an inadequate sentence or two, is based on the relative strengths of supply of skilled and unskilled labour and the possibilities of supply altering by movements between the groups, in times of boom when differentials are narrowing, and at other times when they are not. Employers are assumed to be able to adjust 'hiring standards' so that when labour is plentiful higher skill is required for entry into skilled work. Thus

---

[1] The background and causes of the narrowing of differentials between juveniles and adults, and between apprentices and juvenile unskilled labour, are probably as complex as those which we have been discussing for skill, and cannot therefore be gone into at length here. In the short period the source of narrowing juvenile differentials has probably been the same institutional tendency during inflation to seek wage rate increases which have a bias towards flat-rate changes. In both the short and the long period the competing claims of education, and especially the increased school leaving age, have probably been at the root of higher relative rewards for young people, together with the shift away from young people in the composition of our population.

[2] M. W. Reder, 'Theory of Occupational Wage Differential', *American Economic Review*, XLV, December 1955.

skilled work maintains its price more easily than unskilled through restriction of supply. When labour becomes scarce skilled hiring standards may be reduced. This increases the supply of skilled and reduces the supply of unskilled, so causing a wage movement against the skilled. The argument might also be put differently by saying that in unemployment all unemployed men whether skilled or unskilled become at least potential applicants for unskilled work whereas only skilled can apply for skilled work; thus, a surplus supply is added to the ranks of unskilled men during general unemployment and withdrawn when full employment is reached.

Each of these suggestions offers a special short-period answer to our problem: can they all be accepted? Mr Turner's institutional analysis, and the flat-rate cost of living advance argument clearly apply to wage rates and have much force in that connection. They do not, however, help greatly with earnings except in so far as earnings contain wage rates, and if the gap in wage rates is narrow, it has a due effect in limiting the range of the gap in earnings. If earnings are sufficiently flexible these effects on wage rates can be set aside. In practice, however, it is unlikely, if wage rate gaps are persistently narrowing, that earnings gaps will show a comparable facility at widening, though they may do so a little. In consequence the general institutional arguments on wage rates probably go a long way towards explaining earnings and wage rate narrowing.

Both Mr Reder's analysis, and that relating to the relative movements of remuneration of apprentices and juvenile labour generally, can be applied to wage rates and earnings. If granted they both offer an explanation of why narrowing differential payments for skilled workers become acceptable. There seems to be no obvious flaw in the apprentice/juvenile argument. Mr Reder's analysis however, has more difficulties; indeed, it is probable that it is more applicable to the U.S.A. than to here. It depends on a transference between skilled and unskilled employment as 'hiring standards' are altered. With general unemployment skilled men can doubtless offer themselves for unskilled work, so increasing the intensity of supply of unskilled labour and keeping differentials wide, though this is somewhat different from the suggestion that hiring standards of skilled labour are raised at such times. In times of full employment however, while skilled men will no doubt withdraw from unskilled work, it is less easy to see that the unskilled can in fact crowd in on skilled workers by alterations in hiring standards. In Britain, where skilled men are generally subject to apprenticeship or some other formal training, it is difficult to adjust formal hiring standards which are governed by the possession of recognized credentials. Thus, while the employer may be more selective at some times than others, the range of variation in hiring standards open to him is strictly limited. In consequence full employment may cause extreme shortage of some types of skill which may indeed become

175

the limiting factor on output, and in some sectors skill would appear likely to develop strong scarcity value. Mr Reder's analysis is not proven for Britain.

Our discussion of the short-period forces at work in narrowing skill differentials has been somewhat inconclusive. There are various possible explanations but none are completely satisfying. This may suggest a failure of theoretical reasoning: it is not really so. The essential determinants of the level of skilled remuneration are long period, the kind of forces discussed in the preceding section. Short-period forces may conform to, or make more difficult, the long-term trend; but there is no reason why they should be able to be explained as fitting satisfactorily into the long-term trend. Each of the explanations presented above has relevance to the short-period situation— none completely ties the short period to the long. The least useful is probably Mr Reder's theoretical explanation. Mr Turner's analysis and the general institutional 'flat-rate' arguments are valuable in explaining wage rate tendencies. As to earnings, the real explanation of the short-period movements of the earnings-relation between skilled and unskilled may well be that it is an accidental by-product of payments of overtime and payment-by-results designed for quite different purposes.

THE REWARD FOR SKILL AND FACTORY WAGE STRUCTURES

The method of discussion adopted in this chapter has been to begin with the most general considerations affecting skilled labour, and then to move on to the shorter period and the actual level of the differential for skill in post-war Britain. The concluding stage of this process is to relate the discussion to factory wage structures, and so to bring the case-studies back into the picture. The points to be made can be conveniently itemized.

1. One of the major complicating factors in discussion of the prospective demand for skilled labour relative to other grades is the extent to which the simple division of the manual labour force between skilled journeymen and unskilled workers has been replaced by a more complicated ladder of skill gradations. Lack of clarity in definition of new skill gradations and in appreciation of changes in the ladder of skills may be one factor in producing confusions in relative wage levels in actual factories. The best illustration of this problem that occurs in the factories described in the case-studies is the tendency for turners and machinemen working in the same shop to be treated similarly for wage purposes. It is by no means always clear that the training of a turner in many aspects of his trade is really needed when in practice he is put to work in a machine shop on one type of machine exclusively and so takes his place alongside the machinemen. It is inevitable that lack of clarification of the status and functions of a job should be reflected in lack of

clarity in payment differentials. That the same kind of thing does not happen in the shipyard is a clear indication of the continuation of the old journeyman/labourer tradition in that industry.

2. No recommendation is made in this chapter on the actual size of the skill differential which our economy requires. Indeed, it is suggested that the precise level of differentiation needed cannot be dogmatically asserted. But, nevertheless, there can be no doubt that *some* positive differential must exist if suitable provision is to be made for the economy's skill requirements. Each of the case-studies shows a general tendency for the patterns of average earnings to result in some positive skill differential. But these average figures are determined to a major extent by payment-by-results and overtime, both of which vary for reasons unconnected with skill. Moreover, these payments spread out earnings in such a way that the distribution of skilled earnings, even on an hourly basis, is overlapped by those of the semi-skilled and unskilled. Both payment-by-results earnings and overtime earnings appear to be more important determinants of relative wage levels than differential payments for skill. Despite the average result which shows a skill differential, these wage structures are not therefore directed clearly towards skill rewards, mainly because of the influence of payment-by-results and overtime.

3. Skill is a long-term attribute and one of the functions of a differential payment for skill is to confer a long-term difference in income status on the skilled man. It is not only necessary that the differential should be positive but that it should be seen to be so. This is not true of the case-studies. The average level of skilled earnings conceals many cases in which earnings of skilled men fall below less skilled. But even the average level of skilled payment, and the individual cases above and at the average, are largely founded on conceivably highly unstable and certainly short-term overtime and bonus payments. The factory wage structures do not give long-term status labels to skilled men which set them at a clearly established wage level. All is confusion and uncertainty in a very short-period way.

PART 3. WAGE POLICY

CHAPTER 11

TRADE UNIONS AND EMPLOYERS' ASSOCIATIONS

The central theme of this book has been the many ways in which wages paid in factories may differ both in amount and in structure from the agreements negotiated nationally for industries. Admittedly the case-studies are derived from the engineering and shipbuilding industries, where the national agreements may well be simpler, and the divergence of factory wages more marked, than in other cases; but, divergence between national rates and industry earnings is by no means wholly confined to such industries,[1] and there has been a general tendency for wage rates to advance at a slower rate than earnings in Britain since 1938. It is appropriate and necessary therefore to consider this tendency in relation to the functions of the principal parties to national negotiations, the trade unions[2] and the employers' associations.

TRADE UNIONS AND FACTORY WAGES

The trade unions were created to maintain and improve the conditions of the working lives of their members. As far as wages are concerned this could be interpreted as a three-fold duty to keep the wage level rising, so as to achieve a better standard of life for workers, to achieve a reliable method by which conditions may be altered, and to eliminate underpayment of the least protected workers. In practice this three-fold task has been interpreted as the frequent pursuit of money wage increases (with an apparent disregard at the point of settlement of the real versus money wage controversy), the drive to obtain a recognized status in wage bargaining for the unions and recognized procedures such as collective bargaining, and an adherence to standard rates and the 'common rule', by which uniformity in wage rates is held to keep the individual who is in a weak position secure from exploitation.

It is naturally difficult to obtain a satisfactory set of simple generalizations to cover the wealth of trade union history in the field of wage settlement, but for present purposes the following points may be made.

---

[1] Cf. H. A. Turner, 'Wages, Industry Rates, Workplace Rates and the Wage-Drift', *Manchester School*, May 1956.

[2] The writer's article 'Trade Unions and Wage Policy', *Political Quarterly*, January/March 1956 is relevant both to this chapter and to the following one.

1. The trade unions were not at first recognized as legitimate parties to wage agreements. Wages were a matter for individual determination between workers and their employers, and the superior strength in bargaining power inevitably rested with the latter. In such circumstances trade unions had to try to impose their will by force, through, for example, restrictive practices or strikes, or else had to look after their own workers with their own resources by mutual insurance. The biggest single change in wage settlement in the last century has been the recognition of the right of trade unions to represent workers and their right to be heard and to take part in negotiation with employers.

2. The right of trade unions to represent workers and negotiate on their behalf has found institutional expression in collective bargaining and the variants of it. There are few workers—and those mostly in salaried occupations —who do not now have their wages settled by trade union negotiation or representation in collective bargaining, or in complementary Wages Council or arbitration procedures.

3. One of the most distinctive features of the period prior to trade union organization and organized wage negotiation was the very wide scatter in levels of payment and the existence of seriously underpaid groups. The trade unions made it their objective to eradicate these disparities and insisted on the pursuit of uniformity in payment—the rate for the job, the standard rate, the common rule, etc. This need to defend the underpaid, and to develop maximum defensive power in wage negotiation under conditions of serious unemployment, and maximum aggressive power at other times, led to their wish to develop large-scale wage agreements settling common rates for workers in whole industries. Thus the trade unions fought for, and secured, large-scale national wage negotiations according to established collective bargaining procedures and used these to impose uniformity and standardization in wage rates.

If we now consider these three features of the developed association between trades unions and national collective bargaining in the light of the trade unions' present situation, then we have to note that in recent years the strength of the trade unions has been much enhanced, by full employment especially, but also by more complete organization. Not only do they have the formal right of negotiation but they also have the power to force negotiations through to a conclusion which is biased in their favour. How else can one explain their success, exemplified clearly in 1956 and 1957, in getting wage rate increases beyond the cost of living rise and under conditions of static production? The right to negotiate and the recognition of the trade unions are both now well established; indeed, some would say they are over-established. Collective bargaining procedural forms, or variations of them, are almost universal. There is a fairly adequate mechanism for defending

179

under-privileged wage earners. Besides, such is the present state of labour demand, the persistent tendency is for wage rates even for the poorest workers to be pushed up rather than held down, if it keeps the workers with an individual employer and he can avoid competitive retaliation by others. All these points suggest that the trade unions do not now have to pursue the ends in wage settlement which they have historically sought, for the good and simple reason that they have won them. The important question for the trade unions should be what next?

It is clear that no trade unionist would willingly abandon the national collective bargaining network built up over the years, though this does not necessarily exclude its amendment. But if we accept the general supposition that the network on present principles is approaching completion, then, either the trade unions settle down to a period of mature stagnation, or else they move on to its supplementation. There have been in trade union mythology various beliefs about the 'rate for the job' and 'fair' wages which have given an ethical tone to the desire for national collective bargaining and uniform rates, but, in fact, such bargaining got its chief stimulus from the desire for aggressive and defensive strength, and its chief impetus during and after the First War, when broad industrial policies on wages were needed, and the parallel development of employers' associations was well advanced. If we set aside the ethical atmosphere in favour of collective bargaining uniformity, since ethical statements of this order can conveniently ignore difficulties, surely nobody failed to realize that compression of all wages into a few standard rates left a number of possible causes of wage difference not allowed for. In any case, whether or not, at the time when national collective bargaining was developing, people realized its limitations, the need for supplementation to recognize other factors in wage determination has now found unmistakable and very obvious expression in the emergence of an earnings structure which differs from that created by wage rates. It would seem to be the obvious next step for trade unions to begin to extend their activities towards regularizing this new development. Indeed it is not only a case of national collective bargaining being in need of supplementation, the indications are, and the case-studies confirm this, that if the unions do not attempt to supplement their national collective bargaining activities they will slowly lose control of the actuality of wages in this country in pursuit of a dream. The positive contribution to wage change of national collective bargaining at present (and not always a very fortunate one) is to control the rate of change of wage rates: it does not determine either actual wage structures or their less formal supplementation.

The principal question that arises from the suggestion that national collective bargaining is not now adequate is to ask whether collective bargaining as a method should be continued either nationally or locally. Whatever name

it may be given, negotiation between an organization representing a group of
workpeople with an employer or a group of employers will tend to take the
same general form as collective bargaining, which will therefore certainly
continue to exist. But if the orientation of collective bargaining is changed
from large-scale, highly standardized national bargaining towards more local
decision-taking, how much, if any, of national collective bargaining should
be maintained? Two major functions can be attributed to it.

1. National collective bargaining is necessary to settle minimum rates of
wages. This is the old defensive function of national bargains and of the trade
unions, which trade unionists would certainly wish to keep, and rightly so.
It is also as far as some collective bargains at the national level go at present.
In some cases the agreements relate only to minimum rates. In others, while
the agreements refer to standard rates, the general presumption in the industry
is that they shall be regarded as minima and almost everybody will get more
than the standard rate. In these latter cases, which include engineering, this
arrangement has the result that bargains are concluded and cases argued as
though everybody were on the allegedly standard rate. If the negotiations
were formally confined to minimum rates these examples of 'double talk'
would disappear.

2. National bargaining, provided industries are appropriately defined so as
to include firms with similar problems, is useful as a means of settling uniformly broad conditions of work and general disputes procedures. Such
matters as, for example, the standard hours of work for the industry, overtime
premium percentages, or the duration of holidays with pay can readily and
usefully be nationally determined. It is also both useful and important to
have agreement for the industry on how to deal with disputes which grow
beyond the confines of one firm or factory.

These two functions ought to be centrally dealt with, but national collective bargaining on minimum rates requires to be added to by local negotiation on wages if the present division between agreements and factory
practice is to be mitigated.

The degree to which collective bargains should be localized depends on the
type of industry or occupation in question. In some cases the extent of possible
local variation is not very great. One thinks immediately of the civil service,
the railways or local authority employees. In cases such as these, workers in
each grade are employed on very similar work, under very similar conditions,
by the same employer or by closely related authorities. These circumstances,
especially that of one employer, suggest that national bargaining may be able
in some cases to do the whole job of formulating an adequate wage structure
without much being left to local supplementation, though it is likely that
regional differentials will have to be noted in the national bargain. This
statement does not negative what has already been said, but merely indicates

the exceptional cases in which the two types of bargaining coalesce. The distinctive contribution of national bargaining is to settle the general provisions and conditions of service which apply throughout an industry, while the contribution of local bargaining is to adjust and complement these general provisions with the appropriate local details. If the industry is closely defined, then little local supplementation may be needed. Such close definition will occur most readily when only one employer is involved. It may also occur when the conditions of work, the duties of the workers, the product and the competitive position of the employers are all alike. Clearly such provisions are more likely to be met with in public services than elsewhere, while in manufacturing industry they are unlikely. Nevertheless the general prescription that close definition of the industry will make the national bargain more complete has validity for manufacturing industry as well. An industry such as engineering, which is loosely defined in almost every aspect, can only successfully use a very thin national bargain which must be filled out by local bargains, if the bargaining system as a whole is to be able to specify actual wage structures. If the industry is sectionalized then the chances of producing more adequate national bargains promptly grow. The first step towards localization is therefore the sectionalization of existing national bargains. For the present this may be as far as unions can go with localization of collective bargaining, and the details of such a step are worked out in Appendix 2 for the engineering industry.

Will such a step towards more sectionalized and more detailed collective bargains suffice to bring negotiated settlements into line with actual wage structures, and to bring trade unions closer to grips with actuality in wages? Again the answer depends on the closeness of definition of the section of industry to which the settlements are made to refer. The basic issue here is probably once more the number of employers involved. If there are a number of employers then differences in their labour policy become likely. Three factors in the actual situation suggest that in manufacturing industry more local bargains still must eventually be envisaged. (1) The tendencies for firms to differ in their profitability and rates of expansion or contraction cause differences in need to attract labour and willingness to pay adequately for it. (2) Despite their belonging to the same industry, there is usually some variation in one firm's end-products from those of another, and this causes the intensity of demand for labour and the types of labour required to differ. (3) Firms differ in the methods of payment they use. To overcome these difficulties collective bargains at the factory level would be necessary.

The first two of the factors listed above are fundamental. An industry wage structure will always tend to be subject to modification by particular firms which are more in need of workers, are more prosperous than others, or need different types of workers, being for example, perhaps more prepared to pay for quality or youth than others. It is doubtless true, as wage theory would have it, that in the long run and in equilibrium these factors cancel out through movement of workers between firms, but in the short run they make any industry-wide bargain, no matter how closely defined the industry may be, subject to the constant danger of being superseded at the factory level. It is this type of consideration that makes factory collective bargaining necessary if wage agreements and wage structures are to coincide.

What of the third factor listed? Is the existence of different payment methods a recommendation for factory-level collective bargaining? The use of payment-by-results has been exhaustively discussed in earlier chapters, and the suggestions made there would, if followed out, reduce the need for this type of payment and the difficulties it creates for standardizing, or even comparing, different types of payment in different factories. In existing circumstances, however, payment-by-results schemes have two broad functions. First, by providing generous bonus they can be used as a substitute for adequate wage rates, or to supplement nationally negotiated wage rates in order to get and keep workers. Secondly, they may be used for their designed purpose as incentive schemes. In practice both uses come together. The first use is represented by the generosity of the scheme and the extent to which a proportion of bonus is always earned, while the second use can be found in operation at the margin of work and earnings. Similarly overtime can be regarded at present both as an alternative to wage rates or as a payment for extra time at work. In so far as overtime is a more or less regular part of work regularly paid for, it conforms to the first of these uses; since it is specifically payment for hours worked outside the normal day it conforms to the second use. If factory collective bargaining were established, then the need to offer regular bonus and regular overtime as supplements to negotiated rates, might be presumed to disappear. A more rational solution of the factory's need to pay more money to get suitable workers could be arrived at. Factory negotiation is likely to be a necessity, therefore, to eradicate these anomalies in present methods of wage payment. If overtime were then to become an occasional extra payment there does not seem to be any real reason why special factory negotiation should be necessary. On the other hand, the operation of an incentive scheme in a particular way by a particular factory would need to be the subject of a distinct bargain if the factory's wage structure were to be controlled by a collective bargain. In other words there are several reasons why, in manufacturing industry, detail in collective bargains and the marriage of collective bargaining negotiated rates and actual factory wage structures can only be achieved at the factory level.

What has now emerged from this discussion? First, from the trade union viewpoint the system of national collective bargaining represents the culmination of a long struggle. It is not now, however, an adequate means of giving trade unions control over actual wage payments; nor can trade unions simply rest content with the national structure, which requires supplementation. Secondly, the functions of the national agreements in an industry ought to be to fix those points of the industry's labour arrangements which are common to all its firms. For wages, this generally means minimum rates. Thirdly, the extent to which bargains would have to be localized to make them fully relevant to actual factory situations depends on the industry in question. In manufacturing industry at least factory collective bargains would be needed before negotiated rates and actual payments could coincide. The upshot of all this, as far as trade unions are concerned, is an accusation that they have not followed up their success in achieving national collective bargaining by carrying on to supplement it, and further that they have, therefore, been directing their thoughts and energies far too exclusively towards collective bargaining at the national level and have so encouraged and aided an artificial settlement of wage payments against the background of an artificial wage structure. There is also the challenge that they should try to go beyond the network of national agreements to establish a further network of local, and finally factory, bargains.

If British trade unions accept this challenge it will involve changes in several of their present attitudes. These may be itemized.

1. The tendency to regard the national bargain as the climax of the union's endeavours and the end of a season of wage fixing would, of course, have to give way to much more diffuse activity in settling local and factory bargains. Further, the present uncritical formulation of the 'common rule' dogma as an expression of trade union desire for non-discrimination and uniformity in wage payment would have to be replaced by a more sophisticated attention to the merits and complications of detailed wage structuring.

2. This would produce a most desirable change in the types of argument suitable to the occasion of a collective bargaining discussion. At present trade unions present their cases at national negotiations based on broad general movements of the cost of living, general statements about profits and production in the industry, and broad general statements about the relation of their wage rates to those in other industries. The difficulties of conducting a rational discussion on these arguments are numerous. Even if they are accurately presented they are too general to apply to all the employers in an industry, and in any event they are related to industry wage rates which are much too general to be appropriate indications of the amounts actually paid by different employers in an industry. If a clean split between national negotiations and local or factory negotiations were to be established, this would induce considerable changes in the use of these arguments. The general cost of living argument, accompanied by the type of social examples about living wages, and the lowest level of wage compatible with contemporary ideas on

living standards, which are at present produced by unions at national negotiations, would now be applied to the type of situation to which they are most
relevant, namely, the determination at national level of the minimum wage
rates which can be accepted in an industry. Arguments relating to profits
and production would be most relevant to factory or local conditions; but,
presented at that level they would acquire precision and relevance which they
can never have on a national scale, since at the local level they would be based
on the actual case under discussion. Arguments relating to the cost of living
and to relative levels of wages paid in other factories, or occupations, or
industries would now have to be related specifically to the factory's own labour
force. This would bring into their correct prominence the related questions of
recruitment, labour turnover and the general contentment or otherwise of the
factory's labour force. All the various arguments at present used by trade
unions would therefore gain in clarity and in relevance by such an alteration.
Negotiation might then no longer appear to be based on arguments which
are irrelevant and to which nobody pays much attention.[1]

3. An immediate corollary of the above is that the unions would be forced
by a change in emphasis towards local bargaining to become more interested
in, and more knowledgeable about, the problems of factory managements.
This may seem like a most unfortunate suggestion to factory managers who
resent interference. And yet they already have much interference of this type
in the form of directives produced by national bargaining. If factory bargaining is to be fruitful and helpful it must be informed on both sides of the table.
Indeed, since awareness and appreciation of detail are of the essence of successful factory wage structures it is to everybody's interest to have informed
and trained trade unionists.

4. The development of more local bargaining, and the changes in emphasis
of argument and knowledge of detail which this implies, have important
consequences for the quantity and quality of trade union officials required.
The point has frequently been made that British trade union officials are both
overworked and underpaid. 'By and large the unions are run in such a way
as to impose on their leading executive officers burdens and hardships of a
kind not to be found in any comparable non trade union undertaking.'[2] This
is already true with largely centralized bargaining: how much more true
would it become if detailed local negotiation were to be substituted. A trade
union official whose diary is crammed with meetings and conferences is in no

[1] A most interesting recent article by Lady Gertrude Williams ('The Myth of "Fair".
Wages', *Economic Journal*, December 1956) expresses strong antipathy to the current
tendency to discuss wages in ethical terms as 'fair' or 'equitable' or 'just' to the neglect of
the economic motive for paying them. It is probable that the development of this attitude
on the part of trade unions and public reflects the national bargain and the arguments
appropriate to it, and that it will diminish if local bargains become more usual.
[2] J. A. Mack, 'Trade Union Leadership', *Political Quarterly*, January–March 1956.

position to conduct detailed local negotiation, or to be fully familiar with local details. Wage structuring at the local level requires time and patience. The present number of full-time officials in British trade unions is not adequate to this task. Indeed this is probably the major practical difficulty standing in the way of a more thorough attempt by trade unions and employers in co-operation at producing more adequate wage structures.

The problem of securing an adequate number of trade union officials is intimately related to their payment. There can be no question, with a democratic body of this type, of arguing on recruitment of leaders as a simple supply and demand problem related to salaries paid. Nevertheless the present tendency to associate the payment of officials with varying degrees of closeness to the wages earned by members puts a premium on the enthusiasm of the official, who almost certainly puts in longer hours than members, and certainly carries more responsibilities. It also puts at a discount the prospects of a young man deliberately choosing a career as a trade union official. Moreover, the whole question of remuneration of officials indicates a strong bias on the part of the movement against the costs of organization and administration. Yet, the responsibilities of detailed collective bargaining can hardly be met without more organizational costs, and, while it is right to emphasize the voluntary and elective principles for recruiting trade union officials, again more detailed work may force the issue of a career outlook and prospects for officials. The question of training is relevant here. A purely election method of getting officials means that their training may be less important than their popularity; but to impose long courses of training without career prospects would be difficult. A trade union official in the changed circumstances of detailed bargaining could not very well do without training; yet, a training principle of selection is not easily reconciled with a voluntary and democratic organization.

There is no need, however, to conclude that the issues involved for trade union administration and leadership are necessarily confined by an unbreakable circle of difficulties. There is a clear need for more full time trade union officials with knowledge and time at their disposal. Two basic problems hold back this result. These are the present attitude of trade unions towards officials' salaries and administrative overheads, and the question of reconciling election and training. The first of these difficulties is the exact parallel in the administrative field to the policy issue already discussed. If the trade unions take up the challenge of the step beyond national bargaining in wages, then a further step in administration is an essential. A change in attitude towards policy requires and embraces a change in administrative attitudes. As to reconciling training and election—this is no new problem. Already the duties of the leadership have changed sufficiently to make training generally necessary. Two possible administrative devices may effect the reconciliation.

186

These are recruitment from members by examination into the lowest grade of officials with relatively permanent appointments, and election from this group to higher offices; or, the provision of training courses for membership generally, with election to all offices requiring a minimum attendance at these. In practice both these suggestions amount to the same things—more training, and election only after training.

5. In recent years the literature on trade unions has had much to say on two related matters—apathy and decline in branch life, and developing workshop organizations, controlled by shop stewards, inclined to militancy, and only moderately under union control. The policy towards wage structure here proposed, would greatly alter this problem which essentially arises from a shift in the centre of official union activity from the branches to headquarters.

The developing scale of collective bargaining machinery has had the effect of concentrating decision-taking authority at union headquarters, leaving to the branches the tasks of interpreting decisions, carrying through centrally organized education schemes, and discussing and commenting on union affairs, for example, proposing resolutions, frequently on somewhat extraneous matters, for discussion at conferences. Moreover, this shift in the centre of decision in the union also involves an alteration in the method employed by the union to secure its objectives: large-scale bargaining proceeds by discussion and negotiation rather than by direct action. When a strike is contemplated something has to be done by all members and the branches become important; but official strike action has tended on the whole to be a less important method of trade unionism in post-war years, and so the branches have a less active part to play. A decline in branch life through lack of duties and sense of purpose would seem to be inevitable in such circumstances. The really significant point of interest for students of trade unions must be that the branches have continued to have a live existence at all, other than as administrators of welfare schemes.

Though in existing circumstances branches have little to do, this does not mean that there are no reasons for local activity. The remoteness of the union decision-taking centre, and the general nature of the bargains it concludes, provide plenty of problems of interpretation at the local level, and make possible supplementary activity. But since such activity is in the factory, and since it is supplementary, and is not part of the official or central union policy, it lies outside the jurisdiction of the lowest rung of the regular organizational ladder—the branch—and falls to the shop steward organization. The duty of the branch is to assist in the formulation and execution of the main policy of the union, in this case the conclusion of broad general, and probably national, agreements. The fact that in practice this duty is somewhat nominal does not affect the result that the branch is thereby more or less excluded from pursuing the different policy of settling local bargains and arguing out disagreements with individual factory managements without reference to the union headquarters. This is left to the less official, and less inhibited, shop stewards. Of course in some unions the branch is organized on a workshop basis or is more frequently brought in to factory discussions and this difficulty does not arise to the same extent; but the vacuum in union control of conditions at the factory, provides a natural point for growth of alternative control.

Another reason for the relatively greater activity of shop stewards as against the branch is that in present circumstances the stewards have become the heirs of the militant and active traditions of the unions. The history of British trade unions is bound up with strong loyalty from members and with direct action taken by workers to achieve their purposes. As a result of the development of negotiation rather than direct action, the unions are in the difficult position of wishing to retain this loyalty, but also of being embarrassed by any direct and active manifestation of it without their authority. They encourage members by reference to their history of struggle but prescribe little outlet for local enthusiasm in action of any kind. It is not therefore surprising that activity should be channelled into the less official and less restrained actions directed by shop stewards. These provide the outlet for enthusiasm and action which the more official machinery does not.

If the unions were to move out from behind the protective barriers of national agreements and begin on the task of discussing actual wage practice and payments in a more realistic way, then all levels of the unions would immediately have a job to do. The sterilization of branch life has been due to the mistaken theory that everything that is necessary is being done centrally. If more local negotiation and more detailed work is undertaken, the branches would be required to play a part as decision-takers and in training officials; shop stewards would become more integrated into the normal union machinery; and, members would have a more natural outlet for their enthusiasm.

EMPLOYERS' ASSOCIATIONS, EMPLOYERS AND FACTORY WAGES

The growth of trade unions to a position of power and influence, and the development of national collective bargaining have been accompanied by a strong tendency on the part of employers to associate, and to negotiate as an industry, with the relevant trade unions. Naturally single firm industries do not do this, but they are in any case largely excluded from the distinction between local and national. Most other industries have such associations. Some industries have associations of employers which are purely for the purpose of regulating or advising on trading arrangements and common technical problems. Such associations are most commonly described as *trade* associations. Their function is divorced from labour problems. On the other hand some industries have associations of employers which are specifically designed to represent the industry in negotiations with trade unions and in deciding policy on labour matters. These are commonly described as *employers'* associations. There is a complication in that in some cases the one association serves both purposes, though their activities can normally be divided into these two sections. It is only employers' associations, or sections of general associations which deal with such matters, that are discussed here.

There can be little doubt that such associations owe their present form to defensive instincts. Before trade unions acquired their present stature, employers had the advantage in their dealings with unorganized workers, and there was less need to organize employers against excessive pressure from workers. On the other hand, it was useful even then to have an association which agreed on the broad lines of a common policy towards labour. In later years this motive of convenience in exchanging information and formulating broad policy towards labour has formed one very important part of the employers' associations' functions, but it has been supplemented by a rather greater function, to restore the balance of power in labour relations by confronting an industry-wide trade union, prepared to negotiate from the strength of its monopoly control of labour, with a rather similar body acting as though it were a single employer and exercising monopsony power. The development of an employers' association providing a vehicle for exchange of information and attitudes is one that is to be expected, and seems a faithful reproduction of the source and purpose of countless associations of people or institutions with common interests. The more unusual feature of employers' associations at present is that they can act as though they were themselves the agency employing labour. In order to develop maximum monopsonistic bargaining power employers' associations attempt to fix wages, conditions of work, and methods of bargaining for the employers as a whole. This involves both the arrogation by the association of authority in decision-taking superior to that of individual members, and attempts by the association to control dissenting members. In present circumstances a number of consequences for wage payments follow.

First, since the association has acquired the right of negotiation from its members it tends to impose its own character on the proceedings and result. Since it represents an industry it will lend itself to the belief that an industry with recognizable characteristics and fair homogeneity actually exists. Thus it will be ready to accept a uniform payments structure for the industry tending to minimize actual distinctions. Moreover, like the trade unions, it is an association of these directly affected by the decisions made, but is not, as an association, itself specially involved financially. The officials of the association are therefore likely to approach negotiations as being exercises in power politics or strategy with arguments and threats as the weapons, and not as an economic exercise fixing an economic price. The foregoing has accused the trade unions of tending to conduct their battle on the wrong front with the wrong weapons; the employers' associations have assisted by being willing to fight in this way.

Secondly, just because the association settles wages for all the employers in an industry, the individual employers lose one source of their worry over the consequences, in rising costs and prices, of a rise in wages. Their customers will be displeased, but all their competitors will be affected in the same way. Thus employers may be prepared to put up with wage changes, which are quite unsatisfactory to them on other grounds, simply because they do not directly alter the competitive position in the domestic market.

Thirdly, to maintain the uniformity of payment in the industry and to keep a united front among employers, it becomes necessary for the association of employers to lay down rules of conduct governing the wages paid by their members and their dealings with trade unions. Such rules are of necessity restrictive and lay emphasis on working through the normal channels, which generally means the employers' associations. The effect will tend to be to take away from employers the right to vary the level of their wage rates, and also the right to settle disputes over wages with their own workers. If an employers' association is intent on preserving the unity of the industry to the outsider, then it must insist that it is itself the source of variations in wages and conditions and not the employer, and that the employer should leave the association to do the talking to trade unions when disputes arise. It is a natural consequence of this situation that employers should begin to deny their responsibility for such matters, saying that they are the association's problem. It is, however, most curious that the people who pay the money and employ the workers should be thus hampered in looking after their own interests. This shifting of responsibility by the employers is, as far as wages are concerned, by far the most significant factor in the development of employers' associations.

The final point to be made about the present importance of employers' associations for wages, is that the combination of employers' associations' policies and their regulation of the individual employers, with the failure of national collective bargaining to be comprehensive, is producing for the employers themselves a result which is the worst of both worlds. The employers' associations have been trying to negotiate for industries as units, and in so doing have aided and abetted the unions in producing national wage structures of an unnatural simplicity, which cannot stand the test of actual variations in the market prices of labour. This situation has led on to supplementation and to gaps between actual payments and those prescribed. The employers' associations condition the character of these extra payments by generally insisting on the sanctity of the negotiated rate. Employers are then forced to supplement negotiated rates to get and keep labour; but the obvious way of doing this, by formally altering the rate, is frowned on by the association, and so all manner of other expedients are used. This produces one of the characteristic features of the earnings gap—the confusion of payments which fill it. Further, the employers' associations, by generally insisting on firms working through them, have caused a negative attitude to be characteristic of employers, who let their own wage structure drift without attempting, as they could otherwise do, to take control of it. Disputes, as they arise, are dealt with by the association and not the employer who knows his own affairs. Thus employers' associations by pursuing the national rate, by restricting the freedom of individual employers, and by giving individual employers an excuse for being negative in their attitudes to wages, have been a large factor in producing the situations discussed in this book.

What should happen here? If we are to enter on a period of more purposive construction of wage structures at the local level then the present role of the employers' association must alter. To begin with it is a defensive organization, protecting industry against trade union monopoly powers. In negotiation such a body will tend to say 'no' until pushed into a grudging 'yes'. This kind of attitude cannot produce a directional wage policy and wage structures; and such a negative form of association cannot hold the centre of the stage if more effective wage structuring is to take place. The fact is that, even if trade unions were to become interested in, and informed about, more effective factory and local wage settlement, the burden of the initiative must still rest with the employers themselves. The employers' duty is to initiate and develop his own factory wage structure, since he alone can do this with full knowledge of the circumstances and he alone, being the paymaster, can alter payment levels easily. The trade union's duty is to watch or guide the employer in the interests of its members but without employer initiative the trade union is surely restricted in attempting ambitious changes. The duty of the employers' association is to advise employers, to help with disputes involving a number of firms, and to provide employers with information, but not to dictate to them.

This discussion of employers' associations and employers faced with more developed and more detailed wage bargaining therefore comes down to two statements. First, the employers' associations at present have too much authority; it would be helpful if their position were to be reduced to that of advisers and providers of information. Secondly, much of the present confusion in wages has been due to divided authority between employers and their associations; one of the most hopeful signs for the future would be an increase in management control and initiative in wage settlement.

CHAPTER 12

A COMMENTARY ON WAGE POLICY[1]

Wage policy is concerned with the movement of the totality of wages, the wage level, rather than with relative wages. In consequence, this chapter has a somewhat different context from previous chapters which have been centred rather more on wage structure. In going on to the more general level of wage policy, however, it will be argued that, while movements of the totality of wages can be studied separately from problems of wage structure, full understanding requires detail as well as generality: a wage policy, in the sense of a series of measures or proposals specifically designed to control the general wage level, cannot be fully implemented without attention to structural problems.

It would be possible, and indeed fatally easy, to begin with a digression on the nature and origins of the inflationary process. It will be better to avoid this, and by good fortune some simple scene-setting makes it possible to do so.

There are two separate situations for which a wage policy can be recommended. First there is the case in which excess demand is already in existence, whether as a result of wage rises or other forces, and it is desired, as part of an attempt to correct inflationary pressure generally, to control wage increases so that they do not feed on excess demand for labour and cause a continued inflationary spiral. Secondly, there is the case in which, with prices and demand conditions stable at or near full employment, wage increases in excess of productivity increase can push up costs and hence prices, creating a suitable situation for the generation of a demand inflation. These two cases are of course commonly given the titles of demand and cost inflation: they have their parallel in applied studies in discussions of whether wages have been rising more or less rapidly than prices or productivity in Britain in recent years. For our purposes here it will be sufficient to note that wage policy needs to be discussed both when the existence of inflationary excess demand makes uncontrolled wage increases possible, and when wage increases under full employment conditions appear to be in danger of running ahead of productivity increase and so putting up costs. In other words, discussion of wage policy is needed whether we are talking of demand or of cost inflation: the peculiar properties of these differing interpretations of the inflationary process, in so far as the interpretations can be separately distinguished, will

---

[1] This chapter bears considerable resemblances to an article by the present author in a recent *Scottish Journal* symposium on wage policy ('The Inadequacy of Recent Wage Policies in Britain', *Scottish Journal*, June 1958). The article was written between writing the first and the second versions of this chapter, which it is hoped will be found to be an improvement on the article.

have their effect on judgement of the chances of success of wage policies but need not be separately discussed here. Nor is it necessary to attempt to quantify the extent to which wages have pushed up prices or the reverse, except to note that, at least in the years 1955 to 1957, wages in Britain moved more quickly than prices and productivity, and that through the whole post-war period wages have been among those variables which have shown a continuing upward trend:[1] consequently, whether they may be leaders or followers in the inflationary process, or have been sometimes one and sometimes the other, wage increases are one of the forces which have to be under control if inflation or inflationary tendencies are to be controlled.

THE PATTERN OF WAGE SETTLEMENT

The views on wage policy which are expressed in what follows reflect the pattern of wage settlement which is implicit in the earlier chapters of this book and must now be explicitly set out. The essential feature of the pattern is that of the existence of a distinct gap between national rates and actual earnings levels. This gap has already taken up a large part of our earlier discussion, and its existence as an important factor in post-war wages in Britain may be emphasized by reference to several different sources.[2] The pattern of wage settlement is set out here under these two headings of wage rates and of earnings, with a third heading on the relationship between them.

Wage rates

For the most part wage rates in Britain are determined by national negotiations, or by arbitration or conciliation conducted at the national level. The result of this process is a formal document setting out general conditions as to wages and hours for all workers covered by the document. The scope and applicability of such a document will depend on three sets of factors: (a) whether it refers to one firm or employer or to an industry, (b) whether it refers to minimum or standard rates of wages, and (c) whether the document itself is complex or simple.

(a) While some very large and some very small firms negotiate and settle their wage rates independently of all other firms, in the majority of cases wage rates are agreed for groups of firms constituting an industry. Such industries may be easily definable, or amorphous; but industry-wide national agreements, whether relating to standard or minimum rates, cannot usually cover all the circumstances of the labour forces of all the firms in the industry,

[1] Cf. J. R. Parkinson, 'Wage Stability and Employment', *Scottish Journal*, June 1958, for discussion of wage movements.
[2] E.g., Parkinson, op. cit., G. Penrice, 'Earnings and Wage Rates 1948–1955', *London and Cambridge Economic Service*, December 1955; and Council on Prices, Productivity and Incomes, *First Report*.

and so must inevitably require supplementation in greater or lesser degree.

(*b*) Wage rate agreements nationally negotiated for whole industries may detail either standard rates or minimum rates. Naturally, minimum wage rates require more supplementation than standard rates; but because the negotiated rates have to be such as can be applied by all in an industry, and not just by the better-off firms, standard rates too require to be supplemented. Moreover, the paradox of standard rates which require supplementation produces one of the special features of the rates/earnings gap. A firm which finds its need for labour and for output to be such as to require additional payments does not simply abandon inadequate standard rates and devise new payments. It rather preserves the fiction of standard rates and fills in the differences between such rates and what it proposes to pay with various subterfuges in lieu of a straightforward rate adjustment.

(*c*) The need to fill out national agreements with provision for additional categories and types of workers will vary with the industry and the agreement in question. It is unlikely, especially in the case of semi-skilled workers, that national agreements can possibly reproduce all the detail necessary to a factory wage structure.

Such wage rates are settled in an institutional atmosphere, which may be influenced by economic circumstance but is not determined by it. National agreements are reached by a process of bargaining at the most general possible level by national trade union leaders and officials of national employers' associations, or else by argument before some form of arbitration. The course of bargaining or argument and the power relationships of the participants will partly reflect the economic circumstances of the economy and the labour market; but neither the economic basis of the arguments nor the economic basis of power relationships need be held to determine automatically the amount of wage rate change arrived at in negotiation. This is also the product of institutional attitudes on both sides, of skill in bargaining, of external pressures, of bluff and of other forces. The rates finally settled on, while frequently called standard, generally require some adjustment at the individual employer's level and so individual circumstance cannot be brought rigidly to bear on the negotiated settlement. Moreover, the burden of the increase is shared among all employers: trade may be lost to other products as a result of rising costs, but all in the same industries have to face similar cost increases from a successful wage claim. The more general the round of wage rate increases is, the less any one employer needs to fear, since a general round will bring with it, as well as increases in costs, increases in wage earners' income and demand. This may in turn cause many troubles for the economy and may prove to be the genesis of an inflation. If these troubles are weathered at all, then the wage rate increase is likely to be met without immediate surface strains on the employers' resources.

Earnings

Earnings, on the other hand, are composed of wage rates, supplementary rates, payment-by-results and overtime. Of these only the wage rates are nationally fixed. While very broad prescriptions about the general character of the other payments may be laid down nationally, their size and detail are determined locally. The role of the supplementary rates is clear. By providing a basis in occupational complexity, in differential arrangements, and in amounts of payments, they convert the generalities of the national agreements into each firm's own wage structure. First thoughts might suggest that this is not true of payment-by-results and overtime payments, since each of these appear to be designed solely as payment for differences in individual performance and hours of work. Yet, since payment-by-results bonuses are now frequently much more than marginal additions for above average performance, and are offered as a recruitment inducement, large parts of such bonuses must be regarded as alternatives or as additions to rate payments. The same is true of overtime payments, where overtime is offered, not intermittently as an unfortunate and occasional necessity, but as a regular feature of workers' conditions and as an inducement to recruitment.

Such earnings are much more subject to economic pressures than wage rates. Earnings reflect the ability to pay of the individual employer, and his need for labour. If the demand for an employer's product is not expanding, or if it is actually contracting, he will not be likely to want to increase his labour force or to offer increased payment. He will only be able to do so without his own future actively deteriorating, if all other employers, or at least all in his industry, are similarly experiencing rising wage costs. Many factors will cause variations in the position of individual employers, but the principle that an employer has difficulty in unilaterally increasing the price of his labour under conditions of falling or stable demand for his product is generally valid, and means that control over demand in the economy or an uncontrolled diminution of demand may result in control over earnings levels.

Relation between wage rates and earnings

There are two specially important interactions between national wage rates in general and earnings in general:

(a) An increase in standard wage rates will tend to cause a similar lift in earnings levels. Since standard wage rates are regarded as the proper rate payable to a certain occupation in an industry, then employers in the industry who belong to the employers' association and conform to its rules will also conform to increases in the standard rate, and probably also to increases in minimum rates, though this is more a matter of convention.

Of course, rising wage rates might result simply in a reduction in other

195

sources of income, even apart from the possibility that individuals might display a growing preference for leisure as income rises. It might be argued that other earnings payments, being designed to compensate for the inadequacies of the standard rate, would be adjusted downwards with upward adjustments to the standard rate. The major difficulty involved in holding this view is that the components of earnings other than standard rates are used to fill out wage structures in actual fact, but they still retain their other characteristics as special payments; whether as special rates, or bonus payments, or overtime. Unless a really fundamental change in an industry's whole structure of payments is contemplated and specially negotiated, an increase in standard rates, even if it reduces the need for supplementation, is unlikely to affect the basis of extra payments, nor will it affect their amount if there is no decline in demand for labour. Besides, a change in standard rates applied over an industry will mean an alteration for all employers; unless earnings differentials are maintained, which means earnings levels going up, an employer will lose the relative strength of his demand for labour. It might also be said that employers will be unable to pay an increase in earnings since the existing earnings level reflects their capacity to pay wages in relation to their final product demand. But, while this point may be relevant to a small industry receiving an isolated wage increase, a general wage increase in a fully employed economy can create increased demand and permit prices to rise.

(b) Faults in the earnings structure or unsatisfactory comparisons between the earnings structure and the wage rate structure can be a fruitful source of wage rate claims. If, for example, a wage rate claim is being made on behalf of a group of workers in an industry, then one typical argument would be that of relative position—let us say of group A in industry A to group B in industry B. At its simplest the argument would have four variations, comparisons of wage rates for A and B, of earnings for A and B, of A's wage rate and B's earnings, and of A's earnings and B's wage rate. Naturally, these comparisons can give different answers depending upon the existence of the rates/earnings gap and wide differences in the ranking of groups according to rates and according to earnings.

CURRENT WAGE POLICY SUGGESTIONS

The deep concern about inflation which has been so prevalent in Britain in recent years has naturally produced a number of suggestions on wage policy. No detailed comment will be offered on some of these here. For example, the type of suggestion that trade unions and their leaders can be put off by friendly conversations without policy content must be regarded as being too naïve to require serious discussion. So too is the thesis that if trade unions are allowed, and indeed encouraged, to strike and use up their strike funds they will thereafter be more 'reasonable' even though full employment and unsolved wage problems continue. This thesis ignores several factors. It forgets that trade unionists have not historically been inhibited by lack of funds from taking action where they have felt their interests to be heavily involved. It assumes, unwarrantably, that trade unionists under full employment will necessarily commit themselves to such a struggle, and will be unable to gain their objectives without so doing. Above all it ignores the cost to our long-term industrial relations of the bitterness and the breakdown in industrial cooperation which prolonged and repeated strike action entails. The discussion here will assume throughout that whatever variation on the definition of full employment is advocated, and even if it involves more unemployment than has been usual in post-war years, massive unemployment is not contemplated as a policy objective. The 'industrial discipline through unemployment' type of solution is therefore left out of the discussion. No doubt there is a sufficient degree of unemployment which would reinstate the labour relations of the nineteen thirties. These relations cannot be regarded as either good or desirable, nor is it likely that the same docility under adversity would characterize a recurrence of this situation in Britain. Moreover, self-interest, political expediency, and promises, all force governments in Britain towards accepting the general obligation to try to maintain full employment, though, of course, within this obligation, there are different views about the level of activity which is implied.

The major policy suggestions on wages which have been made in recent years can be roughly separated into two categories. First there is the type of policy which is held to operate indirectly on wages through controlling the level of demand. Since the principal instruments used to this end have been fiscal and monetary, these suggestions on how wages may be controlled can be discussed under the heading of 'fiscal and monetary policies'. The second group of wage policies are designed to operate directly on wages. These may be given the heading of 'wage-control policies'.

Fiscal and monetary policies

Policies involving the use of fiscal and monetary measures to control excess demand are not of course exclusively designed to control wages but, nevertheless, the control of wages is essential to the success of any anti-inflationary policy. If restriction merely creates a vacuum in demand which wage increases promptly fill then the level of demand and prices will rise again and further inflation will ensue. Moreover, wage claims may be influential in originating both internal and external pressure on the economy's resources. Indeed, external difficulties may be induced by a general feeling abroad that wage claims are going to create internal inflation as well as by the actuality of such inflation. Thus, it is vital to the success of restrictive policies that they should

o   197

be capable of limiting wage increases, especially since such wage increases may have been the major cause of excessive pressure on the economy's resources, and also because, so long as restriction continues, opportunities for production increases may be lost.

The influence of restrictive fiscal and monetary policies on wages can be considered in relation to earnings and to wage rates. If the pattern of wage settlement laid out in the previous section of this chapter is accepted, then earnings are controlled by the position of the individual firm. Earnings will, therefore, be responsive to sustained restrictive pressure which will control the demand for the products of each firm, and so earnings can be duly halted or squeezed. If, however, wage rate claims are put forward and are successful, then earnings are increased directly and may also be increased indirectly through increased demand pressure. Thus the efficacy of these policies will depend upon their effects on wage rate changes.

The influence of fiscal and monetary policies on wage rate changes will be exerted at national negotiations. Three aspects of such influence must be considered: (a) their effects on the type of arguments, which, whether justifiable or not, are presented at such bargains, (b) their effects on union attitudes, and (c) their effects on employers' attitudes. On the whole the same set of influences, with perhaps greater emphasis on the arguments, will affect the decisions of arbitrators. The 'national interest', which in these circumstances is likely to mean cutting down on wage increases, will, of course, also influence arbitrators, but they are charged with the settlement of a particular wage claim, and its circumstances must weight most heavily with them.

(a) The most familiar argument for wage rate increase is the cost of living. Presumably policies designed to restrict demand will have some effect in stabilizing prices; but they cannot stabilize import prices. Morover, *fiscal* policy depends either on reduced Government expenditure or increased taxes. Unless there is invariably a convenient scapegoat such as defence expenditure, reduced Government spending is likely to have some impact on living costs. Increased taxes designed to reduce consumption usually have to be placed on articles in mass consumption and so increase a wide range of prices. The cost of living may therefore rise even when excess demand is being reduced.

The argument for wage change 'that profits can stand it', is, of course, much less strong when demand is squeezed. But profits are not squeezed evenly over the whole economy, so while one section of industry may deny high profits, another may have to concede them, and claims granted in any one section lead on to claims in other sections based on relative increase arguments. Rather similar remarks apply to arguments based on the relative strength of demand and supply for labour in any one industry. So long as unemployment is not general, then redundancy in one industry, while it will weaken wage claims in that industry initially, will not be fully effective over the whole wage claim period, since other increases will make way for the relative wage argument. The argument that wages should be increased because production or productivity has gone up will, of course, be invalidated if the economy is so squeezed that general increases do not occur; but, even if this happens generally, some sectors will show increases and the relative wage argument can start again. Finally there is still a whole field of argument based on relative wages. Wage claims here may be based on all the various permutations of rates and earnings mentioned earlier, and also simply on the statement that somebody has had an increase, so why not everybody.

(b) Much can be said about the 'sense of responsibility' of the union leaders which will see to it that wage increases embarrassing to the economy are not pressed. It may even be true that union leaders can be persuaded from time to time that it is their duty to put off wage claims. It is wise, however, to hold three things as axiomatic, first, that the trade union leader will try to do his job; second, that his members will endeavour to see that he does so; and third, that the prestige of his union is a matter of importance to him. The present system of wage negotiation in Britain gives to the union leader as his supreme task the settlement of the national wage negotiations affecting his members. It is his job to achieve satisfaction at such negotiations, and he must ask for an increase as long as existing payments can be adversely represented either against the cost of living or against other wage levels. In other words in existing circumstances a trade union leader may be able to postpone, but cannot forego, a wage claim, so long as any of the above arguments can be brought strongly to bear. If he does not do this of his own accord, then his members will exert influence on him to see that he does, or may even take independent action. Failure in national negotiations, or internal dissension within a union, will damage its prestige, at least in the eyes of the union movement.

(c) Do such policies exert their influence through the employers? Successful restriction of demand will undoubtedly affect individual employers and will control their ability to raise earnings, but in the determination of wage rates the individual employers have their views expressed collectively. Moreover, difficulties in meeting higher wage rates become most apparent after the rate increase has been granted. The individual employer may be said to have influenced a decision on wage rate change through the expression of his views to his association or his representatives in negotiation, but the decision when it comes is an obligation handed down to him from a source outside his direct control. While the influence of restrictive policies on employers' attitudes and actions with regard to earnings is therefore undisputed, their influence on wage rate increases must be considered at two levels, (i) their effect on the employers' attitudes and actions at wage negotiations, and (ii) their effect on the actual abilities of individual employers to pay the increase.

(i) Restrictive policies can be influential in stiffening employers' attitudes to wage claims. Individual employers will feel increased pressure on their resources and will be influenced by a strong general atmosphere of restraint, and this feeling will be responsible for stronger collective determination on the employers' side to resist wage claims. But this determination may not be wholly successful. It may lead on to strike action on a large scale which, even if the employers are successful the first time, will produce bitterness in industrial relations and can hardly be contemplated as a constantly repeated exercise. Whatever may happen during the first year's resistance, the more likely long-term result of increased employer resistance will be compromise, either by arbitration or direct settlement. But, given that restrictive policies restrict output, a compromise settlement may be strongly inflationary.

(ii) Would individual employers be unable to meet a general wage rate increase or be forced to contract earnings by the amount of the increase? The structure of earnings payments makes it difficult to deduct from them the amount of a wage rate increase. Besides, as fiscal and monetary policy have operated in recent years in this country, an increased wage rate has been paid and increased costs have been associated with increased wage earners' demand. It is, however, possible that *monetary* policy could become much tighter in its effects on the individual employer. If the money stock is kept low and the liquidity of the monetary system is reduced, then increasing demands for money coming up against a rigid money supply must, unless velocity can increase mightily, eventually result in someone going short. Industry's working capital will be affected and there would come a point at which the wage-bill would quite generally not be met. This seems to be much further than we have got with monetary policy up till now; but it is a possible result of the continued use of a restrictive monetary policy. If such a situation were to arise the immediate effect would presumably be unemployment of the labour and collapse of the firm concerned. It might then be argued that monetary policy of this degree of severity could act as a massive deterrent to wage rate increase, since the consequence would deter unions from making, or employers from giving, increases which would bring on this effect. This seems doubtful. The wage rate increase comes into being before the deterrent and the unions would now direct their opposition to the government who created the monetary policy and endangered full employment. The individual employers likely to be put in this position would try to have the wage rate increase stopped, but not all employers would be in financial trouble, wage increases would go through and become a fact and an obligation before the consequence became apparent. If any substantial number of firms were in danger of collapse, then employers too would fall back on the political authority and ask for a change. Such a situation would in other words lead to a political crisis which a government could only sustain with great difficulty.

We may then conclude that policies aimed at restricting demand can have a direct effect on earnings, but they cannot in themselves be guaranteed to control wage rate increases which may lead on to earnings changes and to excess demand. Restriction of demand, so long as we are working within any of the moderate quantities of unemployment which can be held to be compatible with any definition of full employment, will not by itself suffice to hold back wage rate changes. Two further conclusions may be thought to follow from this. First, we must clearly look further for a solution to our wages problems. Secondly, without such a solution, the policy of demand restriction loses some part of its justification. It may be needed for other reasons, but cannot be justified as a wage policy alone, indeed it can be said to contain no *direct* policy for wages at all. And, while an economy can undoubtedly show output increase and health while running normally at a lower level of activity than that which has been typical of post-war British experience, constant restriction and constant pushing back are not the best methods for encouraging output increase. If wage increases do take place in such circumstances they are fed by smaller output increases than might otherwise have been available.

Wage control policies

If demand restriction which takes excess demand for labour out of the economy cannot be guaranteed as sufficient to control wage change then it is natural that thoughts should move on to policies designed to control wages more directly.

The first and most essential point that should be made about such policies is that they must by their nature be directed principally at the control of wage rates and not of earnings. Policies of this type are institutional in character and so are aimed at the national bargaining level and at national wage rates. They therefore tend to miss the other level of wage payments, where wages are actually determined in particular factories. They will be unable to do the whole job of wage control so long as earnings are determined by separate processes from the institutional forces which determine wage rates, and must therefore be discussed with this major reservation in mind.

While there are many differences in detail, 'wage policy' suggestions generally reduce to three types. These are (*a*) purely advisory bodies, such as the Cohen Council, (*b*) 'wage freeze' policies, and (*c*) wage-controlling authorities legislating on relative wage rates as well as the wage level. We should perhaps also add Mr Flander's recent suggestion of the 'key bargain' or 'master agreement' approach.[1] Of these the advisory type of suggestion can probably be ignored here, since it is either purely advisory, and so comes into line with all other sources of economic advice, or else it hardly differs from the wage-controlling authority in the duties put upon its administrators, since

[1] A. Flanders, 'Can Britain Have a Wage Policy?', *Scottish Journal*, June 1958.

they have to consider all the same problems as the controlling authority, differing only in that they give advice and not instructions. It will be convenient to consider first the problems that face a wage-controlling authority, since this will enable the 'wage freeze' and 'key bargain' suggestions to be dealt with more rapidly thereafter.

Since the wage-controlling authority has to make recommendations for the movement of wage rates throughout the economy it will naturally tend to look for some kind of convenient formula which will provide reasonably automatic guidance about the changes in general conditions to which wages have to be adjusted. The most usual version of such a formula is price change. But it is by no means invariably true that price increases should be the signal for compensating wage increases. Increased import prices or indirect taxes are more likely to suggest wage reductions than increases. If increased investment or increased government activity are planned, then again it is arguable whether wages should rise or should be held steady to permit competing claims upon the nation's resources. The same type of difficulties apply to the suggestion that wage alterations should be tied to movements of the overall level of productivity,[1] and indeed to any automatic linkage between wages and some general indicator.

This problem of selecting a general indicator to which to attach wage movements illustrates an even more general difficulty of such a controlling authority. Any body which has the duty of controlling, or advising on, all wages must be at the centre of a nation's economic life; it has to take decisions about, or form judgements on, all the central problems and policies of the economy. In effect, therefore, it has either to take orders from the government on the assumptions it is to make about the state of the economy (or be strongly influenced by general government pronouncements on these things), or it has to risk its own assumptions, knowing that action on wages taken on the basis of these assumptions will tend to move the economy and the government in the direction of making the assumptions true. Thus a wage-controlling authority must always take up an uneasy compromise position between being the servant or the master of the government and of the economy. It seems correct to say that this kind of responsibility should only be placed on government itself. But can government take it in a democratic community at peace? The alternatives would seem to be to place a wage-controlling authority in an impossible position, or to give wage-determining power to government itself, or to revert to government working in its more usual ways to control the economy while seeking some more decentralized way of decision-taking on wages. Of these only the third seems possible. The second is, nevertheless, a constant danger of wage inflation and of authority suggestions; the government may itself decide to take control. But this must

[1] Cf. Council on Prices, Productivity and Incomes, *First Report*, pp. 44 and 45.

be recognized as a desperate step, since it involves riding rough-shod over all existing institutions and practices in the labour market, including trade unions and the existing structure of collective bargaining.

The attitudes of trade unions to wage authority suggestions cannot be ignored, and in normal circumstances their agreement would be essential. The trade unions are likely to point out that there are several variables which govern applications for wage increases, and that, if they are to accept control, some guarantee about control of these other variables will be necessary. Thus they may reasonably ask for control of prices, or at least price stability, and expect that otherwise they will be given increases fully commensurate to price rise; they may want profits to be controlled in some way; and they are likely to want some guarantee of a due share in production increases. Neither price nor production movements provide a convenient formula for wage change, nor can profits be controlled without distortions and hindrances to innovation. Besides, the whole idea of a wage-controlling authority is at variance with many of the personal interests of union leaders who would to some extent be deprived of their functions while the unions themselves would lose credit for wage changes.

The major difficulty which a wage-controlling authority would have to meet is its obligation to determine wage structure as well as the wage level since it has to determine every wage rate change. This would be a task requiring considerable courage even without the earnings complication. As it is the authority would require to decide between wage rate claims on the basis of the many different forces, of supply and demand especially, which govern the wages of particular groups of work people, as well as try and determine to what extent each wage rate was actually operative or subject to additional earnings, and in what way a given wage rate change would affect actual earnings. The complexity of our wage rate structure would in itself make the authority's knowledge and competence doubtful: the actual lack of knowledge of earnings patterns in our economy would ensure that an authority would not be able to reach satisfactory judgements.

The 'wage freeze' is not so much a positive policy for wages as an attempt to prevent wage change. Since it makes no effort to provide for any alterations of wage rates, either as to their level or their structure, and does not control earnings, it can only be regarded as a temporary expedient.

Mr Flanders' 'key bargain' or 'master agreement' suggestion proposes 'introducing a new procedure into our system of wage determination which would enable the government and representatives of the two sides of industry to settle the amount of the annual round of wage increases in central negotiations'.[1] This suggestion meets one of the difficulties of the controlling

---

[1] Flanders, op. cit., 121.

authority type of proposal. By providing for direct government participation it removes the possibility of a clash between government and wage authority. Moreover, it has more attractions for the trade unions since it provides them with at least some function and bargaining power. But it is not clear who finally makes the terms of the bargain, nor whether the unions may not want, and get, more than the economy can conveniently bear. Moreover, despite Mr Flanders' insistence on the need to preserve the sanctity of national agreements, there are no sanctions to prevent 'drift' in wage rates, and there is no control of earnings patterns. Finally, one master agreement is a quite inadequate basis for the varying circumstances that comprise a wage structure. This solution ignores the issue of wage structure or simply leaves it to be determined outside the policy.

A summary of wage control proposals must therefore record that such policies do not control earnings or meet the problem of 'wage drift' or the gap between rates and earnings. They are likely to be unacceptable to trade unions. Most importantly, partly because of the gap between rates and earnings, or national and local wage patterns, and also because of the complexity of the present wage rate structure, they are unable to attend to wage structure as well as wage level.

ALTERNATIVE POSSIBILITIES[1]

This discussion of present policy suggestions invites a gloomy conclusion, since neither demand restriction nor wage control policies appear adequate. More radical changes in the structure of wage settlement are therefore necessary; but such changes, even if they can be brought about, will take time to develop, and in the immediate future there is likely to be no alternative to the existing policies. Since restriction of demand seems able to control earnings but not wage rates, while wage control policies are more likely to control wage rates than earnings, the obvious suggestion for current emergencies is to use both these policies together. There are, however, some difficulties here. Demand restriction can mean output loss, and therefore pressure for reduced demand ought preferably to be temporary. Acceptance of any form of wage control policy by the trade unions is problematical, and the process of getting it will be likely to involve bargaining and compromises, of a political rather than an economic nature. The combined failure of these policies to deal with wage structure problems will cause a cumulative build up of structural difficulties in their application which must make the use of such policies no more than a temporary expedient. It is right to be

[1] Somewhat similar views are to be found in B. C. Roberts, *National Wages Policy in Peace and War*, Allen and Unwin, London, which appeared in July 1958 just after this book was completed.

204

gloomy about the chances of success of wage policy at present, and it is highly necessary to look for some more permanent solution to wage problems.

The proposals which the logic of this book leads to are set out in the following two points. These continue to advocate a trend towards local bargaining which was recommended and discussed in Chapter 11 for structural and institutional reasons. Since the stability of the wage level is in essence also a structural matter, it is natural that the wage policy recommendations made here should broadly follow and repeat from a different angle the structural recommendations of Chapter 11.

First, national negotiations on wages ought to be confined to the settlement of minimum wage rates, though possibly conditions of work such as holidays could be left to national decision. The wider and more general discussions on minimum wages become, the more satisfactory they will be. They certainly ought to be divorced from the affairs of individual employers, and even individual industries and occupations, except in the widest possible groupings. There is something to be said for them being conducted on an overall national scale. Changes in such minimum wages should not be regarded as automatically affecting the payment of those above the minimum. In such negotiations about minima social arguments are relevant and very important. The movement of the cost of living should be a specially important indicator for changes in minimum wages.

Secondly, negotiations about the standard wage rates of workers in particular industries, occupations and firms should be shifted to the local level and should become much more detailed. The definition of 'local' must be left vague since it is affected by particular circumstances. The major criterion is from the employers' side. If negotiation is conducted by a group of employers they ought to be very similarly affected by market conditions, which implies close identity of product, and size and type of production process. This may frequently mean negotiation by single plants or single employers, and 'local detailed negotiations' should certainly be interpreted as meaning separate settlement of the rates of distinct occupational groups within a firm.

The first and most important question to be asked about these proposals is on the extent to which they can be expected to fulfil the aims of wage policy. The task of a wage policy could be thought to consist of keeping wages steady when an inflation is already well under way. No wage policy can alone bear the burden of ending an inflation. Just as commodity price controls are found to be increasingly inadequate the greater the degree of excess demand for the commodity, so wage controls can hardly be expected to hold down the price of labour when it is strongly in excess demand. Attempts to do so in such circumstances can only result in the establishment of an imperfect market

205

situation with two price levels, the controlled level and the actual level.[1] An alternative and more appropriate version of the task of a wage policy is that it should arrange wage settlement procedures so that wages do not take the lead in initiating or continuing an inflation. This means that wage policy recommendations should be constructed so that at the point of full employment, or at least where there is no strong tendency to excess demand, there should be stability of wages, and so that under inflationary conditions wages are no more out of control than other variables.

A necessary corollary of this attitude to the task of wage policy is to say that wage policy is not a substitute for a general attack on inflationary excess demand. It may be thought that this lands us squarely back with restrictive policies of the monetary and fiscal type as the cure for wage inflation. It is true that, when an economy is suffering from inflationary excess demand, restrictive policies will be necessary to control wage increase. But there is a big difference between a situation in which wages are rising in response to excess demand for labour and that in which wages, almost as an independent variable, are rising so as to create excess demand, from a situation of general price stability; or, under existing inflationary conditions, are rising at a rate in excess of other variables in the inflationary complex. The use of policies designed to restrict demand, because demand for commodities is in excess of their supply at the prevailing price level, differs from their use specifically against wages for three reasons. First, there is now no suggestion that reduction of demand is a *wage* policy, and so wage policy and the structural functions of wages are left open for further discussion. Secondly, the level to which demand restriction is pushed need only be sufficient to reduce excess demand, and the reactions of trade unionists and employers to wage claims need no longer be the guide to the correct degree of intensity of restriction. It seems probable that on this kind of criteria the policies for restriction of demand which were enforced in Britain in 1957 and the first half of 1958 were too severe. Thirdly, continued restriction of demand as a continued process of discouraging wage claims is no longer appropriate. Once excess demand has been removed, if demand restriction is no longer designed to stabilize wages

---

[1] Something of this sort was probably a principal reason for the marked growth in the gap between rates and earnings in post-war years. In the 'wage freeze' period wage rates were held down while earnings rose with excess demand for labour. General propaganda for wage restraint may also have operated at other times to the same effect. Of course the artificial nature of the national wage rates made such a situation likely and the separation of the earnings *pattern* from the rates *pattern* was in any event a necessary response to structural needs. Moreover, the lagging behind of rates at some periods does not mean that rates cannot at other times, as excess demand is restricted, take the lead and push up the earnings structure as has been suggested here, nor can we be sure that granting rates increases even under conditions of rising earnings and a widening gap between earnings and rates was not a primary cause of 'jacking up' both the rates and earnings structures and injecting fresh excess demand into the system.

then expansion of output can again be undertaken. This type of demand restriction is a temporary corrective to excess commodity demand not a weapon against wages.

The main thing that has to be asked of policy recommendations for wages is, then, that they should provide for wage stability. Moreover, since full employment is a stated, and surely generally desirable, end of our present economic policies and a central part of our philosophy of economic wellbeing, it is desirable that policy recommendations should be directed at adjusting wage settlement procedures towards permanent stability under full employment conditions. This surely means more radical changes than *ad hoc* proposals of the wage authority type. How do the two changes put forward here meet this test?

The most important destroyer of wage stability in our present situation is the independence of national negotiations from direct economic pressure. The positive and fruitful function of national negotiations is to determine minimum wage levels and so to secure protection at the lowest level against exploitation and against adverse economic forces; their pernicious effect is to increase and interfere with the payments of individual workers without actually determining them, and to do so by reference to social argument and through institutional bargaining which is not sufficiently controlled by economic circumstances or by economic policies. It is a positive virtue of national negotiation, when it is applied to the settlement of general minimum wage rates, that it should stand somewhat aside from the market place and should consider social factors and the effect on minimum incomes of cost of living changes. The proposal that national negotiation should be on minima has positive merits in the determination of minima, while the only way to prevent the present relation between national negotiations and the actual wage level of all wage earners is to cease to use national negotiations to negotiate standard increases.

The second most important destroyer of wage stability is the rates/earnings gap, which is the joint creation of 'standard' rate determination by institutional forces and the further determination of actual payment levels in an uncontrolled market in which payments do not serve the purposes for which they are allegedly designed, and which is characterized by lack of that knowledge which is the most essential condition of effective free-market operation. This gap results in two separate determinations of payment which provide a prolific source of wage demands even when general economic forces are stable. It also means a situation in which one version of payments can go ahead even when the other is being controlled, as happened during the 'wage freeze' of 1948–50. The only way to avoid this is to bring the two versions together; to determine wages at the level at which supplementation, except for individual differences in rate of work or extra hours, is not necessary; and to try, by going into sufficient detail, to work towards a more effective wage structure responsive to changes in labour demand. This means wage determination at the local level. Moreover, at the local level social arguments are of less moment, even the cost of living argument is subdued, and the relevant points are the profitability, ability to pay and demand for labour of particular employers. Since the issues of wage determination are here related directly to the economic position of firms it is possible to bring wages into line with other rewards in the economy in being subject to, rather than almost controlling, the economic policies of the government. There is a very big difference between employers in general saying 'no' to an increase while taking part in an argument round a table about a few hundred thousand workers, and an employer with an expanding business and an expanding demand for labour doing the same thing. On the other hand an individual employer affected by credit restriction can more effectively demonstrate his difficulty than can a whole industry at a quasi-political negotiation.

If we talk in wage structure rather than wage policy terms, then the major source of instability in the present dual system of wage settlement is its failure to work out clear differential relationships. If a structure is not adequately designed to do this then relative wage claims to which no clear answer can be given are a continuing, and a grievous, possibility. Such differential relationships can only be worked out in detail at the local level where all differences can be recognized, and the wage system can be stripped of complicating national rates and of payment-by-results and overtime payments which are actually serving structural needs.

This point can also be put more positively in terms of labour mobility as an aid to output. One of the arguments used by those who favour restriction of demand as the principal weapon, both in correcting inflation and in holding back wage increases, when they wish to show that restriction is compatible with, or even necessary to, greater economic efficiency, is that reduced general demand for labour will help to increase labour movement into the under-manned sectors of the economy. But if the present national wage rate structure continues, then the most positive aid to labour mobility, a well-designed pattern of relative wages, will be automatically put out of commission. To achieve any considerable desired change in labour mobility it is surely necessary to use to the full the positive directional incentive of differentials as well as the negative push of losing an existing job.

One of the difficulties of the policies for wage control discussed in the previous section is their failure to give the unions a functional part to play in wage settlement. Chapter 11 has discussed the increased load which the present type of suggestion puts on the unions and the long-term advantages of it to them. It seems possible that, given a clear lead, the unions would accept orientation of the framework of wage settlement towards more local wage

determination. It must be stressed, however, that the issue of union participation is not one of initiation of such an alteration but of acceptance. One
of the more attractive features of this kind of change is that it places much
more initiative in forming wage structures upon the employers. At present
employers create the actual pattern of earnings by their extra payments of all
kinds, and the wage structure brought into being by the incidence of such
payments is much more real than the formal creation of national agreements.
Employers are after all those who pay the money and so might perhaps be
expected to be as much interested in the detailed results of wage payment on
the labour force as are the workers themselves; but their present actions are
not so much deliberate planning of wage structures as action by default. The
future pattern of wage structure and of wage policy depends primarily on
employers' initiative.

The position of the government in relation to this type of proposal must
also be considered. There is of course a general responsibility on the government to ease industrial relations along the path which leads to the best interests
of the economy. Thus it is appropriate to suggest that the government should
be willing to assist the type of development suggested, perhaps especially by
a willingness to foster the general determination of minimum wage levels.
A further government duty is to aid the flow of knowledge necessary to
decision-taking. Here we are in the field in which the British government have
shown quite insufficient initiative. Statistical and descriptive information is
necessary to the successful functioning of any wage structure. The statistics
made available in Britain deal far too much with average movements, of
earnings by industry groups for example, and are much too general to provide
the detail needed to allow the labour market to work in full knowledge. Yet
knowledge of prices and conditions is necessary to the working of any market.

The government is also a very important direct employer of labour, and,
moreover, sets the broad policy objectives, and the limits on the funds, of the
nationalized industries. Devolution of bargaining to a local level or a single
employer, as it has been described here, is really only a recommendation to
undertake more detailed wage structuring in the case of the very large section
of the labour force employed by the government itself and the nationalized
boards. The attitude of the government to wage settlement in these cases
could be of vital importance. Direct government employees are required, as
wage followers, to conform to patterns set by outside industry; but the position of the nationalized industries is much less clear. Both the miners and the
railwaymen, for example, have recently appeared to be wage leaders. If we
argue that it is necessary to revise our present system of wage fixing because,
amongst other things, national bargaining is at present leading to quasi-
political decision-taking on wages, then we can hardly leave the large nationalized sector alone in an atmosphere in which the decision to grant wage

increases is made politically. If a new dispensation for wages is to have any chance of working, the government must make its economic relations with the nationalized industries quite clear, and quite obviously fixed for long periods, so that here too negotiations are based on the economic position of the concern in question. In the ends-and-means controversy about nationalized industries, wage policy favours having both the ends and the means, in so far as they are provided by government, fixed with some strong appearance of permanency.

It will be useful now to conclude with a very brief summary of this section on alternative possibilities. Neither methods of controlling wages by deliberate reduction of demand for labour nor those which are specifically based on wage controls are adequate to their task; in present circumstances, however, we can only try, not very hopefully, to deal with inflationary tendencies in wages by using both together. This is a very temporary expedient and we must look for a method of giving stability to wages so that stability in the economy as a whole can be maintained: this means a permanent alteration to methods of wage settlement. The biggest disruptive forces are the artificial settlement of national agreements and the gap between rates and earnings, both of which indicate inadequate attention to wage structure while the former creates a situation in which wage rate determination is set aside from the direct influence of economic forces. Wage stability is only possible when wages are settled more closely in harmony with the economic pressure bearing upon employers and with the forces which bear upon and determine wage structure. National agreements should be conducted at a very general level and confined to determining minimum wages and general conditions. Wage structures, and wage stability, should be built up by much more local wage determination.

PART 4. WAGE THEORY

CHAPTER 13

WHAT KIND OF WAGE THEORY?[1]

This concluding chapter takes the form of a commentary on current wage theory in the light of the preceding discussion. This has been preferred to the more usual type of conclusion which catalogues the various conclusions of the separate chapters, because theoretical discussion provides the right level of generality for a conclusion and theory is, or should be, a unifying influence. There is, however, no intention of producing a new wage theory, or even elaborating in detail the construction of existing theories: the task is rather to re-weight existing theories and to place them alongside that aspect of the wage situation, as it is seen here, to which they appear to refer.

A STATEMENT OF THE POSSIBILITIES

During the period of what has been called, however inappropriately, the Keynesian Revolution, the theory of the determination of relative wages gave way to theories which considered the general wage level as a variable in the determination of income and employment. Since these seemed to suggest that the general wage level was the important thing, and since unemployment was sufficiently great to make it appear that the labour market was perpetually in a state of excess supply, there grew up a tendency to say that the theory of the determination of relative wage rates had nothing to offer. In recent years there has been an agreeable re-awakening of interest in the study of relative wage rates, a field which, it may be asserted, has more right to be regarded as the proper province of wage theory than has the money wage level.[2] This re-awakening has found that the difficulty is not that there is no wage theory

---

[1] A recent notable contribution to the analysis of wage structure produced by Professor Lloyd Reynolds and Miss Cynthia Taft, while very different in many ways, has the basic similarity of being composed of case studies and broader discussion. It ends with a chapter on 'The Dynamics of Wage Structure', which gives the theoretical inference of what goes before, and has as the title of one of its sections—'What Kind of Wage Theory?' This title has been borrowed for use here. (Lloyd G. Reynolds and Cynthia H. Taft, *The Evolution of Wage Structure*, New Haven, Yale University Press, 1956.)

[2] Excellent examples of this renewed interest are K. W. Rothschild, *Theory of Wages* Oxford, Basil Blackwell; *The Theory of Wage Determination*, edited by John T. Dunlop, London, Macmillan; and Reynolds and Taft, op. cit.

but that there are too many in current existence. Can they all be used—and especially can they all be used in the study of factory wages?

Very broadly, current theories concerned with the determination of relative wages fall into two distinct categories—those which favour supply and demand explanations of wage movements—economic theories—and those which are set out in terms of the behaviour of the institutions which take part in the labour market—'institutional' theories.

Economic

Supply and demand explanations of wage movement have found their most developed expression in the 'marginal productivity' theory. This theory relates to the demand for labour and can be combined with a number of alternative supply explanations. Put at its very simplest it states that an employer will not employ a worker or pay for work if it is not worth his while to do so. In its actual theoretical formulation this proposition is put in terms of the product to be expected from the marginal workers and the relation of its value to the wage that has to be paid. Under perfectly competitive conditions, each individual employer will employ workers until their marginal product is no greater than the wage fixed by the market. The aggregation of the numbers of workers employed by all the employers will constitute the demand for labour which will, in conjunction with labour supply, determine the market wage. This theory has been used to argue the general wage level as being fixed in conjunction with supply by an accumulation of the demands by employers for all types of labour. It is less used on this scale nowadays because of the influence of Keynesian thought, but is still put forward as an explanation of the demand for any given type of labour. It is most frequently expressed in terms of perfect competition but this need not be so. Where an employer enjoys a monopolistic position in respect of his product, then a further variable is introduced in wage determination, in that the marginal product of labour in physical terms is subject to a correction in value terms to allow for the monopolist's need to reduce his price to sell more of his product. If the employer is a sole purchaser of one particular type of labour, then the marginal product of labour has to be related to a schedule of wages which rises as the employers' demand for labour grows, since as a monopsonist the employers' demand for the labour will immediately affect its price. But in both these cases the idea of marginal product continues to exist as the prevailing factor in labour demand.

The marginal productivity explanation of demand for labour has been relatively undisputed at the theoretical level; but theoretical explanations of labour supply have been much less favourably received. Indeed the most obvious lack in marginal productivity thinking on wages, even considered on

212

theoretical grounds alone, has been the absence of a strong explanation of labour supply.

The most long-term factor that can play a decisive part in labour supply is the supply of population. Since subsistence-fund theories have been abandoned, the general view is almost certainly that, while population is relevant to the supply of labour, and is indeed the most relevant factor of all, there are so many other factors involved in population supply that it must be left out of wage theory. Such theory is therefore faced with solving the shorter-run problems of what determines the proportion prepared to work out of any given population, and how hard that labour will work.

There are a number of obvious factors which have an important influence on the ratio of working to total population; but, on the whole such factors are not capable of much variation. The level of the school-leaving age is prescribed by law. Many people of retiral age are not fit to continue working. The need to permit and encourage a proportion of the population to continue their studies full-time well beyond the legal school-leaving age is an important one. Strong social forces may help to limit the proportion of married women at work; and in the case of mothers with young children there are all manner of difficulties to prevent their going out to work. Among the rest of the population there are few who can afford not to work. In consequence, except for a movement into and out of the labour force by married women, and relatively small movements by retired people, and by the fortunate few whose other income permits them a choice, the supply of the majority of workers to the economy's labour market is relatively fixed. Despite this, theories relating to variations in the supply of workers have been put forward. These usually emphasize that work is unpleasant and has disadvantages, or alternatively contrast work and leisure, and so put forward supply-schedules of labour, relating disutility of work to wages or relating preference for leisure to wages. As it happens both these ways of looking at the matter apply with considerable force to the only substantial group of people who do supply and withdraw their labour: the married women do almost certainly react in this way, though easy availability of work is another factor in their decision. But this, as an approach to the supply of workers, was not thought of as simply applying to this rather special group of married women, and when used more generally it fails because most potential workers are from recruits permanently attached to the labour market. It is, however, more acceptable in explaining the supply of work from any given worker rather than the supply of workers. Here, ideas of the disutility of marginal increments of work, and of marginal preferences for leisure, have considerable usefulness, or the issue of the labour supplied or effort put forth by a worker may be put more positively in terms of his demand for income.

If, then, no attempt is made to explain the forces that bring workers into the labour force, but it is simply accepted that, apart from some exceptional cases, they are present and available for work, the analysis of labour supply becomes a discussion of the factors that govern the supply of workers to particular occupations. There are, of course, many variations of such theories. In the main, however, they work with such factors as differences in ability, differences in training, differences in attractiveness of jobs, and the immobilities that arise from geographical or social difficulties, or as a result of time lags.

There is however a further obvious and most important consequence which follows from the statement that the labour force is in the labour market and available for work; it is that this extreme inelasticity of supply makes an analysis of the labour market in perfectly competitive terms not sufficient, since labour starts at a disadvantage. If the supply of labour can be taken as fixed, then, except for particular occupations where special circumstances may apply as a result of immobilities, the determining factor in arriving at the wage is demand. This gives a specially strong position to the employers, as those demanding labour, and creates a situation in which wages may theoretically fall very low indeed if demand should be less than supply. If the much smaller number of employers, which gives them something of a monopoly position, is added to the picture, then the potentially extremely weak position of labour relative to the employer is made clear.

Response to the consequences of this situation was one of the main motivating forces in the development of trade unions. Theorists have used the functions of trade unions to correct the imbalance of the supply and demand for labour, since they are held to prevent the wage level falling to its theoretically possible extent by securing agreed minimum wages. The action of trade unions on the wage bargain is that of monopoly sellers of labour: their presence greatly strengthens the supply side of the relationship between demand and supply. The limits to their power to influence wages are suggested in theory as being set by various restrictions on the demand for labour's services as its price rises. Such limit theories cite, especially, restrictions which the elasticity of demand for the final product, and the availability and cost of substitute ways of producing, place upon employers' demand for labour.

Institutional

On the whole the awakening of theorists to the presence of the trade unions has been slow, and characterized by a tendency to remember the existence of the trade unions as an afterthought, requiring the addition of a few remarks about their influence on wages at the end of the discussion, in rather the same way as it is done in the above subsection. The distance that such theories stood from the hurly-burly of the market place did not commend them to those of a more inductive turn of mind. In consequence there is a further group of explanations of how wages are set which centres on actual arrangements made for fixing wages, and on the institutions taking part in wage fixing. In practice this approach has concentrated specially on the trade union and its characteristics. The results of wage bargains are ascribed to the motives and characteristics of the trade unions. Economic forces are not denied, but the actual process of wage settlement is seen to be determined by institutional and social forces. The whole approach is much more empirical than the theoretical economic approach, since it demands detailed knowledge of trade unions and of the methods of wage settlement used.

A generally empirical attitude to wages has also been the characteristic of other contributions, which have stressed either the lack of evidence that the workings of the labour market have produced anything in any way as orderly as the theorists suggest or the many forces other than economic which influence the wage earner's actions. Approaches of this type are concerned to demonstrate the failings of economic theories of wage settlement by drawing attention to the anomalies of existing wage structures or pre-union structures, and by pointing out that social and accidental factors are most important in determining what jobs people take, since knowledge of opportunities is severely limited.

FACTORY WAGES AND WAGE THEORY

Even the brief account given in the previous section reveals the tendency for there to be too many wage theories, rather than too few. It is difficult to work with all these different theories, especially since their protagonists tend to spend at least some of their energy in denying each other's case. Yet, it is also difficult to see how any of them can be dismissed. Theories, whether they are admittedly inductive or proceed largely by deduction, must draw on some facet of their subject as the reason for their continued existence. The continuance of a theory suggests some continuing applicability for it, even though it may be misguided. It can sometimes be argued that the answer is simply a division into periods—that one theory relates to the earlier and the other the later period. In this case this would mean economic theories being regarded as pre-union and institutional being related to the period since unions have become important and powerful. But such a compromise would be in difficulty in explaining the *continued* currency of these divergent theories.

This study of factory wages has concentrated attention on the diversity of aspects of wages as they appear to the factory worker. It has emphasized constantly that the total pay packet is composed of a number of different elements which may be combined in differing proportions and are fixed in differing ways. It therefore leads on quite naturally to the contention that a number of apparently conflicting wage theories can be quite relevant and useful, provided it is remembered that they apply to different aspects of the wage. The broadest division in theory is between economic theories and purely institutional theories. The broadest division in practice is between nationally negotiated wage rates and actual earnings. It is also broadly true that the settlement of nationally negotiated wage rates is to be thought of in terms of institutional analysis, while the pattern of earnings is most clearly understood using the methods of economic theorizing.

Nationally negotiated wage rates are settled in an atmosphere of bargaining. To understand the result it is best to think of such things as bargaining techniques, and the conflicting pressures put upon the institutions and people involved. Some of these pressures may be economic, but many will not be. In any event economic theory cannot provide an analysis of the rate which will be fixed, since national bargaining involves a debate between monopolist and monopsonist and the result is theoretically indeterminate. An institutional approach is needed to understand national bargains.

In fixing actual factory wage rates, or a national bargain where there is only one employer, the fact that employers will be unwilling to exceed a wage level which can be squared with the demand for their product, and the availability of alternative capitalistic methods of production, suggests that here an institutional approach to understanding needs to be supplemented by the use of some version of the limit theory. The applicability of these economic limits is much more obvious in the type of case where the union is dealing with an economic unit, a single employer, than in the large-scale national bargain, where individual differences are averaged out.

In contrast to the settlement of wage rates, the only way to understand fluctuations and variations in earnings levels is by reference to economic analysis. Earnings variations between districts or between occupations can hardly be explained by institutional analysis since they do not conform to institutional arrangements. For example, analysis of wage agreements for signs of the prescription of a lower wage rate for Scotland as against that set for England will generally produce a negative result, while examination of average earnings levels will show that in most cases similar occupations and similar industries show lower average earnings in Scotland than in England. There is even some constancy in the proportion of Scottish to English averages at about 95 per cent.[1] The explanation of this rests on the strength of demand for labour generally in the two areas, and on the specially strong demand from the high-paying industries in some English areas, which causes a need to pay higher all round so as to get and keep labour. This demand factor coupled with the supply factor of some, but not sufficient, rectifying movement of labour, gives meaning to a divergence which lies completely

[1] Cf. Chapter on 'Wages' by D. J. Robertson in *The Scottish Economy*, ed. A. K. Cairncross, Cambridge, 1954.

beyond institutional analysis. The factors governing the long-term reward of different occupational groups require to be thought of in a similar way in terms of economic analysis (as in Chapter 10), though here social factors are also important. Indeed, in thinking of the relationships and movements of broad earnings averages, the forces other than economic which have to be considered are social rather than institutional.

At the factory level variations between earnings levels are dependent on many chance factors such as the department in which a man works, the easiness or tightness of a piece-work price, or the possibility or lack of overtime. These variations make it difficult to ascribe any rationality to relative earnings at this level. Certainly *on average* such earnings appear to form a broadly intelligible pattern, but the individual case shows up the anomalies more clearly. It can, however, be emphasized that variations are not simply the result of institutional forces, unless in the special sense that it is the failure of the institutional bargain to be adequate to the circumstances that has produced the present earnings situation. The case for tidying up the use of payment-by-results and overtime has been argued at length in this book. As individual earnings variations stand at the moment no very clear theoretical analysis at all can be applied to them. Nevertheless, the only possible theoretical approach is through economic analysis, which can yield some useful results. For example, the theories relating to disutility of work and leisure preference are of considerable value in understanding the marginal incidence of overtime working.

This attempt to show that the relevance of institutional and economic theories of wages is to be interpreted in relation to different aspects of the wage, completes the argument of this book—with but two further points that require some exposition. First, a consideration of how institutional and economic theories are connected—since one accusation that is outstanding from what has been said up till now would be that the argument here suggests that institutional forces have no influence on earnings. The second and final task is to attempt to show the relation of the theories expounded here to the suggestion, made earlier, that bargaining should be more local in its emphasis.

A. Do institutional forces influence earnings? Of course they do, but this is not the same thing as saying that they determine actual earnings levels. Reynolds and Taft talk of 'the rebound of wage differentials under the influence of market forces'.[1] This phrase well conveys the general atmosphere of the relation between institutional forces and economic pressures. The process of adjustment of institutional decisions to market forces occurs both in the very long-period influences on wage rates and in the short-period divergences between rates and earnings. Where necessary, earnings provide the

---

[1] Reynolds and Taft, op. cit., p. 371.

countermoves to institutional change, though, given the imperfections of the market and the systems of payment, such countermoves may be slow and incomplete in present circumstances.

The interplay between earnings and institutional determination of wage rates may be summed up in four points.

1. Where institutional pressures push payments out of line with economic forces, the action of earnings is to adjust to economic forces.

2. Institutional determination of minimum wage levels alters the power relationships in the wage bargain, and ensures that earnings levels cannot follow supply and demand strictly, if supply should be greatly in excess of demand, and are less subject to the monopoly influence of the employer as a single purchaser of labour.

3. Large increases in wage rates secured by institutional bargaining naturally lift up the level of the earnings structure, and may also alter the relative levels of the earnings structures of different industries. The effects of these alterations on the pattern of relative earnings, though not the general effect on the level of earnings, may be slowly eroded by changes in earnings.

4. Because of the slowness of factors altering the broad streams of labour supply, institutionally settled wage rate changes may make major alterations to the average levels of differentials in earnings also, though small scale variations about such levels will exist. These factors are mainly social, and the best examples of them occur in the determination of appropriate occupational differentials. This issue is therefore discussed at some length in Chapter 10 on the reward for skill. Actually the point here is not just one of slowness of reaction in supply factors, though in the case of differentials between regions the slowness of social response to the need for mobility is explanation enough, but of social variation in the size of acceptable differentials. If institutional arrangements result in heavy pressure towards alteration of differentials, in time society's opinion of the appropriate differential may also change and the relationship of earnings levels may settle down to stability at new relative positions.

B. What are the inferences for wage theory of the policy suggestions contained in Chapters 11 and 12? The general attitude expressed there was that at present both trade unions and wage policy exponents place too much emphasis on the national bargain and too little emphasis on local wage settlement; and, that an attempt should be made to increase the scale of local bargaining, while retaining national bargaining on minimum rates and conditions of work. The suggestion was that this would make possible the reconciliation of wage rates and earnings, since at the local level bargains could be related to actual conditions in the place of employment, making earnings differences a matter of differences in individual behaviour only. This would appear to be in broad conformity with the prescriptions of economic

218

theories of wage settlement, which stress the beneficial effects of exposing wage settlement as closely as possible to market forces; but evokes the criticisms of that type of theory, which, mainly drawing on pre-union examples, stress the failure of the labour market to achieve balanced equilibrium and to avoid anomalies. This type of criticism can be held to take two forms. It may stress the view that the trade unions have been responsible for achieving orderliness in the labour market, implying thereby support for national bargaining and a contrast with the workings of an untramelled free market: or, it may doubt the existence of a general labour market altogether. How do these criticisms affect the proposals made?

'The countries with the strongest union movement appear to have a wage structure which is more orderly and defensible than the wage structure of countries where unionism has been weak.'[1] This view sets the scene for those who favour union-negotiated wage structures. It might seem possible to extend this thought to infer that since Britain has an exceptionally well-developed trade union movement it also has an excellently well-ordered wage structure, which should not, at this late date, be subject to a reversion to local bargaining. Unfortunately this does not necessarily follow. It is undoubtedly true that the first effect of trade unionism in Britain was to shake out many traditional anomalies and inconsistencies arising out of disorganized local labour markets. The drive towards uniformity got rid of the worst anomalies and narrowed the spread of payments. Thus, as trade unionism became accepted the contention that it brought with it a more orderly wage structure was most reasonable, both for Britain and, no doubt, for other countries also. But uniformity as well as reducing anomalies can be an over-simplification, which leads to new anomalies, through stress between an over-simplified wage structure and economic pressures. Wage negotiations can become formalized and wage structures can become set in a new traditionalism. There is nothing to show that the initial reduction in anomalies achieved by trade unions is followed by continuing success, indeed formal national bargaining may breed new wage structure problems. Thus local bargaining may be represented as a further stage in the efforts to remove anomalies rather than as a reversion to old practices.

The disorganized labour market which appears to have preceded trade unionism in most countries suffered from so many defects, that it may be doubted whether it is correct to speak of a market at all. Any suggestion that wages should move back towards local settlement will undoubtedly raise the ghost of this pre-union market and its inconsistencies will be paraded. Two features were primarily responsible for the peculiarities of the pre-union labour market. It was a market in which wages were governed by social convention and the motives for seeking work were conditioned by social

[1] Reynolds and Taft, op. cit., p. 195.

factors. To some extent nothing can be done to alter this feature, which still exists. Wages are in part the product of social forces, which influence the volume of labour supply to different jobs. But the economic forces are there too. The social forces are only alone in importance when the economic forces, especially wages, are obscured. Clear-cut local bargains would see that they were not obscured. The most important reason for inadequacy in the pre-union labour market was, however, the lack of the knowledge without which no market can operate with success. Based on completely local or individual wage settlement it provided no general source of information. Wage earners, especially, had to form their judgement about opportunities available to them in alternative employment on hearsay evidence. No market can work successfully without the clear use of its most important agent—price. But, this is precisely the factor in the local labour market which would be altered by increased local bargaining in the present trade union era. An extension of bargaining to the local level would not be the same as a reversion to pre-union local markets. The union itself would be a unifying factor, and local bargains would provide much more adequate knowledge for the functioning of the labour market than that provided by the present mixture of national rates and local confusion. Local bargains backed by the interchange of knowledge in the market could make possible a wage structure working in the way which economic theorists have always wanted, but which, up till now, has been denied to them.

APPENDIX 1

VARIABLE EARNINGS AND WAGE EARNERS' EXPENDITURE

The analysis of factory wages contained in this book produces some illuminating results when used in discussing wage earners' expenditure. There are of course, plenty of theories relating to consumption behaviour, both in macro-economics (the consumption function), and in micro-economics (theories of demand and individual consumers' behaviour); but, the influence of the type of wage income on the pattern of expenditure of its recipients has not been much discussed.[1]

THE SOURCE OF VARIABLE EARNINGS

The characteristic feature of present-day factory wages as evidenced in the studies in this book, and almost certainly to a greater or lesser extent in most wage earners' payment, is a wide gap between rates and earnings.

The wage rate may be prescribed by national agreement to be paid to a worker of a certain occupation or grade for a certain length of time. It can usually be related to a 'standard' week, similarly prescribed by agreement, giving a certain fixed sum payable for a standard week's work and conditional only on the worker being of the occupation or grade in question and turning up for his work for the hours appropriate to the standard week. This agreed rate has a quality of certainty about it. It is contained in a written agreement and is dependent only on occupational grade and appearance at work. All other payments which fill the gap between rates and earnings are less certain to be paid and are more dependent on circumstance.

Factory earnings differ from nationally agreed rates as a result of three additional sources of income. These are additional rates, payment-by-results and overtime.

Factories may decide to supplement the national rate by various forms of additional rate payments. Some of these may be offered 'without strings', simply to increase the rate, but others may take the form of merit rates, or incentive rates, or some other special rate payment made conditional on some additional requirement. Only the rate payments 'without strings' can be classed with the national rate as being secure and certain to be paid to a worker provided he comes to work. The others may be paid regularly enough,

---

[1] These matters are also briefly discussed by the writer in 'The Present Complexity of Wage Payment', *Scottish Journal of Political Economy*, February 1955.

but, since their payment depends on special conditions they can never be absolutely relied on. If an additional rate is, for example, dependent on the bonus level remaining above 80, then even though it is most unusual for the bonus to fall below 90, the rate has still an element of uncertainty. A merit rate can be withdrawn. A rate for special conditions of, for example, hardship or danger goes out of existence when the conditions change. Such additional rates as these may have a fair degree of certainty but do not have the same certainty as the rate itself.

Payment-by-results and overtime, as has been fully discussed elsewhere, generally fill the major part of the gap between rates and earnings, and can either be paid fairly regularly or else fluctuate considerably. In post-war years each of these payments has been used as a regular addition to the pay packet, and has also been used in its original function as a payment varying according to the achievement of a higher rate of output, or for working at times additional to the standard week. Despite the use of such payments with some regularity as supplements to rates, their very nature precludes their being regarded as really secure parts of the pay packet.

The major distinction between factory wages and national agreements is then the distinction between rates and earnings, and while rates are characterized by certainty in payment, earnings, with the exception of some local additions to the rates, are uncertain. Even though the earnings have tended to occur regularly they cannot be counted upon. A consequence of this is that the certainty of income payments to wage earners, which usually only comes up in discussion at the national level in terms of employment or unemployment, actually is much more widely relevant and is a problem internal to the pattern of wage payments. The magnitude of this problem of certainty and uncertainty in the pay packet cannot, in the existing state of wage statistics, be stated adequately. The case-studies suggest that proportions of irregular payments in total pay packets varying from one-third to two-thirds can occur, and that the irregular payments do show their irregularity in sudden fluctuations from their more usual level.

The result of this distinction in the certainty to be attached to different types of wage payment is that wage earners cannot regard the whole of their pay packet as being equally secure. Income security is not therefore the same thing to wage earners as job security, since fluctuations in income may occur even when employment is secure. The wage earner's position at its most extreme may be put by considering the reactions of a prospective employee to a personnel manager's account of the pay prospects attached to a job. The personnel manager may begin by explaining that the job is for a particular occupation, and that the national rate for the job is so much, but that in practice the factory rates the job rather more highly. Up till now doubtless the man will believe what he is being told. The job is rated at more than the national rate. Then the doubts begin. The personnel manager may go on to explain that the factory pays an incentive rate of one penny an hour for every 10 points by which the bonus exceeds 80, and that it normally runs at 100. The man may well wonder how much stress to put on 'normally'. Then he may be told of merit rates and wonder how you come to merit them. The payment-by-results scheme is most generous and most people have little difficulty in keeping up a 100-per-cent bonus: here too, despite the personnel manager's assurance, the prospective employee may wonder whether he will get 100-per-cent bonus—and how often. Finally, the personnel manager may point to the advertisement, with its mention of unlimited overtime, and assure the man that this can add several pounds a week to his pay packet. The man may wonder how long the overtime will last. To a new employee unfamiliar with the factory or its management, the only certain thing about this account is the wage rate. The rest is all somewhat problematical and uncertain.

The uncertainty which attends on the act of taking a new job is something which is probably inevitable. The present way in which payment is made does, however, aggravate it. Moreover, even though the personnel manager in the illustration has spoken the truth, there *is* some uncertainty attached to payments which 'most people normally get'. The extent to which earnings are insecure differs from factory to factory and industry to industry. Some factories, notably those where little use is made of payment-by-results or overtime, will be relatively free from uncertainty in payment, others will have a great deal of uncertainty. Similarly some industries, such as the docks, or iron and steel, will have a tendency to cause a lot of uncertainty about the size of the pay packet. The wage earner, therefore, takes on a job when in some doubt about the size of income he may usually expect from it, and then, while in the job, is in doubt from one week to the other about the size of pay packet he may expect to receive and whether, and for how long, it will remain stable.

WAGE EARNERS' EXPENDITURE IN RELATION TO VARIABLE EARNINGS

It is possible to think of a classification of the spending of income according to whether it is regular or irregular, defining these terms loosely to mean by 'regular' those outlays which tend to recur at stated intervals, and by 'irregular' those which are either not repeated at all or which recur erratically. Regular expenditure may be further subdivided to indicate whether it is continuing, terminal or terminable. Continuing regular expenditure is that which is not likely to stop during the spender's lifetime or, at least, goes on for a sufficiently long number of years to appear to be in that position. Terminal regular expenditure is incurred for a fixed period of time. If the fixed period is for a long number of years, terminal expenditure will shade into continuing expenditure, and it is therefore best to think of terminal expenditure as lasting for a few years only. Terminable expenditure has no fixed time-period on it, but can, if need be, be stopped. Within the categories of continuing and terminal expenditure another distinction may be made, between those expenditures which are contractual and those which are not, the latter presumably being more capable of postponement than the former.

An attempt to relate these categories of spending to the actual pattern of consumer expenditure must of necessity be difficult and full of borderline cases. But while precision is quite impossible, something useful can be done on an impressionistic basis, using what appear to be broadly the most important items in the usual consumers' budget.

1. Continuing regular contractual expenditure is probably best exemplified by expenditure on housing. Expenditure on house purchase by mortgage is possibly less easy to get out of, or appears to the timorous spender to be so, than renting a house, and so house purchase may be a more contractual item than house rent. But since house room is an essential, a regular contractual outlay on rent or mortgage is an important example of this type of expenditure. A further example is expenditure on life assurance.

2. Continuing regular non-contractual expenditure has as its most obvious example daily spending on food and consumable domestic items. Of course, food expenditure is inevitably continuing and regular, but since variations in standard of feeding are possible it could be argued that there is in food and consumable domestic expenditure an element of terminable expenditure. While this cannot be denied, it is probably best to think of this type of expenditure as continuing, for two reasons. People tend to set themselves a standard of feeding to which they become accustomed and to which the household cook adjusts her ideas. Clearly this standard can be varied but it is a matter of strong habit and is possibly relatively fixed for fairly long periods of time. Then too, this type of expenditure is the major element in the payment between husband and wife. From the man's point of view this is a fixed claim upon his pay packet which, while not formally contractual, has a priority and importance similar to contractual payments. Besides this obvious case of continuing regular expenditure we might list such items as fuel and light which again can be varied greatly but have a valuation for each household which does not vary very much over short periods of time.

3. Terminal regular contractual expenditure has hire purchase of consumers' durables as its most obvious example. Hire-purchase debts bind the contracting party to repay in fixed regular amounts over a defined period of time, which is usually not more than two years and may be considerably less. Hire purchase may, however, also be thought of as being irregular expenditure since the financing of the deposit, usually required for goods bought on hire

purchase, involves the once-for-all spending of a lump sum. Thus a single lump sum expenditure—irregular—may acquire the article. If the deposit is fairly large or if the immediate accumulation of a deposit presents a greater obstacle to the potential purchaser than the smaller and less immediate regular repayments, then hire-purchase expenditure may be regarded as irregular.

4. Terminal regular non-contractual expenditure does not suggest any very important items of expenditure. Childrens' upkeep and schooling might be mentioned as a possibility, but the time period involved here is somewhat long and the family man probably regards the family expenses as continuing.

5. Terminable expenditure covers all the items on which people habitually spend their money but are not contracted to do so and can stop doing so when necessary. A most obvious example is regular spending on entertainments. While some clothing has to be bought and so is continuing regular expenditure, quite a lot of variation in standards of dress is possible and some of clothing expenditure can be thought of as terminable. Again, while food expenditure is continuing and should be thought of in that way, at least a proportion of it is terminable.

6. Irregular expenditure is represented by all those purchases which do not require regular repetition—a present, or an unusually expensive holiday, a specially expensive item of food, a heavy night's drinking, an unusual expenditure on entertainment, and so on through a thousand variations.

This classification of types of expenditure can now be related to patterns of wage income to show what pattern of expenditure may be expected to follow from different patterns of income. It is not proposed to enter into a discussion of different levels of income here but to compare incomes of the same level though differently constructed. The variables that have to be considered relate to the security of income, the certainty that it will be forthcoming. In the long-period sense this brings into consideration the security of employment, job security, which is needed to ensure security of income. Security of income in the long period may also be affected by whether or not an incremental scale is in operation. Those who expect a regularly increasing income can hardly fail to feel secure in the present level of their income. In the shorter period a man's income security depends upon the regular expectation of a regular income from his employment. This expectation has two aspects both that the income is certain to arrive and that it arrives in regular amounts.

Suppose then we assume that we are concerned with incomes of about the size we expect wage earners to get, which come to the same annual total and so *average* out each week to the same weekly amount, even though in actual practice week-to-week variations may occur. What effect will changes in the composition of such incomes have on the pattern of expenditure? Will the proportions of income devoted to the different types of expenditure differ if the pattern of income differs? The effect of long-term job and income security will be to make possible expenditure similarly based on a long-term outlook, and, given security in income, a contractual obligation in expenditure will be possible. Thus such security means that, other things being equal, a higher proportion of income can go on continuing regular expenditure, and contractual obligations will be acceptable. If the income is subject to regular increments this will increase the willingness to incur contractual obligations, since they will as time goes on become a diminishing proportion of income. In the shorter period a secure and certain income will make possible a higher proportion devoted to continuing regular expenditure than when income is inclined to be irregular and fluctuating. If there are factors in the income situation, which keep a quantity of it uncertain, but which nevertheless permit a reasonable hope that it will not decline much in the relatively near future, then terminal contractual expenditure will be possible. Highly fluctuating and insecure income will favour terminable and irregular expenditure.

These points can be put more concretely. The pattern of income payable to an employee on an incremental scale and with high job-security favours a high proportion of income devoted to regular outlay on house-room and domestic expenditure on food and fuel and so on. It suggests a low proportion of income spent on irregular items, both because a high proportion is regularly committed, and because irregularity in expenditure is not easy to adjust to regularity in income. If terminal regular expenditure (hire purchase) is undertaken it will tend to be kept in proportion, again because of high proportions committed elsewhere, and because a variable proportion would not adjust easily to regular income. An employee with fairly secure employment, such as full employment has given to most workers in regular employment, and with a regular weekly pay, will be in a position to spend a high proportion of his income on continuing regular expenditure on food and on house-rent, though he may find difficulty in undertaking house purchase. Again having committed himself here he will not be in a position to spend much irregularly or on hire purchase. In contrast, even though he has the security of employment which full employment provides, the man with a fluctuating income will find it hard to commit a high proportion of his income on continuing regular expenditure and will find it easy to spend on terminable and irregular expenditure which accords well with his fluctuating income.

The comparison of possible income patterns with possible expenditure patterns suggests that a particular income pattern will tend to create a particular expenditure pattern. The gap between rates and earnings which is typical of the pay packet of so many factory workers is characterized by lack of certainty about whether or not earnings will come up to expectations from week to week and by an actual lack of stability in earnings. Even though full employment has minimized the factor of job security, this uncertainty in earnings will tend to produce a pattern of expenditure which favours terminable and irregular expenditure at the expense of continuing regular expenditure.

In recent years the earnings of the more highly paid wage earners have been overlapping those of the more lowly paid salaried workers, and the earnings through payment-by-results and overtime of some less skilled men have reached a par with the more stable payment of skilled maintenance workers. Thus placing people of these three types on the same income level is not totally against the facts. If the suggested expenditure pattern resulting from the types of income appropriate to these three groups is examined it bears a rather close resemblance to the popular conception of these groups. The salaried man will devote a high proportion of his income to house purchase or rent, will give a high proportion to his wife, will keep his hire-purchase commitments small, will have little left over, and will have parcelled out what is left over into various regular extras rather than occasional erratic bursts of spending. The man earning 'a steady wage' will be similar except that he is likely to be renting and not buying his house. The typical wage earner will be thought to be spending too little on house-room, to be giving his wife too low a proportion of his total earnings, to be overburdened with short-term hire purchase and to waste too much money on casual spending.

If these illustrations are granted then the patterns of income which produced these expenditure patterns have considerable social importance. There can be little doubt that popular estimation gives higher social standing to the salaried worker in his own house or in a good rented house, eating well and spending carefully. Yet wage earners often nowadays have as much money income, which being differently acquired and differently spent produces less social result. There is a lot of truth in the idea that the major source of difference between working- and lower-middle-class people with the same size of family in Britain today is not how much income they have, but how it comes along. Since, for better or worse, our society tends to place high standards on the middle-class type of existence, it therefore follows that many wage earners have the same incomes as lower salaried workers but have higher expenditure on the less essential ingredients of accepted standards and are regarded as having a lower standard of life.

Various possible sources of dubiety about this discussion must however be mentioned. The most obvious is to enquire about the possibility of a bank account ironing out income irregularity. Secondly, it is, of course, necessary to enquire if the suggestion is that income irregularity is adequate excuse for a wasteful expenditure pattern. Thirdly, does hire purchase fit in as neatly as is suggested?

The argument relating to the use of bank accounts in the circumstance of irregular income would say that the obvious way to balance an irregular flow of income against a regular flow of expenditure, or indeed to adjust any pattern of income to a pattern of expenditure totalling the same amount over a period, is to use the facilities of the banking system. A current account (working between zero and positive or negative balances representing the maximum tendency to diverge from the average level of income) will allow an individual to work to a regular pattern of expenditure, even though his income flows in unevenly. Examples might be quoted of people who receive income very unevenly, authors are an obvious possibility, and yet maintain regular expenditures. The difference between working class and middle class might be said to be a difference in the pattern of their incomes, plus the fact that the former make less use of banks.

Let it be admitted that this view of the matter has some foundation. Undoubtedly a prudent use of a bank account can minimize the difficulties of irregular income, and working-class people are very slow to think of banks in this way. But, this is not the whole story! More is involved than in an averaging problem. The argument put forward here is that earnings are not only variable but that there can be an element of uncertainty in them. If regular expenditure commitments are made against an average income which is uncertain then a banking account cannot help very much if the uncertainty results in a fall in income and an accumulation of debt. Further, it is not fair to consider all magnitudes of irregularity of income as being the same problem. A man faced with no regular pattern of income receipt at all may be forced into working through a bank account since he has to budget all his expenditure against an irregular income. Another man with a regular source of income and also a number of irregular receipts may base his regular expenditure only on his regular income source and may treat the irregular flow of receipts simply as 'windfalls' to be spent in a different way and according to a different set of values. It is, of course, possible to make an effort to get some regularity out of 'windfalls' in income; but, it can hardly be said that it is a thing which any middle-class person with any common sense would automatically do. The contrast between social classes here is not as strong as that.

Is the suggestion in this discussion that income irregularity is an adequate excuse for a wasteful expenditure pattern? Clearly it would be difficult and unwise to try and prove a complete causal relation. But if severe difficulties are placed in the way of one course of action, it is never very surprising to find people taking the easier alternative. All that is being said here is that variable earnings for wage earners make it easier for them to go in for terminable and irregular expenditure and put grave difficulties in the way of their spending a very high proportion of their average income (an average which they only discover *ex post*) on continuing regular expenditure. A man who has earned fifteen pounds a week on average but has considerable week to week variations in it will find himself in difficulties if he tries to maintain the same quantity of continuing regular expenditure as the man who gets fifteen pounds a week with regularity and certainty. Suppose for example we consider the problems of house rent and of the allowance to the housewife. Is it not excusable only to be prepared to spend on rent what can *with certainty* be regularly met? And this may for the first man be a considerably lower amount than the second can afford.[1] Then the housewife will want to know how much money she can count on having for food and domestic requirements. Even a perfect husband and wife relationship would find difficulty in working on a fluctuating food budget. There is therefore some explanation for a man with variable earnings keeping his wife's share down to about the point which he knows he can afford every week—though undoubtedly this can be altogether too conservatively assessed. If this is the position then the destination of the variable earnings is already mapped out. They become available for 'extras'. They are treated as 'found' money, or as 'windfalls' uncommitted to any specific line of spending. In the existing state of British society the ways of dealing with unexpected acquisitions of money undoubtedly include high expenditure on drink, or entertainment, somewhat useless presents, and the other ways of getting rid of money, which are laid at the door of the working class. Besides, is this attitude to extra income so very different from that taken by all sections of society? Do we not all itch to find something to buy with an unexpected bonus, or a legacy or whatever it may be? 'Found' money is generally related to a quite different scale of values than other income. Since after all the regular commitments of the household are already dealt with, this type of income can be disposed of more lightheartedly. It is perhaps the misfortune of workers that so much of their income can come in this way.

The place of hire purchase in this discussion requires a little elaboration. It was classed as the main example of terminal regular contractual expenditure, and yet it was given as one of the items of expenditure, which would show a low proportion in the budget of those with a regular income, and a high proportion in the budget of those with irregular income. Can this be justified? As far as those with regular incomes are concerned the argument would stress that their budget is built on proportions related to a fixed income. Each hire-purchase repayment is related to a specific item of equipment, and its period of repayment runs on for a year or two. If a number of items are bought in this way at the same time the expenditure naturally grows and then falls off afterwards. To keep a due proportion to a regular income it is necessary to plan hire purchase carefully and to limit it at any one time. The terminal expenditure is converted into a continuing item taking a steady proportion of income. This proportion is likely to be fairly low, both because

[1] It is tempting to wonder whether the extreme reluctance to accept rent increase in postwar Britain has been due to increasing income irregularity. It would appear absurd to say that increases in council house rents, for example, cannot be afforded by industrial workers with high earnings. If, however, it is remembered that the rent has to be related to the regular wage and not to total income then the above normal resistance to increases in this particular price becomes more understandable, though not necessarily fully justifiable.

it is continuing and represents a gradual process of acquisition, and, because it has to compete with other lines of continuing expenditure.

A number of points may be put forward to explain the contention that variable incomes for wage earners tend to be associated with a high proportion of spending on hire purchase. First it should be stressed that a marked feature of variable income is its lack of definition and plan. The income earner has no clear idea of planned destinations for his income. This is an atmosphere in which acquisition of goods 'the easy way' beloved of hire-purchase salesmen, becomes attractive. The consequences follow but are not planned or predicted. Secondly, hire purchase generally, though not invariably, requires a deposit. This deposit which secures the goods presents a ready way of disposing of the excess in a high-earning week. Thirdly, while hire purchase involves regular expenditure, it is terminal. Thus it may be undertaken when things are going well and does not commit the wage earner permanently. Earnings are uncertain and variable but a man may consider that present prospects are reasonable, and start on hire purchase, whereas he might hesitate at a permanent alteration to his expenditure pattern. Then, finally, hire purchase of goods one at a time does not represent too great a possible sacrifice if repayments cannot be met. There is a gamble on the future but the stakes are not too high or the period too long.

SHORT NOTES ON RECRUITMENT POLICY AND 'IRRESPONSIBILITY'

This discussion of the links between variable earnings and wage earners' expenditure patterns provides some helpful ideas on recruitment policy for wage earners and on the alleged 'irresponsibility' of wage earners. This Appendix may therefore be usefully concluded by short notes on these two matters viewed from the standpoint of variable earnings and of their effects on expenditure patterns.

Recruitment policy

The picture given above of the personnel manager's efforts to 'sell' variable earnings to a prospective employee, can be used to show the consequences to recruitment policy which variable earnings involve.

Put at its very simplest a wage is the price of labour expressed in units of work. In practice, since work involves workers, a distinction may be made between the actual work and the worker. An important way of making this distinction arises in the practical contrast between the function of the wage in keeping the existing labour force contented and at work, and its function as a price which will attract a potential new recruit to the labour force. In the first case the workers may be assumed to be already in the labour force and the task of wage payments is to keep them turning out to their work, to keep up a satisfactory output from them, to retain their services, and to keep them generally contented. In the case of the new recruit, the wage has the sole function of attracting him so that he takes the job offered.

Even if we accept that payment-by-results and overtime are invariably successful in their aim of increasing the work done by an employee, their particular influence is entirely directed towards the existing employee. The issues of rate of work or extra hours of work do not arise specifically until a man has become a worker in the factory in question. Thus, the supposed positive advantages of payment-by-results and overtime have little direct effect on the recruit. The recruit does not know the internal workings of the firm he is joining, and so he will be inclined to discount offers of payment which are conditional or uncertain. He is selling his services for a period of time, the reward he will be looking for will be a clear promise of a payment based on the length of time for which his services are bought, a wage rate. All forms of payments will, of course, come into the employer's wage bill; but those payments which are uncertain and variable, principally payment-by-results and overtime, will not be fully accepted by new recruits. The employer, by keeping variable some part of this payment to existing employees, is only able to offer a recruitment wage which is less than the average amount of his wage payments. In this aspect of the wage, as a recruitment agent, variable earnings payments do not yield an equivalent return to the employer.

The same point can be made in terms of workers' expenditure patterns. When a man takes on a new job he is automatically involved in a process of revaluation of his standard of living. He has to do this so that he can compare the prospects offered by future employments against his present or past conditions. If the argument of this Appendix is accepted, then this long-term revaluation of standard of living will focus on regular expenditure of a continuing nature. In consequence, certainty in income payments will also be emphasized by the job-seeker.

The influence of this type of reasoning on recruitment policy is obvious. It is to suggest that, where possible, employers who are engaged in recruitment programmes would be best to reduce the variable element in pay packets, and to provide the best possible offer of a wage rate type of payment.

'Irresponsibility'

The influence of patterns of expenditure may be important in relation to the 'irresponsibility' in their attitude to work of which workers are often accused. If either working hard or working extra hours are associated in the workers' mind only with extra, and less essential, expenditure, then it is easy to see that a transference of attitude from the type of expenditure to the work itself may take place. If the expenditure is lighthearted, so too may be the workers' acceptance or rejection of the work, as his fancy dictates. In contrast, all the salary-earner's work is bound up with all his payment, and there is no break in the 'responsibility' of his work or spending.

At present systems of payment are used for wage earners which make the bond between worker and employer dependent upon a short-period reckoning of work and rewarded by short-period payments, so that the worker's action in behaving responsibly and producing a satisfactory output is rewarded by a variable payment-by-results bonus. Since these variable payments may be related to variable and less important expenditure, it may follow that the worker holds his responsibility for an adequate output lightly, and is capable of 'irresponsible' slacking when he feels so inclined.

This short-period attitude to work may mean that the way to get 'responsibility' with such types of payments is to ensure a steady flow of short-period goals for expenditure which keep attracting workers' efforts. This however is not something that a factory can readily do on its own, but depends rather on the surrounding society and the type of worker. This point can be well illustrated by the remarks of a manager employing a large number of semi-skilled girls. He began by pointing out that the problem of ensuring continual high output from such girls is specially connected with short-period expenditures, since they have few long-term family expenditures to meet. The job is easy if society provides plenty of short-period expenditure objectives, and very difficult if they are lacking. He went on to ascribe a large part of the credit for his having girls who were good bonus workers to the influence of the glossy women's magazines. These provided ample short-period goals and his girls worked hard. They were advised to keep up a regular flow of terminable expenditure on cosmetics and the like, and in addition were set specific recurring tasks, the holiday on the Continent, then the winter rig-out, the spring suit, etc. It should be recorded that the manager's evidence was that the girls had been successful and that a higher proportion of them than of the staff took holidays on the Continent.

APPENDIX 2

NATIONAL AGREEMENTS IN THE ENGINEERING INDUSTRY

Chapters 11 and 12 have emphasized that the only way to get away from the confusion that presently exists between national agreements and actual factory wage structures is to reduce the importance of national agreements, and to increase their generality, by negotiating only extremely broadly based minima, while substituting local, and even plant or firm, agreements as the main vehicle of wage structure. Such a suggestion may however prove much too radical for the practitioners of wage settlement. The situation which is outlined in this book will then continue to bedevil wage structures and industrial relations in Britain. In particular, the disparity between wage rate structures and earnings structures will continue. Nevertheless, some improvements in the existing situation could be effected by improvements in existing national agreements which would bring them closer into line with actual conditions in the industries with which they deal. The present wage agreements in the engineering industry afford a particularly bad example of the consequences of inadequately detailed national agreements. This Appendix is therefore devoted to discussion of possible improvements to the existing fabric of engineering agreements, on the assumption that the present emphasis on national negotiation and national agreements will continue.

THE STRUCTURAL FAULTS OF THE PRESENT AGREEMENTS

The engineering industry's post-war wage agreements have been responsible for several important national debates and crises. A Court of Inquiry proved necessary to settle a dispute in 1948. The wage claim of 1949–50 lasted for 17 months and 'severely strained both the Confederation of Shipbuilding and Engineering Unions and the negotiating machinery'.[1] The wage claim submitted in May 1953 resulted in a widespread token one-day strike in December 1953. This was followed by the Confederation's recommendation of a ban on overtime and a limitation of piece-work. In January 1954 a Court of Inquiry was set up which reported in February 1954,[2] and the dispute was settled shortly thereafter. After negotiations which began late in 1955, an increase was agreed in February 1956. This was followed by a wage claim submitted

---

[1] A. Tatlow, 'The Underlying Issues of the 1949–50 Engineering Wage Claim', *Manchester School*, September 1953.
[2] Cmnd. 9084.

in August 1956, by a series of meetings between the parties without agreement being reached, and by a national strike, which however was started in some districts only and was called off before all parts of the country were affected, since by this time a Court of Inquiry had been set up. This Court reported in May 1957[1] and the dispute was settled shortly thereafter.

In these documents and debates may be found, implicit or explicit, an awareness of the problems relating to wage structure to be answered by the industry. The three major problems may be listed.

1. 'There was disagreement as to the basis to be adopted in assessing the workers' standard of pay. The Unions contended that the basis should be the workers' minimum wage rates. The Engineering and Allied Employers' National Federation claimed that the basis should be the pay packet, in other words total earnings.'[2] Clearly one of the most important problems is that of the relationship of wage rates and earnings and how it is to be resolved in the engineering national agreements. In this connection the level of the percentage, given in the agreements, as that by which the earnings of the payment-by-results worker 'of average ability' should exceed the basic rate, has from time to time been under discussion.

2. The evidence presented to the various Courts of Inquiry was quite largely statistical. On the 1954 occasion, for example, the debate at the public meetings was largely concerned with interpretation of statistics. The two sides disagreed on the meaning of the figures relating to earnings, and this disagreement was in fact partly responsible for the differences in attitude mentioned above. The Chairman quite properly insisted on the figures presented to him being defined and on his being shown clearly to which section of the industry the figures related. This created constant difficulties. By the third day of the Inquiry both sides were reluctant to put forward any statistics and were embarrassed by the difficulties of the statistics they had already presented.

The problem of the engineering industry's wage agreement is in large part a problem of definition. The statistical difficulties reflected an inability to define the mass of engineering activities within the compass of a single industry. 'The engineering industry is so complicated and varied both in its structure and in the occupations of the constituent companies and firms that it is impracticable to set any clear limits to it. The terms "engineering industry" and "engineering products" are used loosely, and may mean different things in different contexts. Statistics about the industry require to be used with some care and reservation.'[3]

3. The large group of semi-skilled workers in the industry has been the cause of suggestions for the revision of the wage structure to include more

---

[1] Cmnd. 159.   [2] Cmd. 9084, p. 41.   [3] Cmd. 9084.

occupational groups. This has been a fairly constant theme of union discussion of the agreements since the war. The National Committee of the A.E.U. raised this issue in 1944, and joint discussions were entered into with the employers in 1946 but these broke down in the next year. In 1949 the A.E.U. proposed a division into six grades 'appropriate to the various degrees of skill',[1] but again negotiations broke down.

Evidence of structural deficiencies in the agreements can be followed out in more detail from the case-studies of Chapters 3 and 4. They provided evidence

(1) that the time workers are not necessarily all on the agreed time rate nor the payment-by-results workers on their basic rates;

(2) that there are many types of workers (amounting to a large proportion of the labour force in the factory) besides fitters and unskilled; but, apart from a few special skills such as patternmakers, the agreements make no direct provision for these;

(3) that the 45-per-cent piece-work standard has little meaning;

(4) that the differentials established by the agreements need not necessarily apply either in the rates actually established or in the earnings achieved in factories either in gross or for like periods of time; and,

(5) that overtime payments may be so large and usual as to be an integral part of earnings rather than an extra.

More general information seems to confirm these statements. Evidence detailed at the 1957 Court of Inquiry[2] suggested for example that only 10 per cent of time-working fitters were on the agreement rate. Other engineering factories tend to display the same complexity of occupations and the same contrasts with the simple occupational structure of the agreement. Chapter 2 verifies for industry averages that the minimum piece-work standard has little relevance to actual earnings and that differentials established in wage-rates can be upset in terms of earnings. Average hours worked in the industry lend support to the contention that overtime is a usual feature of its working.

Two further general points may also be made.

(6) The agreements reached nationally do not refer to a number of firms. These fall into two categories; the smaller firms who, while they are not members of the Employers' Federation, will generally have to pay the recognized rates; and, secondly some very large firms which negotiate separate agreements. There seems little reason to doubt that the latter have separate agreements because the existing agreements fix rates that are too low to be meaningful for them.

(7) The agreements do not give more than the most general advice (related to

[1] Cf. Tatlow, op. cit.   [2] Cmnd. 159.

the 45-per-cent minimum piece-work standard) about payment-by-results earnings.

The first major revision required is that of the list of occupations for which rates are to be fixed. An arrangement which concentrates attention only on skilled and unskilled is obviously insufficient for an industry where large numbers are semi-skilled. Further, neither skilled nor semi-skilled are homogeneous groups; each requires further differentiation.

Chapter 3 showed that the wage rates of skilled workers in the factory studied were subject to considerable variation, and the rates given to semi-skilled employees were generally on a par with skilled rates. The reasons for this situation in this particular case need not concern us in our present discussion, but it is necessary to note the intermingling of rates which occurred. In another engineering factory (discussed in Chapter 4) which classified its labour force in much greater detail than the agreements, it was found necessary to specify rates for twenty or thirty different engineering occupations to keep different groups distinguished. Undoubtedly the failure of the agreements to specify the exact position of different groups has created confusion. The greatest confusion has arisen with semi-skilled grades.

The difficulties of the status and wage rate position to be accorded to semi-skilled groups have been growing along with the growth and changing pattern of the engineering industry itself. When the work of the industry was largely conducted by skilled craftsmen assisted by a 'mate' or a labourer, then semi-skilled workers were generally 'mates' whose position relative to their tradesmen could be readily decided. In such circumstances, the question of wage rates for semi-skilled workers presented few difficulties since their status was known. In shipbuilding the position of semi-skilled workers is still largely of this kind, or else semi-skilled operatives are workers whose role is ancillary to the production process (such as cranemen); as a result, the problem of semi-skilled wage rates has not been great in shipbuilding. In engineering, however, increasing use of machines has meant a change in the role of the semi-skilled and a considerable increase in their numbers.

This change in the position of the semi-skilled workers in engineering may be said to have four aspects. First, there has been an increase in the number of semi-skilled operatives relative to total employees in the industry. Secondly, along with this there has been an increase in the number of types of semi-skilled workers in the industry. Thirdly, the semi-skilled workers are no longer either assistants to workers engaged in production or ancillaries to the production process but are themselves largely directly engaged in the process of production. Finally, the semi-skilled worker has become associated closely

236

with the operation of machinery and the distinctions to be drawn between semi-skilled operatives are frequently distinctions based on the types of machines they operate.[1]

These changes in the semi-skilled group in the engineering industry provide the major grounds for an increase in the number of occupational groups defined and separately treated by the wage structure of the industry. At present there is no uniform treatment of the semi-skilled. Along with this clearer delineation of semi-skilled groups would go an increase in the number of skilled groups receiving separate treatment.

The second major revision which appears to be required is to bring the level of rates prescribed by the national agreements closer to the levels of rates and of earnings actually payable in the industry. The engineering industry has adopted payment-by-results systems of one kind or another to a very considerable extent, but despite this there are still large numbers of workers who are officially classified as time-workers. Because of the existence of both time-workers and payment-by-results workers, the use of the term 'rate' introduces a perplexing confusion. For the time-workers, the rate fixed nationally is a time rate intended to be the full payment for time worked in the normal working hours; while, for the payment-by-results workers, the rate fixed nationally is a basic rate which is payable to the worker for hours worked and which also frequently forms a base for payments schemes. Moreover, though time-workers are probably in a minority in the industry,[2] the rates normally discussed and quoted for the industry are the time-worker's rates.

The narrowest issue that arises in this discussion of the contrast between the wage rates fixed by the engineering agreements and the actual level of earnings in the industry, is that of the difference between the levels of wage rates fixed in the agreement and the actual wage rates set up in the various factories in the industry. This issue refers to the time rates in the agreements and the rates actually paid to time-workers, and also to the basic rates for payment-by-results workers in the agreements and the basic rates which are actually applied to payment-by-results workers in the industry.

The habit of paying rates in excess of those agreed upon nationally is by now widespread. There can be little doubt that it originates from a shortage of engineering workers. When labour is short managements are prepared to take the initiative in pushing rates above those negotiated. Local negotiations designed to increase rates in particular factories above the level of national rates do not meet with vehement opposition from managements. When total

---

[1] Thus some firms get round the lack of guidance on semi-skilled rates by putting a rate on the machine irrespective of the type of operative working it.

[2] Cf. 'Earnings in Engineering 1926–1948' (op. cit.). Time-workers are in a minority in skilled groups, in a very definite minority of semi-skilled, but are the majority of the unskilled.

wage rate payments are less than total earnings, whether because of the existence of various compensatory additional payments to time-workers, or because of bonus payments to payment-by-results workers, or because of the frequency of overtime for both groups, managements are likely to feel that the marginal increases requested are less heavy in relation to earnings than they are in relation to rates. When rates are lower than earnings managements may easily have some desire to lessen the gap in the interests of clarity. In brief, the present tendency for factory rates to be higher than national would seem to be a clear indication that the national agreement rates in the industry are at present too low relative to earnings.

The result of the present low level of rates, and the established practice of better firms rating workers above them, has been, naturally enough, to reduce the negotiated rates which were thought of as standard rates to the status of minimum rates. If the principle of negotiating only minimum rates is now accepted, then the present negotiations are quite hopelessly misleading, since they prescribe increases to be given to all workers, not only to those who are at the minimum; while if the negotiations are to continue to be thought of as concerned with revisions of the standard rates in the industry, then there is every reason to suggest that they should be standard, in fact as well as in theory. Provided the circumstances governing levels of wage payment in the industry are sufficiently taken into account in fixing the standard rates, then it is likely to be to the advantage of the unions, and to the advantage of the majority of employers, that those paying less than the standard should be brought up to scratch. This means, however, that the rates presently given in the agreements will have to be increased.

Since wage rates are the principal means of payment of time-workers, adjustment of factory and national rates to bring them together, would (with the exception of overtime which is not discussed here) eliminate the discrepance between rates and earnings of time-workers. In the case of payment-by-results workers, the gap between nationally agreed basic rates and earnings, other than differences arising out of overtime, is created by the payment of basic rates above those nationally agreed, and by payment-by-results earnings. As far as payment-by-results workers are concerned, the biggest area of possible change is therefore that of payment-by-results.

The agreements in the industry talk only of a 'minimum piece-work standard' of 45 per cent above basic rates (though this should probably be called a minimum payment-by-results standard since straight piece-work is almost certainly less common than other types of payment-by-results schemes). The 45-per-cent figure represents what a worker of average ability is expected to be able to earn above basic rates. The apparent glaring contradiction of a 'minimum' which is to be earned by an 'average' worker can be resolved when it is realized that this is an injunction upon the firms in the industry to preserve adequate remuneration in their incentive scheme—the 'minimum piece-work standard' refers to firms not to individuals. There is by now sufficient information to substantiate the view that the 45-per-cent gap does exist and indeed that it is distinctly on the low side as a description of the actual situation in the industry;[1] though the extent to which it is exceeded does vary. The important question here relates to why a gap of this kind is necessary.

The first reason which is likely to be given as justifying 45 per cent (or the higher figures which exist in some cases) as a working base for the payment-by-results system of a factory is what may be called for convenience the 'doctrine of the whole bonus'. By this is meant the tendency on the part of employers to believe that the worker responds more readily to a high figure of bonus percentage. The suggestion is that the total bonus has to be large before the worker bothers about extra effort. To anybody brought up on the idea of the margin this notion is very difficult to follow. Is it necessarily an added incentive to a worker to work for an extra little output when he knows his bonus is already sizeable? Would it not rather be the reverse since an increase in output on a small bonus percentage would appear proportionately greater? Moreover, from the point of view of the worker this high bonus percentage makes an unnecessarily large part of his pay packet appear to be uncertain and subject to chance.

Of course, the existence of a large percentage bonus gives to the employer the impression of a wider range of possible variations in actual bonus percentages earned by individual workers. It seems to provide for the possibility of a very inefficient worker getting very much less than 45 per cent. In actual fact, agreements in the industry would prevent a variation by the inefficient worker below about 30 per cent, since there is an agreement whereby payment-by-results workers who cannot make more than the time rate revert to that rate, and it becomes operative at about a 30-per-cent bonus level. In other words the agreements themselves preclude use being made of the complete range of bonus percentages. In the case of factories where the actual level of the bonus percentage is much above 45 per cent, somewhat different considerations apply. In a factory where the average bonus percentage was, for example, 80 per cent, then the agreements would permit individuals to earn percentages ranging from 30 per cent upwards. The relevant question here is whether a factory management would permit this latitude to a worker who is so much slower than the rest, and who is likely to be an outsider among his workmates, since he does not conform to the normal behaviour of his work group. If the management is prepared to keep such a person in employment, is it not further relevant to enquire whether such a person, who is so manifestly not responding in the normal fashion to the

[1] Cf. Chapters 2, 3 and 4.

incentive should not be dealt with apart? It must be admitted that there is a good reason for a management to want some range of possible bonus below the 'average worker' level—but it must be doubted if this amount of range is required.

It may also be suggested as a second reason for retaining the 45-per-cent 'minimum piece-work standard', that, from the management's viewpoint, it is easier to get out of than an increased basic rate would be, if a reduction were to become necessary. Such a suggestion would infer that, for factories where the 45-per-cent standard is a relevant description of wage conditions, the agreements for payment-by-results were less binding or more easily adjusted than agreement on rates. In fact, however, an alteration of the 'minimum piece-work standard' would require negotiation on the agreements just as much as an alteration to basic rates; moreover, the provision for reverting to time rates if payment-by-results earnings fall to the level of time rates, is also in an agreement.

In the case of factories where the actual average level of the bonus percentage is much above 45 per cent, alterations to bonus levels could conceivably be made without infringing existing agreements. Such alterations would require either an alteration in piece-work prices or in the time allowances of the payments system, or a reduction in the rate of working (and of bonus earning) of the workers. A downward alteration in prices or times would hardly fail to produce a mirror at factory level of the sort of trouble which would ensue at national level from a reduction in rates. It is hard to see that the local nature of the trouble would make it any less unpleasant. The alternative of allowing the workers to reduce their rate of bonus working would appear to be not very likely, since financial stringency would increase the need for high output per worker not reduce it.

Neither the idea of the 'whole bonus', nor a belief that bonus percentages are easier to reduce in hard times, seem adequate to justify the very wide gap between the 'average' or 'minimum' level of the piece-work standard and the basic rate. A possible explanation of how these percentages became so large is that their growth has been to an extent unnoticed and not the result of deliberate policy: this is probably the true explanation in factories where levels are well above 45 per cent, while the 45-per-cent level itself was altered to this point from 27½ per cent by an agreement of 1950 which was mainly attending to other things. If the preceding argument is accepted, and the effect of a bonus is regarded as marginal, then there would seem to be grounds for reducing the gap between basic rates and payment-by-results earnings by raising of the basic rate and appropriate emendation of prices and time allowances.

This suggestion that the new basic rate for payment-by-results workers should be much closer to the norm of actual bonus percentages in factories

240

meets with one big difficulty. The tendency of factories to outdistance the 45-per-cent standard has already been discussed, but appropriate levels at which to set basic rates in relation to the levels of bonus percentages actually existing in the industry have still to be established. In other words having suggested an upward revision of basic rates for payment-by-results workers and an upward revision of time rates to bring them closer to the actual situation, we now find that the actual situation is unknown.

It is clear that an investigation by the engineering industry is required to discover what are the actual levels of time rates of occupations in factories in the industry, what are the actual levels of basic rates for payment-by-results workers and what are the actual norms and averages of bonus percentages in the industry. Such an investigation would certainly produce wide variations which might make any general level very difficult to fix. Two features of the industry are however of relevance here, and it may be suggested that when the information from the various factories is subdivided in accordance with these features a clearer pattern will emerge. These features are that the engineering industry covers a very wide assortment of different engineering activities, and that it is located in all the regions of the country.

The engineering industry in Great Britain is not now so much a single homogeneous industry as a collection of highly diverse industries selling a very wide range of machinery and metal products and employing broadly similar types of workmen. This is the basis of the second main (and statistical) problem which was suggested at the beginning of this Appendix. It is the tendency for the various sections to use the same types of workers that has mainly held these industries together and has given them a single wage agreement. But, it is only partly true to say that the workers in the various sections of the industry are of the same type. A fitter in a marine-engineering shop has a very different job from a fitter in a mass-production automobile factory. The sections of the industry differ in the extent of their use of machinery and in the extent of their use of semi-skilled workers. They differ greatly in the size and type of their final products. They differ in their suitability for, and use of, payment-by-results schemes. Perhaps most importantly for the present discussion, they differ greatly in their ability and willingness to pay high wages.

It seems probable that this sectionalization of the industry, which is not reflected in its present wage agreements is the greatest single contributor to the present unrealistic position of the wage structure. It is therefore essential that an investigation of the present levels of rates and bonus percentages should be analysed in terms of these sections, and that a revised wage structure should specify time rates and basic rates for each section. While it may be argued that this would be a retrograde step in that it will lead to the re-establishment of differentials between one section of the industry and the other, a much more sensible attitude would be to say that it constitutes a recognition of the fact that such differences already exist and provides solid ground from which to study their possible reduction.

Similar considerations apply to regional differences in the engineering industry. While it is possible that the regional differences in earnings levels in the industry may prove on investigation to be merely reflections of the different sections of the industry which occur in some areas rather than others, it may also prove necessary to specify wage rates by regions.

CONCLUSIONS

The suggestions put forward may now be set out in summary form.
1. Two investigations should be undertaken by the industry,

    (*a*) to discover the extent of occupational diversity in the industry; and
    (*b*) to discover the actual levels in factories in the industry of,
        (i) time rates paid to time-workers,
        (ii) basic rates paid to payment-by-results workers, and,
        (iii) the bonus percentages actually earned by payment-by-results workers of average ability.

These investigations should be analysed by sections of the industry and by regions.

2. On the basis of these investigations the wage agreements of the industry should be revised to specify time rates and basic rates for payment-by-results workers for more occupations. These rates should be given for each section of the industry, and (possibly) for each section in each region.[1]

[1] T. P. Hills and K. G. J. C. Knowles, in 'The Variability of Engineering Earnings', *Bulletin*, May 1956, published the results of a detailed investigation of the average hourly earnings in the early part of 1952 of fitters and labourers in each of over 2,000 firms who were members of the Federation. As a result of this investigation they rejected the suggestion of separate region and section bargains. Their conclusion seems to the present writer to underemphasize three factors.
1. They have concentrated, at least in this article, on time-workers rather than payment-by-results workers and so have made the whole situation simpler than it is. In consequence, they have felt able to recommend that the job of revision of the engineering wage structure could be carried out on a national scale. Add the complication that most of the industry's workers are on payment-by-results and the task looks much more formidable; and probably requires more detailed consideration than an industry-wide negotiation could achieve.
2. They appear to underestimate the extent of differences in the level of economic well-being of regions of the United Kingdom. If this separateness is granted, separate regional agreements in engineering seem more sensible.
3. They analyse the engineering industry in sections and discuss its sectional characteristics; but in the end they fail to pursue this to the logical conclusion that the engineering industry is not one but a number of industries. If this is appreciated then separate agreements for the separate sections of the industry do not seem a complication but a clarification of the existing situation.

3. The time rates given should correspond closely to the actual levels of time rates paid in the industry. This need not necessarily be made the occasion of an all-round wage increase.

4. For each section in each region of the industry basic rates for payment-by-results workers should be adjusted such that actual bonus earnings are a much smaller percentage above basic rates than at present. The minimum piece-work standard should also be adjusted appropriately.

APPENDIX 3

MEMORANDUM TO THE COUNCIL ON PRICES, PRODUCTIVITY AND INCOMES

In the spring of 1959 the Council on Prices, Productivity and Incomes asked for a number of comments on wage policy in Britain from those who were known to have been writing in this field. The Council incorporated a summary of the views it collected in its Third Report published in July 1959 and expressed the hope that discussion of what they regarded as 'a major problem of our time' would be stimulated. I was invited to submit a memorandum amplifying my article in the *Scottish Journal of Political Economy* on which Chapter 12 above is based. In view of the importance of the topic I have decided to add this memorandum (at the proof stage) as an Appendix to this book.

NOTES ON A WAGE POLICY FOR BRITAIN

I

The following notes are intended to amplify the discussion of wage policy in Britain which I put forward in my article in the *Scottish Journal of Political Economy* in June 1958.[1] I began that article by setting out my views on the structure of wages in Britain by stating them as assumptions. Since my opinion on appropriate wage policies for Britain follows directly from these assumptions, I repeat and to some extent reformulate the main ones here.

I assume that wage rates in Britain are for the most part settled by collective bargaining processes, by statutory wage regulation (Wages Councils), or by arbitration carried through at a national level for 'industries' composed of a number of 'firms' or independent employing units. I am aware that there are a number of cases in which this assumption is not true. The major exceptions are probably the nationalized industries and the Government itself, since in these cases the 'firms' and the 'industry' are the same. These are important exceptions which must be discussed later. There are also some very large firms, and a larger number of small firms, who do not participate in national collective bargaining. At present the large firms who are outside these arrangements are not sufficiently numerous to affect the general pattern of wage settlement processes, while the small firms are probably very definitely followers rather than leaders in all wage matters.

I assume that these national agreements cannot in the nature of things cover all the detailed needs of individual employers and all the varying circumstances of particular workers. I therefore consider it proper to assume the existence of an earnings structure in Britain which in present circumstances

---

[1] 'The Inadequacy of Recent Wage Policies in Britain.'

244

is generally above, and frequently substantially above, the wage rate structure, and that, further, this earnings structure can differ from the wage rate structure not only in level but also in pattern. In saying this I am doing no more than giving formal recognition to the 'earnings drift' and the 'earnings gap', which are statistically recognizable parts of our post-war wages scene.

It is sometimes suggested that earnings differ from the wage rates contained in national agreements because of personal distinctions in effort, or ability, or hours worked. For example, it may be argued that workers receive payment-by-results earnings only if they work *especially* hard, that they receive overtime payments only if they work *especially* long hours, or that they receive extra rate payments only if they are *especially* meritorious. At the margin of earnings I have no doubt that this is true and that some workers do receive specially high earnings for personal reasons and personal performances; but this cannot be applied to the generality of earnings, since the average, and in many cases the minimum, level of earnings in Britain would appear to be above that of agreement rates. For the most part the earnings structure can only therefore be regarded as more individual or personal than the rate structure in that being localized it is more complex and takes more differentials into account.

It is also sometimes suggested that, while earnings are different in level from the wage rates laid down in national agreements, the seeds of the differences are created and controlled by provisions of the agreements. This kind of approach emphasizes that national agreements are concerned with much more than settling wage rates and contain recommendations and agreements on many other aspects of work and payment. Thus, for example, we could suggest that overtime payments are regulated by agreements on overtime premia and possibly limitations on the volume of overtime working, or that payment-by-results can in some cases be governed by recommendations about the volume of earnings which ought to be made available from this source to 'average' workers. It is true that this kind of thing can restrict the freedom of earnings movements but it seems to me to be an exaggeration to suggest that earnings are completely *controlled* in this way. Besides it is specially important to remember that in many agreements only *minimum* rates are settled and the bulk of wage rate determination is therefore automatically excluded from their scope.

I therefore make a fairly clear-cut distinction between two systems of wage determination in Britain at present—the process which takes place at the national level and fixes agreement rates, and the process which takes place 'locally', and determines a pattern of average earnings or an earnings structure. It follows that I consider that only a method of wage control which is able to keep in check both forms of wage movement can be adequate for British wage policy.

R   245

II

There are two possible sets of circumstances in which wage control may be advocated. Without going into the controversy about the meaning of these terms I would suggest that they roughly correspond to what people mean when they talk of (a) demand inflation, and (b) cost inflation.

Demand inflation

In the 'demand inflation' case there is excess demand for both products and the resources (including labour) used in production, and prices of both products and factors tend to rise in response to demand pressures. Control of the earnings structure in these circumstances may be regarded as a problem in price control under conditions of excess demand, and we may judge its feasibility in the same kind of terms as we would judge any price control proposals. The relevant points seem to be as follows.

1. The first essential of a price control policy is to be able to sort out the existing price structure of the commodities to be controlled. Any earnings structure must necessarily involve a large number of prices for different sections of the labour force and would make the provision of adequate knowledge very difficult. Besides, no machinery designed to give us this kind of information exists in Britain. In any case, the nature of the present earnings pattern would make problems of definition very difficult: for example, the use of regular overtime and payment-by-results earnings as substitutes for more conventional forms of wage increase would in present circumstances cause many disagreements about existing price levels for labour.

2. It is normally easier to control the prices of goods which are produced by a small number of sources: the 'producers' of labour in Britain number over twenty millions. Alternatively, price control is helped if the number of outlets for the goods is small, or if the number of purchasers is small: every separate employing unit is an outlet for labour's services and every employer is a purchaser.

3. Controls always create problems of enforcement. While it is not necessary that everybody should willingly accept the control, it is generally necessary that those who break it should be the exception. In the case of a control on earnings, most people, as employees or their dependents, will have a marked inclination to break out of the control in their own interest, while employers, faced with a shortage of labour, will be under strong temptation to get round the frustrating restrictions, and informal ways of doing so will be readily available.

I conclude from these points that control of earnings in conditions of demand inflation will not work. Since I require control of both wage rates and earnings for a successful wage control I can therefore say that, whether or not wage *rate* control could work in the circumstances of demand inflation, a total policy of wage control will be a failure. I discuss the possible success or failure of wage rate controls later in this paper, but I must mention here two factors which make such controls specially unmanageable under demand inflation.

(i) Under demand inflation, unless it is very effectively suppressed, we can expect indicators of retail prices and of profits to show substantial increases. These are two of the indicators most frequently used to justify wage rate increases and changes in them would severely strain any wage rate control.

(ii) If wage rates were controlled while earnings were free to move, numerous stresses would be set up which could overthrow the wage rate control. For example, earnings increases would widen the gap between earnings and wage rates and would therefore force union leaders into the awkward position of refusing to push forward wage claims when payments were obviously capable of rising. Moreover, there would be an acute danger of wage rate agreements becoming more unrepresentative and so of both them and the union and its leaders losing influence. Wage rate claims based on comparisons with the earnings pattern would become highly likely. Earnings would tend to respond to changing market circumstances and so differentials in earnings, and differential comparisons with wage rates, would alter and provoke wage rate claims. Moreover, the extent of earnings possibilities available to particular groups of workers varies, and wage rate claims on behalf of those with no, or few, earnings opportunities would be inevitable.

I can myself therefore see little or no hope of instituting wage control under conditions of demand inflation. I must in any case confess to grave doubts about the appropriateness of singling out wages for special treatment in such circumstances. If it is a question of seeking to punish or control those who are to blame for initiating an inflation, then, unless the inflation is caught near its beginning, I fear it becomes wellnigh impossible to sort out those wage increases which can be regarded as initiating forces and those which, like other price rises, are merely consequences of inflation. If wage control merely forms part of overall controls then I think it is much more sensible to try to reduce demand than to try to control everything.

Cost inflation

The other situation for which wage controls are advocated comes about in conditions of general price stability where excess demand for neither products nor labour exists. If in these circumstances wages increase by more than productivity then we can infer pressure upon costs which can lead on to general price increase. The increase in costs and prices will be met by a similar increase in the income and operating powers of wage earners, is likely to be responsible for an increase in real demand in the economy, and may eventually lead on to demand inflation, but in the first instance at least cost and demand inflations may be usefully distinguished.

In circumstances of price stability without excess demand so long as wage rates are unchanged I would consider that the earnings structure will be controlled by the level of demand in the economy. Earnings are fixed by the circumstances of the particular employer and if there is no increase in the demand for his product he will tend to be automatically excluded from increasing his wage bill. This does not of course mean that the earnings *patterns* of individual employers or of the economy as a whole will not alter—indeed they will certainly do so in response to changes in structural needs in the labour market. Nor need it follow that there will be no trend upward in earnings with productivity changes, or long-run upward trends in the wage bill if labour-using innovations should be introduced. But, if wage rates are unchanged and there is no excess demand the earnings level in an economy will tend to be stable in the short period.

If wage rates are increased, the present convention is that such increases, whether applied to standard rates or to minima, will be passed on to all workers in the category covered by the increase. Further, it is usual to find that most, or at least a large proportion, of the wage claims in our economy are brought to fruition within a relatively short period each year, and wage rate increases are usually applicable to a whole industry at once. It will, therefore, generally be true that demand for a firm's products, in money terms at least, will be built up at approximately the same time as its costs, and its competitors will be similarly affected. Thus, wage rate changes will tend to be passed on into and increase the earnings level.

Two factors are therefore of special importance in the cost inflation situation: the conviction that wage rate increases are passed on, and the ways in which wage rate changes take place. I will later discuss possible alterations to these factors but let me first consider wage control under cost inflation with the existing conventions and methods of wage rate change. Since earnings begin by being under control in cost inflation the main problem is wage rate control.

Wage rates in Britain are presently settled for the most part by national bargains. This means that discussion of wage rate control must go far beyond the workings of the economic system to consider 'political' and institutional factors. There is no automatic mechanism of wage rate control in the economy. The very idea of cost inflation by wages involves an assumption that wage rates can be increased even when the demand for labour's services is steady (or even declining). A wage rate policy must therefore rest on the agreement of the institutions who are parties to the bargain—in practice the trade unions. It can only last as long as the trade unions agree to it. Since trade unions are explicitly bodies which are concerned to raise the living standards of their members, and they regard wage rate increase as essential to this end, we may expect that any form of wage control which makes no allowance for wage change (for example, a wage freeze) will have to be a very temporary expedient. Any longer term form of wage rate control will need to have provision for wage rate change. What difficulties stand in the way of such wage rate control?

(i) The most general difficulty is that of uncertainty. If we allow freedom to institutions in the labour market, and it seems likely that we must, then we have to be prepared for constant alarms and crises in any wage control system. Even if it did last, it would still be necessary to think of its operations in a short period way.

(ii) A wage control policy could place the unions in a difficult position. Any social institution must have a function if it is to survive and wage control (say by some kind of central board) comes dangerously near to depriving unions of their reason for existence. Of course such a controlling body would be likely to operate with the help and advice of the union leaders. This could embarass the union leaders in several ways. It would divide their loyalties between their members and the central control. It might involve their supporting a policy of inaction and so depriving themselves of their function. In the kind of situation in which we might expect a union leader to be active (and in which his members will certainly expect activity) the union leader may be forced to do nothing. This could be bad for his prestige and control over his members. Indeed there is a real danger that acquiescence by union leaders in wage control will lead to unofficial leadership and unofficial action within the unions and to loss of official control. Similarly, continued support by the T.U.C. of a controlling body could result in the alienation of member unions. In circumstances of this type both the T.U.C. and individual unions would be forced to back out of control and close their ranks by moving nearer to their members' views. Moreover, even if for a period this did not happen, the threat of its happening would act as a constant cause of uncertainty and compromise.

(iii) The controlling body would be faced with the task of making decisions on wage claims presented to it. This would be a considerable duty. The present complex wage situation in Britain as I have outlined it above[1] leads to many confusions of terms and to comparisons which are founded on uncertainties. Not only would it be difficult to work out criteria for wage advances but it would be difficult to find solid ground on which to base evidence on existing relative and absolute wage levels. Further, the existence of a central board charged with duties of this kind implies that a general overall view of the wage rate pattern in Britain is a possibility, and so infers

[1] Cf. my article 'The Present Complexity of Wage Payments', *Scottish Journal of Political Economy*, February 1955.

that the board will be able to make order out of disorder and to impart an atmosphere of rational decision taking. This kind of inference may expose the board to criticisms which exist and are justified now, when there is no such board, but cannot at present be directed at so convenient and central a scapegoat. I think it is also important to emphasize that a control of this kind is exposed to a cumulative build-up of anomalies and criticisms: a series of approximately right decisions can cumulate the errors in approximation into real grievances. Moreover the earnings pattern in the economy will continue to change with changing circumstance and this will provoke comparisons which a board will have to heed and a wealth of detailed problems which no one body can tackle.

I may now sum up the discussion of this section.

1. I do not consider that any wage policy is likely to be successful in controlling wages, whether earnings or rates, under conditions of demand inflation.

2. Under conditions of price stability without excess demand I consider that the earnings level of an economy will be stable, and that earnings may therefore be said to be 'controlled' in this situation.

3. The avoidance of cost inflation by wages rests on the possibility of control of wage rates, combined with the observance of the convention that all wage rate increases are passed on. In discussing the present situation we must assume the existence of this convention.

4. The possibility of a successful wage rate control policy depends on political or social, and institutional factors, and these present many difficulties.

5. A wage rate control policy at present will be temporary, subject to crises, and based on compromise. The type of policy (wage freeze) which does not permit wage changes will be more temporary than the type that tries to work out wage changes.

III

The main results of my review up to now are to suggest that a wage control policy cannot be combined with demand inflation, and to suggest that present methods of wage settlement can only at best be made to provide a *temporary* means of wage control against cost inflation if circumstances are favourable. This is a depressing result because we all hope that full employment is to be a permanent feature of our economic life. We can contemplate with equanimity neither the levels of unemployment which might suffice to rule out all possibility of 'cost inflation', nor yet the lack of price stability and incipient or active inflation which has characterized our post war experience. I think that we can and should deal with demand inflation by monetary and fiscal means, and I will not discuss this type of situation any further, but, if we are to have both full employment and a reasonable degree of price stability then we must also have some permanent feeling of security against cost inflation. The present dual rates and earnings structure and present methods of wage settlement in Britain can only provide temporary solutions; therefore we must work towards new types of wage structure and new methods of wage settlement.

The chief difficulties in the present situation are as follows.

1. Wage rate movement is governed by a social/political/institutional process which depends on arguments which need not necessarily have an economic content. Wage rate control therefore involves compromise and has to be set up in a political and institutional context. There is no certainty that a change in economic circumstances which reduces demand will necessarily restrict wage rate claims or their success relative to production movements. Even moderately high unemployment will not necessarily mean wage rate stability.

2. Wage rate increases are passed on to all who are nominally covered by them, whether or not they are actually being paid at the rate or are being paid, possibly by other methods, above the rate. This seems usually to be true whether the rates in question are standard rates, minimum rates, guaranteed payments, legal minima or any other variety. In consequence we have a situation in which increases are determined for workers in every variety of circumstances, and firms in every degree of economic viability, throughout an industry by one negotiation, where social arguments, more appropriate to minimum levels of remuneration, take precedence over the economic considerations that affect the majority of workers and firms.

3. As a result of confusion of purposes between the wage rate and earnings structures, and overemphasis on the wage rate structure, the earnings structure is not at present operating to its full effect in creating purposive labour mobility in response to differential rewards.

The ideal way out of this situation would in my view be to have two levels of wage settlement. The first level would consist of very large scale negotiations covering industries or groups of industries and settling minimum wages only, without any tendency for increases here to be passed on to the generality of wage payments. At this level we could expect, and approve of, much social argument. The second level would consist of much expanded settlement of wage structures and wage levels by managements in consultation with unions at the level of individual employers, or individual employing units. At this 'local' level decisions would of necessity have to relate to the economic circumstances of particular firms. I would hold that this type of development in the settlement of wages would result in wages coming within the normal orbit of economic policy. We would still have, and properly so, pressure by unions to raise the living standards of their members, but such pressure would now occur at the level of the individual employer and within the context of economic conditions. There would be a desirable strengthening and clarification of what I have here described as the earnings structure, which would now become the wage structure of the economy and would have a fuller role in encouraging desired mobilities. Social argument and debate about the 'under-dogs' would of course continue but it would be addressed to its proper level—the settlement of minimum wages.

Now, of course, I realize that this description has a ring of the fanciful in relation to the possibilities of the actual situation. But I believe that something of this type must in the long run develop if we are to have both stability and full employment. We ought now to develop our wage policies towards this end as fast as we can. The following are my practical proposals.

1. The first step is the establishment of Government sponsored minimum wage negotiations covering very wide sections of industry. There are broadly two possibilities here. The first is that the Government should approach industrialists and trade unionists and encourage them to form this type of negotiating body alongside their present negotiating machinery. The second, and more likely, possibility is that the Government itself should create minimum wage fixing bodies to cover large industry groups. I would favour for these a constitution rather similar to that of Wages Councils at present. Indeed it would probably be sensible to propose the amalgamation of groups of the present Wages Councils so as to take them further back from the detailed problems of sections of industries. An alternative here would simply be to pass a single piece of minimum wage legislation setting up one minimum wages board. My fear here would be that such a single body would be forced too low in its wage determinations to be of any relevance to most industries. I am in fact aiming at bodies which would be away from detailed problems of industries but still close enough to take account of all the social arguments for minimum payments which arise in each section of industry and commerce.

2. The second step is to encourage employers to begin to settle their own wage patterns outside the context of present negotiations. This would involve their being prepared to make positive proposals and to take the initiative in wage formation and in proposing wage changes. It would also involve considerable reformulation of present earnings structures and willingness to co-operate with the unions in detailed discussion and consultation.[1] It is my belief that the initiative in creating adequate local wage structures rests with the managers and that with encouragement we might see a strong development in this direction. I think that one factor which holds managers back at present is their feeling that they ought to stand by the industry and not go too

---

[1] I discuss this kind of issue at greater length in an article entitled 'Managerial Control of Wages' which is presently awaiting publication in *The Manager*. (Published in *The Manager*, September 1959).

far on their own. The substitution of minimum wage fixing for industries in place of present arrangements would I feel allow managers a greater sense of freedom here. I also think that this kind of development could be attractive to unions since it would bring them closer to the operative levels of wage payments and would help to end their present difficulties over dissensions between national and local union levels. I therefore suggest that managements should be encouraged to make this move.

3. The third step is to increase the flow of information. If we are to make local negotiations work without creating a disordered wage structure, and if we wish the wage structure to encourage mobility, then we must ensure that there is a free flow of information on wage patterns. The Government should therefore be encouraged to supply all concerned with the maximum possible information, and propaganda should be directed at managements to show the benefits of a freely operating and well informed labour market fed by adequate data from managements. This would require a considerable expansion in the industrial relations and statistical sections of the Ministry of Labour.

IV

I have now put forward my main proposals. I wish however also to mention briefly two complicating factors—the meanings I attach to 'local' and to 'no excess demand'.

'Local'

Without going into the structure of every industry and of every firm it is impossible to avoid some ambiguity about the precise meaning to be attached to the suggestion that wage settlement should take place at the 'local' level. Because I am concerned to point out the significance of the gap between rates and earnings and of the divorce of the present bargaining machinery on wages from the economic and financial units of our economy, 'local' wage settlement must for me meet two tests. First it must be at a level which will allow the wage structure which results to take account of all necessary differentials, such as those which may exist for particular types of labour in particular regions or localities, or special requirements which certain processes may demand from the labour force over and above its being of the requisite skill or training. Secondly, it must be at the level of the individual employer.

There are roughly three types of employers of special interest in this connection. I presume that the medium-sized employer could form a natural single bargaining unit, and need not be discussed here. But there are some employers working on a very large scale with many plants and departments under their control. This group may be divided into large multi-plant concerns in private hands and those in public hands—the nationalized industries

253

and the Government itself. Then at the other extreme there are a very large number of small employers with only a few workpeople.

There might be justification for a number of small employers grouping together to settle their terms for employing their labour. But I suspect that in these cases workpeople and their jobs are considered individually and wage structures are so closely related to the particular needs of particular employers and workers that a common policy would be very difficult to formulate. I think it is likely that very small employers at present use national wage agreements as minima and arrive at their actual payments by following behind the levels of payments of their larger neighbours, adapting them to suit their individual workers. I would expect this kind of situation to continue.

I see no particular difficulty in arranging 'local' agreements in the case of very large private employers. All that is necessary is to sectionalize their agreements and indeed some of them already do this. The criterion on the degree of sectionalization must be the level at which all necessary differentials can be taken into account. Thus a firm with plants of many different types or situated in many different regions will naturally require more, and more detailed, agreements than a less diversified concern.

In my view the present Government policy, by which Government employees' payment is determined by comparison with, and following trends in, the private sector, is the logical and correct one for it to follow. I think, however, that present wage policies in the nationalized industries offer very real difficulties for any form of wage control. The nationalized industries are both large and important and cover many grades of labour. It is natural that from time to time they should be regarded as 'wage leaders' or at least as important factors in the determination of the size of a 'wage round', and that their actions are capable of profound effects on the course of wage movements in the economy. This can have unfortunate results in present circumstances, since we have no great long term clarity on the extent of Government help to nationalized industries, or the extent to which a loss on their current trading at any time is acceptable. In consequence, employers and workers seem to have some tendency to wait on the nationalized industries before deciding on wage increases and the nationalized industries are sometimes given increases which do not seem to conform to the prior expectations formed about particular 'wage rounds'. This situation is unfortunate even in the context of the present bargaining set-up which is already full of 'political' and arbitrary factors: it would be disastrous if the rest of the economy were to be tied in its wage movements to the economic prosperity of particular firms and the nationalized industries were alone to be exempt. If we were to have a new bargaining set-up it would be essential that the position of the nationalized industries should be more clearly known in advance. The Government would doubtless insist on retaining some control over the rate of capital investment of these industries, and the right to vary it. But wage policy requires that the Government should lay down the extent of its current help to nationalized industries, if any, and there should be the greatest possible clarity for a few years ahead on the current economic position of these industries, and on the extent of their responsibility for balancing their books. I realize that this would require a degree of political abstemiousness which political parties of all colours would find difficult, and it would require both courage and a strong will to lay down clear-cut rules on current balance and then to exercise such restraint, but I hold that it is quite essential for any form of successful wage control.

'No excess demand'

I have taken the point at which there is 'no excess demand' as my dividing position between demand inflation, when earnings will tend to run up quickly, and the situation where wage rate movement can upset stability. 'No excess demand' is however a difficult term to define and it is not necessarily true that a position of no excess demand in the product market means that there is none in the factor market either.

I would regard a position of no excess demand in the product market as being generally achieved when there is price stability in relation to the total pattern of demand and supply of goods, and when there is no strong tendency to lengthening of delivery dates or waiting lists beyond what is regarded over a long period as normal in each trade, and no tendency to run-down of stocks. We must, of course, expect that within this general stability there will be price movements, and changes in waiting lists, due to structural changes in the patterns of supply and demand for products, and the price stability may be disrupted by costs movements originating outwith the economy or in wage rate claims.

There are several reasons for supposing that a situation of this kind may involve a condition of over-full employment in the labour market where there will be a strong tendency for the price of labour to rise and a sufficiency of shortages of types of labour as to produce symptoms of fairly widespread, though perhaps not overall, excess demand for labour.

1. Demand for labour and the supply of labour's services may take two forms. It may mean extra hours and extra effort accompanied by extra bonus and overtime payments for existing labour, or the acquisition of extra workers. Now, attempts to get specially high output or hours from labour are costly and involve irregularities in work routine, so while some extra output may be achieved managements will also be in the market for more workers. So we can have here both a position in which supply of the product is being met and a position of excess demand for extra workers accompanied by willingness to raise the price of labour.

255

2. The labour market in an expansionary phase can draw from stocks and from substitutes. I know of course that this is also true of the product market, but since the reserves of labour, or substitute labour, produce the same final products, the situation arises in the labour market before it occurs in the product market. A very large part of post war increases in the supply of labour has been due to the use of married women and also people of retiral age. Now some part of this is obviously suitable and helpful but at the margin it involves special arrangements for irregular part time work and special facilities. Thus at the margin of pressure on the labour market we can create a marked growth in management preferences for the normal run of workers as against these special alternatives which can be regarded as an emergency stock of substitutes. The same is also true in the case of the partially disabled or otherwise handicapped workers who may be drawn into the labour force at the margin. Again therefore we can have a position in which the goods are produced but excess demand for normal grades of labour also exists.

It may be said that both this point, and point 1 above simply amount to saying that costs rise when an economy becomes over-strained, and demands for goods are met by high cost production which will inevitably throw over price stability, that in other words this is another form of cost inflation. This is true when the situation becomes noticeable, or chronic, as it will be when the product market also moves into excess demand, but I would be inclined to feel that price movements do not always result in the early stages. In this situation the change in employers' costs occurs for each of them individually: there is no such unanimity of cost increase as results from a wage rate increase passed on to all firms in an industry at the same time. Employers may well hesitate, therefore, in putting up their prices relative to their competitors. Moreover, we are of course talking of an economy which, though without excess product demand, is in a condition of buoyant production and demand where some overhead costs per unit may tend to be minimized and where productivity increases due to technical change are likely. There is therefore some chance at least that increases in labour cost may be offset against other cost reductions.

3. In any type of market we must expect that general price stability and no shortages will be accompanied by some structural maladjustments. In the labour market, however, such structural problems can be much more deep seated than in the product market and may, therefore, though primarily specific in character, aggregate into the appearance of general excess demand in wide sections of the market. The reasons for these greater structural problems in the labour market are as follows.

(i) Strong social forces slow down the rate of adjustment of the labour force to regional alterations in the structure of demand for labour.

(ii) In the case of skilled men, or those with any form of expert or professional knowledge, reaction to a decline in demand is slow, being hampered by the tendency of those already in the market to resist losing their skilled standing. Reaction to an expansion in demand depends quite largely on expansion in training facilities, the length of the training process, and on the slow growth of new recruits as social and economic attitudes towards the skill alter.

(iii) In recent years there have been signs that employers have 'hoarded' scarce types of labour against their future needs.

(iv) The somewhat confused wage rate and earnings structures at present have not facilitated structural re-allocation of the labour force.

I draw the following conclusions from this discussion of the condition of 'no excess demand' in the labour market.

1. If we were to reformulate our methods of wage settlement as I have suggested something would be gained for wage policy if the economy were kept very slightly below the maximum which can be achieved without producing instability in the product market.

2. The degree to which the labour market can be pushed without instability is closely related to its ability to adjust itself structurally. Encouragement of structural adjustment is therefore an important matter of practical policy. This suggests that the following lines of policy should be pursued.

(i) Training and re-training schemes should be fostered by the Government, and the Government should be persuaded to engage in re-training on a larger scale than at present both in regard to the provision of facilities and to payment of subsistence.

(ii) The problems of housing for workers moving from other regions are central to issues of regional differentials.

(iii) The payments structure should be made as effective as possible. A general move towards clear local patterns of payment would greatly help to make differentials operative.

(iv) Attempts should be made to persuade employers not to 'hoard' key groups of skilled workers. A more mobile labour market and more flexible payments structure would reduce the need for, or possibility of, hoarding.

(v) Workers should be encouraged towards purposeful mobility where it is needed. Redundancy payments and greater Government assistance to those who are unemployed for a short time in changing jobs would be most helpful in achieving this, since they would reduce fear of lack of income security in changing jobs, and, by creating a more suitably adjusted structure in the labour market, would greatly aid the prospects of long-term security.

INDEX

The whole of this book is about wage rates and earnings and the relationship between them, and these topics are mentioned on practically every page. This means that any attempt to provide comprehensive indexing of general references to wages and earnings would be both extremely difficult and quite futile. In consequence this index follows the convention of only mentioning wages, earnings and types of wage payment when there is some special reason for doing so.

259

For EU product safety concerns, contact us at Calle de José Abascal, 56–1°,
28003 Madrid, Spain or eugpsr@cambridge.org.